THE BEDFORD SERIES IN HISTORY AND CULTURE

America Views the Holocaust, 1933–1945

A Brief Documentary History

Related Titles in
THE BEDFORD SERIES IN HISTORY AND CULTURE
Advisory Editors: Natalie Zemon Davis, Princeton University
Ernest R. May, Harvard University

THE BEDFORD SERIES IN HISTORY AND CULTURE

America Views the Holocaust, 1933–1945

A Brief Documentary History

Robert H. Abzug

University of Texas at Austin

BEDFORD/ST. MARTIN'S   Boston   New York

To the memory of my father

For Bedford/St. Martin's
History Editor: Katherine E. Kurzman
Developmental Editor: Charisse Kiino
Editorial Assistant: Molly Kalkstein
Production Supervisor: Dennis Conroy
Marketing Manager: Charles Cavaliere
Project Management: Books By Design, Inc.
Index: Books By Design, Inc.
Text Design: Claire Seng-Niemoeller
Cover Design: Donna Lee Dennison
Cover Photos:
"German 'Ultimatum' Aimed at All World." *The Boston Globe,* April 1, 1933. Reprinted with permission from The Boston Globe and Associated Press.
"Mobs Wreck Jewish Stores in Berlin" by Sigrid Schultz. *Chicago Daily Tribune,* November 10, 1938. © Copyrighted Chicago Tribune Company. All rights reserved; used with permission.
"Germany to Seize All Property of Jews, Goebbels Discloses; Curley Calls Hitler 'Madman.'" *The Washington Post,* November 14, 1938. © 1938, The Washington Post. Reprinted with permission.
"Roosevelt Holds Nazi Brutality Incredible: Calls on American Nations to Arm in Defense." *The Washington Post,* November 16, 1938. © 1938, The Washington Post. Reprinted with permission.
"American War Chiefs See Concentration Camp Atrocities in Germany." *The New York Times.* April 24, 1945. *The New York Times* (U.S. Signal Corps) photo. Copyright © 1945 by The New York Times. Reprinted by permission.
Composition: ComCom, an R. R. Donnelley Company
Printing and Binding: Haddon Craftsmen, an R. R. Donnelley Company

President: Charles H. Christensen
Editorial Director: Joan E. Feinberg
Director of Editing, Design, and Production: Marcia Cohen
Manager, Publishing Services: Emily Berleth

Library of Congress Catalog Card Number: 98-87517

For information, write: Bedford/St. Martin's, 75 Arlington Street, Boston, MA 02116
(617-426-7440)

ISBN: 0-312-13393-6 (paperback)
    0-312-21819-2 (hardcover)

Foreword

The Bedford Series in History and Culture is designed so that readers can study the past as historians do.

The historian's first task is finding the evidence. Documents, letters, memoirs, interviews, pictures, movies, novels, or poems can provide facts and clues. Then the historian questions and compares the sources. There is more to do than in a courtroom, for hearsay evidence is welcome, and the historian is usually looking for answers beyond act and motive. Different views of an event may be as important as a single verdict. How a story is told may yield as much information as what it says.

Along the way the historian seeks help from other historians and perhaps from specialists in other disciplines. Finally, it is time to write, to decide on an interpretation and how to arrange the evidence for readers.

Each book in this series contains an important historical document or group of documents, each document a witness from the past and open to interpretation in different ways. The documents are combined with some element of historical narrative — an introduction or a biographical essay, for example — that provides students with an analysis of the primary source material and important background information about the world in which it was produced.

Each book in the series focuses on a specific topic within a specific historical period. Each provides a basis for lively thought and discussion about several aspects of the topic and the historian's role. Each is short enough (and inexpensive enough) to be a reasonable one-week assignment in a college course. Whether as classroom or personal reading, each book in the series provides firsthand experience of the challenge — and fun — of discovering, recreating, and interpreting the past.

Natalie Zemon Davis
Ernest R. May

Preface

America Views the Holocaust, 1933–1945 offers a selection of original documents that illustrate the varied texture of Americans' reactions as they witnessed what we now call the Holocaust. It may seem startling that less than forty years ago (fifteen years after the end of World War II), a book about America and the Holocaust would have been inconceivable. The term *holocaust* was not yet used to describe Nazi Germany's murder of five million to six million Jews during that war. Nor had scholars or the public even begun to make historical sense of the myriad policies and events that had led to the killing of two-thirds of Europe's Jews, half a million Gypsies, and millions more people who were slave laborers, Nazi-defined mental and physical defectives or social undesirables, and political opponents of the Nazis. Least of all, until about 1968, postwar Americans viewed their own country in relation to these horrors as simply a noble liberator. America and its allies had defeated Nazi Germany and brought the slaughter to an end.

Times have changed. The Holocaust has become the topic of college courses and a vital research area in Jewish and European history. New discoveries make front-page news. Indeed, the Holocaust has become not only a topic for historical or sociological study but also a metaphor for ultimate evil. It has sparked theological reformulations among Christians and Jews; inspired works of art, literature, and music; and become a staple of popular culture. The use of the word, once so necessary to fix a distinct historical consciousness on an extremely complicated story, ironically now tends in many minds to reduce a horrific and complex history into a single event.

Nowhere has this tension between historical complexity and moral judgment been more vexing than when broaching the topic of America and the Holocaust. Careful research has opened painful questions of national conscience and reputation and has led to a profound rethinking of the past. Historians have long since disproved the heroic view of the Allies as simply innocent liberators. Clearly, the Allies had fairly complete knowledge of the Nazi genocide as it happened, and only a few scholars have argued that the Allies could not have done more to save at least some Jews before the end of the war. They generally differ over the motivations of historical actors, the practicality and significance of rescue opportunities, and the moral characterization of Allied actions. The historiographical epilogue at the end of this book introduces students to the basic history of that debate.

All too often, however, in the popular media and in historical circles, the nuanced work of Holocaust scholars has been compressed into anachronistic moral judgments and analogies that have more to do with present-day concerns than with historical context. *America Views the Holocaust* recreates, through a series of carefully chosen and varied documents, part of the social and political world within which Americans reacted to and acted on news of what we now call the Holocaust. Furthermore, it follows the story from 1933 and the rise of Hitler to the liberation of the concentration camps in 1945. It does not attempt to replay debates over Allied guilt or innocence or to assess the practicability of one or another rescue plan. Rather, it allows the reader to gain a sense of the ways Americans of the Holocaust era thought and felt about these events in the context of their times. The documents are presented with background for each selection and within a narrative of key events for the period 1933 to 1945. A historiographical essay (epilogue), chronology, and bibliography reinforce the selections presented in the main text. Together, they should bring students to a new understanding of the tragic dimensions of the Holocaust and provide a vital sense of the times in which it occurred.

ACKNOWLEDGMENTS

Whatever usefulness this work attains will be due in no small part to the extraordinary efforts of a number of individuals. First and foremost has been the engaged presence of Chuck Christensen, Katherine Kurzman, Molly Kalkstein, Donna Dennison, Emily Berleth, and especially Charisse Kiino at Bedford/St. Martin's. I very much appreciated the careful supervision of Nancy Benjamin at Books By Design. Among my fellow historians, I want to recognize the appreciative and thorough critical readings of the first version of this manuscript by Susan Curtis, Purdue University; Leonard Dinnerstein, University of Arizona; Lewis Erenberg, Loyola University of Chicago; Daniel Horowitz, Smith College; and Mike Stoff, University of Texas at Austin; as well as the equally appreciated comments and criticisms of an anonymous reviewer. They all responded to the strengths and weaknesses of my initial foray in the best traditions of scholarship.

Robert H. Abzug

Contents

]

THE BEDFORD SERIES IN HISTORY AND CULTURE

America Views the Holocaust, 1933–1945

A Brief Documentary History

Introduction:
Facing the Horrors

This book sheds light on grave and complex questions: What did Americans know, and how did they respond to the Holocaust as it unfolded before and during World War II? Not only an important historical question, it is also crucial to an understanding of the moral dilemma that continues to haunt our own world: What are the responsibilities of nations and individuals in a world of conflict when common social, political, or military struggles escalate to almost unimaginable, genocidal bloodshed? In the 1990s, the world has witnessed mass slaughter in Bosnia and Rwanda. These were not the first, nor will they be the last, outbreaks of such ethnic "cleansing," but they illustrate something common to most such cases—the slowness or unwillingness of people outside the area of conflict to intercede quickly and effectively to end murderous violence.

Once, when the world was without advanced electronic media and had only the dimmest conception of what transpired in other societies, the question of moral responsibility for events in distant lands hardly had meaning. Photography, motion pictures, radio, television, and now the computer have brought distant places and events into detailed immediacy, breaking through barriers of politics, culture, and language. When viewing the Olympics from a foreign land, with great pleasure we feel drawn into a world community. When viewing mass graves in Rwanda, we feel horrified and disoriented, helpless and almost wishing not to see what the camera has brought us.

The psychological, political, and moral dilemmas created by such confrontations with once obscured human tragedies began in the nineteenth century but reached a watershed at the end of World War II. Widely disseminated photographs and motion pictures taken by Allied troops at the liberation of Nazi concentration camps left an indelible mark on the human consciousness as they made unavoidable our confrontation with the long-reported but largely avoided record of Nazi genocide. We live in the aftershock of that revelation.

More than any other atrocity of this century, what we now call the Holocaust has come to represent the epitome of human evil. Between 1933 and 1945, Nazi Germany set as one of its goals the destruction of Jewish culture in Europe and the murder of every man, woman, and child of Jewish descent. The Nazis almost succeeded. They destroyed centuries-old centers of Jewish life and killed between five million and six million Jews, two-thirds of the continent's Jewish population. Only Allied victory over Germany in World War II ended the slaughter. As we have discovered since, the Nazi racial extermination policy extended to the Gypsies of Europe, as many as half a million or more of whom were killed. Millions of other civilians marked as racial inferiors, as well as thousands of homosexuals and political enemies, also died in and out of the concentration camps. In all, eight million to nine million people perished as a result of the Nazis' slave labor and extermination policies. The crime was so immense that the lawyer Raphael Lemkin felt the need to coin a new word in 1944 to describe attempts to murder whole peoples or races: genocide.

Fifty years after the Holocaust's end, it haunts our vision of the present. Nazi genocide remains the yardstick by which modern examples of mass murder are measured. This is so in part because of the total number of people killed and because the Nazis emerged from a modern Western culture not unlike our own. In addition, the fate of the Jews has been a central theme of the dominant Christian religious vision of Europe and the Americas.

Perhaps most of all, the startling photographs and newsreels taken at the liberation of the camps in 1945 (and other images discovered later) marked a true loss of innocence for Western culture. Pictures of the Holocaust became icons of horror, standards against which to judge and through which to shape our sense of later scenes of mass deaths. Thus color videotape of starving human beings or mass graves in Bosnia or Rwanda seems to echo those permanently fixed black-and-white photos and newsreels taken in the Warsaw Ghetto, at some outdoor mass execution, or at the liberations: vacant, deep-set eyes staring through barbed wire; leathery corpses stacked, as it was said, "like cordwood"; a bulldozer pushing piles of bodies into a mass grave. Whatever the details of their individual histories, across the decades these images have merged into what has almost become a cliché: man's inhumanity to man.

The Holocaust's power to inform the present has moved beyond visual imagery. "Never again!"—a grim phrase heard first among Jewish survivors—has become a clarion call to the world to prevent future mass murder and genocide. The force of that declaration comes from the recognition that Hitler and the Nazis could not have carried out their genocidal policies without the fearful passivity, indifference, and outright support prevalent among Germans and citizens of occupied countries.

In recent years, scholars and writers of popular history have extended the accusation of indifference to the Allies themselves. While recognizing the military sacrifices of Britain and America that brought Nazi Germany to defeat, many argue that these countries could have more vigorously engaged in actions to rescue Jews and to destroy the means by which they were slaughtered. Indeed, the dominant image of the Allies' response to the slaughter of European Jewry today emphasizes inaction and even passive complicity.

The emergence of such a view in the late 1960s began a remarkable reversal of Allied reputation concerning Nazi genocide. This turnabout involved substantive questions of historical interpretation and moral expectation. It also illustrated the ways in which historical understandings evolve not only through new research discoveries but also through the passage of time, generations, and perspectives. Nor is it surprising that, most recently, some scholars have tried to move the debate full circle, returning to the view that little could have been done to save the Jews except to win the war.

My aim in this book is not to lead the reader to some final conclusion about America's moral responsibility in the Holocaust. Nor do I seek a final word on whether, realistically, the Allies could have done significantly more to end the killing of Jews while World War II raged. The historical record has supported several different interpretations, and some of the most important differences have arisen because of the varied philosophical assumptions writers have brought to the debate concerning the ways in which human beings and governments do or should function in the world.

Rather, I hope this book fulfills two purposes. First, through a set of documents from a variety of sources, it reveals how Americans came to view what we now call the Holocaust as it was unfolding from the early

1930s to the end of World War II in 1945. Represented are press accounts, editorials, personal letters, government reports, and other contemporaneous documents. They focus on three periods: the rise of Hitler (1932–1935), the crescendo of prewar persecution of the Jews (1935–1941), and the wartime grappling with the knowledge of the mass murder of Jews as it began to be revealed in 1942. These sources give the reader a vivid sense of history as it happened and illuminate some of the complexities of historical interpretation and moral judgment concerning this central tragedy of the twentieth century.

Second, the Epilogue tracks the changing views of historical reality and moral responsibility that have developed over the years since 1945. In this section, the contrasting approaches of historians are themselves placed in historical and cultural perspective. I hope not only to make sense of this remarkable evolution of views but also to provide a handy starting point for further reading.

PART ONE

The First Years of the Nazi Regime, 1933–1935

In the spring of 1933, with Hitler's coming to power, the Jewish community's thousand-year history in Germany began a precipitous decline toward extinction. Through legal means, the press, and extralegal force, the Nazis launched a ferocious attack on Jews and the Jewish community. It was a cruel and unexpected blow. German Jews had made themselves an integral part of German society and culture. Many had assimilated into German Christian culture, while others who still practiced their faith did so in a modernized form that symbolized their deep commitment to becoming a part of Germany proper. German Jews were innovators in both commerce and industry. Most visibly to the world, they were prominent far beyond their numbers in German science, philosophy, the arts, and popular culture.

These very achievements, however, made Jews suspect among Christian Germans. Not only were they viewed by many through the lens of traditional anti-Semitism, which highlighted the Jews as killers of Christ, "stiff-necked" holdouts against conversion, and ruthless financial parasites. Jews also were now seen as contributors to, or even architects of, a modernity that many conservative, traditional Germans believed was destroying all that was good in their culture. Thus, simultaneously, the

Jew could be seen as a threatening capitalist, a menacing radical, or a debauched and perverted modern artist or actor.

The appeal of such views intensified in the aftermath of World War I. The Treaty of Versailles had left Germany stripped of its former imperial glory and weighed down by reparations payments to the Allies. The immediate postwar years witnessed the forcible suppression of revolutionary movements on the left, as well as the formation of extreme and bitter nationalist movements on the right. Among the latter was the National Socialist, or Nazi, party and its leader Adolf Hitler. Even as a fledgling Weimar Republic experimented with democracy, the Nazis and others on the right flailed against those who, they argued, had stabbed Germany in the back by accepting a ruinous peace.

The problems of postwar recovery were magnified by a disastrous inflation in the early 1920s. The Nazis and other Germans blamed "Jewish bankers" for both the cause and an initially painful cure. In addition, a permissive "Weimar" culture centered in Berlin gave many Germans the feeling that society was out of control and headed toward moral disintegration. It did not help matters that some of the best-known (though hardly a majority) actors, writers, and musicians of this culture were Jews.

Nor did it help that the democracy put in place after the war had only shallow support among Germans, many of whom saw the Weimar Republic itself as the cause of instability. Parties on the left and right organized extramilitary forces even as they participated in the democracy. Chief among these were the Nazi and Communist parties.

The strong economic recovery of the late 1920s did not last long enough to bring true stability, and with the stock market crash of 1929 and the Great Depression that followed, Germany sank into economic and political chaos. Millions lost their jobs, and unemployment reached close to 50 percent of the workforce by 1932–33. The government was paralyzed. Nazis fought Communists in the streets and began to attack Jews, Jewish businesses, and synagogues with relative impunity. Nazi propaganda linked both greedy capitalism and communism with the Jews.

Most important, the once marginal Nazi party gained dramatic electoral support among those who feared communist revolution yet wanted unity, economic recovery, and renewal of national pride. In the mid-September elections of 1930, the Nazis garnered six million votes and 107 (up from 12) seats in the Reichstag, the German parliament. They were now the second most powerful political party in the nation. In the presidential election of June 1932, Hitler lost to the great war hero General Paul von Hindenburg but received 36 percent of the popular vote. In July 1932, the Nazis increased their seats in the Reichstag to 230. Although by the end of the year another election had reduced this number, the inability on the part of Social Democrats and Communists to agree on a coalition government allowed the center and right-wing parties to form a government. They agreed to appoint Hitler as chancellor, and the Nazi leader took office on January 30, 1933.

How much of a role did anti-Semitism play in Hitler's victory? Clearly, the Nazis gained prominence because they provided simple and compelling solutions to complex problems. Nazi propaganda braided typical anti-Semitic arguments—Jews as "un-German" racial outsiders, as heartless "international" financiers and businessmen, as perverted artists and writers, and as dangerous communist revolutionaries—into a single indictment that painted the Jew as one of Germany's principal enemies. Yet during the elections that led to his triumph, Hitler purposely toned down attacks on Jews and instead stressed anticommunism, national unity, and the need for strong leadership to meet the crisis at hand. He portrayed himself as a statesman and peacemaker, leaving brutality to the Nazi street fighters.

Once elected and in power, however, the Nazis wasted no time in implementing their ideology and turning the power of the state and their paramilitary organizations on their political enemies and the Jews.

The documents in this section reflect the discomfort Americans felt as they viewed the first major persecutions of German Jews. They tried desperately to make sense of events and to foresee the future. Within a decade, the Nazi war against the Jews spread as German armies conquered most of Europe and set in motion the final and most brutal chapters of what we now call the Holocaust. What in retrospect seems like a logical progression of events, however, was impossible to predict or even imagine in 1933.

AMERICAN JEWISH COMMITTEE

From *The Jews in Nazi Germany*

1933

The Jews in Nazi Germany was the first comprehensive attempt by Jewish or other groups to make Americans aware of the fate of Jews under Nazi rule and the reactions of various American officials, organizations, and newspapers. The American Jewish Committee, an organization created in the early part of the century to fight anti-Semitism, was in the forefront of efforts to inform the American public and leadership of the situation in Germany. Probably few in the general public read the report, but it contained information that was disseminated in bits and pieces by the press. It was also circulated in government circles.

The pamphlet provided a valuable and accurate history of the Nazi's anti-Jewish campaign, as well as important background concerning anti-Semitism and the status of Jews in Germany. Interestingly, although the American Jewish Committee forthrightly publicized Nazi brutality, it refused to join some other groups in a protest boycott of German goods. Its logic was that such a boycott might make matters worse for the Jews in Germany and that only more subtle diplomatic pressure might ease their fate.

The excerpts included here illustrate the breadth and intensity of the pressure put on German Jews in the first days of the Hitler regime, as well as the depth of information available at the time in the United States. We have no way to judge how the various readers of this report, Jews and non-Jews, felt about the American Jewish Committee as an unbiased source of information. Nor can we measure what importance individuals placed on these facts and stories, whether read in the report itself or in the daily newspapers. The spring of 1933, after all, was a tumultuous time in America. Americans were simultaneously in the depths of the Great Depression and anxiously following the round of New Deal executive orders and legislation that the new president, Franklin D. Roosevelt, was proposing to solve the economic and psychological crises of the nation.

American Jewish Committee, *The Jews in Nazi Germany: The Factual Record of Their Persecution by the National Socialists* (New York: American Jewish Committee, 1933), 1–2, 6, 8–31, 37–39, 41–49, 51–54.

What we can say is that Americans had information about the Nazis' initial actions against German Jews readily available.

THE OFFICIAL DECREES AND MEASURES AGAINST THE JEWS

This particular section of the report quotes some of the laws the Nazis passed that effectively stripped Jews of their ability to make a living as civil servants or professionals—doctors, lawyers, judges, and accountants. The new laws put strict limits as well on the education of Jews. These codes also contained the first attempts to define a "Jew" or "non-Aryan." Note the exceptions given to those who fought at the front in World War I or who lost a father in the war, an attempt to make such restrictions acceptable to those who knew "loyal" German Jews. Note as well the racial definition of "Jew," one that caught in its net many "Christian Jews" who had converted to Christianity or whose families had long been Christian. Such definitions meant that the laws had an impact on literally millions of Germans, not just the 600,000 Germans who identified themselves as Jews. Later laws would elaborate on distinctions to be made among such "non-Aryans."

Civil Service

... (Reichsgesetzblatt* Nr. 34). April 4th, 1933.

Par. 1— (1.) For the restoration of a nationally minded Regular Civil Service, ... there may be dismissed those who come under the following rules, even if, according to the general laws valid at present, there is no legal basis for such action: ...

Par. 3— (1.) Civil Servants of non-Aryan origin must retire; as regards the honorary officials they must be dismissed.

(2.) The above section does not apply to officials who were already employed as officers of the civil service on the 1st of August, 1914, or who, during the Great War, fought at the Front for Germany or her allies, or who lost their fathers or sons in the War. Further exceptions may be granted by the Minister of the Interior, in cooperation with the competent heads of specific Ministries, or by the States' authorities, regarding civil servants working abroad. ...

*Official Federal Law Gazette.

... (Reichsgesetzblatt Nr. 37). April 11th, 1933.

To Paragraph 3 of the above law:

1. Non-Aryan descent means descent from non-Aryan, and especially Jewish, parents or grandparents, even though only one of the parents or grandparents was of the Jewish religion.

2. If a civil servant was not already a civil servant on the 1st of August, 1914, he must prove that he is of Aryan descent, or that he fought at the Front in the War, or that he is the son or the father of a man killed during the War. . . .

3. If the Aryan descent is doubtful, an opinion must be requested from the authority on race questions (Sachverstaendiger fuer Rasseforschung) of the Ministry of the Interior.

No exception is granted to sons of War combatants in general. Only if the father was *killed* may the son be a civil servant. . . .

Education

... (Reichsgesetzblatt Nr. 43). April 26th, 1933.

Par. 4.—The number of non-Aryan Germans, within the meaning of the Law for the Restoration of the Regular Civil Service, who may be admitted to Schools, Colleges, and Universities, must not exceed a number proportionate to the Aryan students in each School, College, or University as the total number of non-Aryans in Germany is to the total population of Germany. *This proportion is fixed uniformly for the whole of the German Empire at 1.5 per cent.* If, in certain schools the number of non-Aryan Students has, in accordance with Law, to be reduced, the proportion of non-Aryans may be 5 per cent.

These rules do not apply in the cases of non-Aryans, whose fathers have fought during the War at the front for Germany or her Allies, or to children whose parents were married before the adoption of this Law if the father or mother or two of the grand-parents are of Aryan origin. The number of these students may not be included when calculating the quota of the non-Aryans. . . .

Medical Profession

... (Reichsgesetzblatt Nr. 42). April 25th, 1933.

Article 1.—The work of panel doctors of non-Aryan descent . . . must cease. Further admissions of such physicians as panel doctors in the national health insurance service is forbidden. . . .

> Article 2.—The registration . . . is permitted only if the physician is of German nationality and is of Aryan descent. . . . Non-Aryan descent does not cancel a doctor's registration, if that doctor has done military service during the War on the side of Germany or her allies, or if his father or sons have fallen in the War. . . .

EXECUTION OF DECREES

This section of the report documents the atmosphere in which such anti-Semitic laws were passed and carried out. Especially in the realm of education and scholarly life, Nazi sympathizers led the direct assault on Jewish intellectuals. Jews at the universities, students and professors alike, were physically attacked and books by Jews and other undesirable authors burned. Note that the excerpted news stories here, when not from German publications, are mostly from English newspapers. One may draw the inference that, in these earliest stages of the Nazi revolution, press coverage was more complete in England than in the United States.

In a public appeal dated Nuremberg, April 7, a group of Nazi physicians and lawyers in Bavaria favored the complete elimination of Jews from *all* the liberal professions. Similar appeals were made by many other groups during the month of April. On April 21, under the leadership of persons close to the Government, a demonstration took place in Munich at which Minister of Justice Frank and others voiced the same demand.

In the *Voelkischer Beobachter*[1] of March 23, 1933, the Union of National Socialist German physicians publishes an appeal to the entire body of German physicians as follows: "Purge the leadership of our organizations, wipe out everybody who will not understand the signs of the time! Make our profession in leadership and in spirit German again, just as the Reich and the people have become in recent weeks."

Before and especially following this appeal, many Jewish physicians were expelled from public health offices; these expulsions increased greatly in number following the publication of the Civil Service Law of April 7, 1933. . . .

In the *Voelkischer Beobachter* of April 22–23, 1933, under the headline "Against the un-German Spirit — Enlightenment Campaign of the German Student Body," there is published an official announcement of the head office for press and propaganda of the Deutsche Studentenschaft[2] of a

---

[1] Nazi party newspaper, literally, "National Observer."
[2] German student fraternity.

"campaign of the enlightenment" to last until May 10th. In the course of this announcement, twelve theses are set down, including the following:

4. Our most dangerous antagonists are the Jews and their satellites. . . .
7. We would respect the Jew as alien and we would treat our national being seriously. We therefore demand censorship to see to it that Jewish writings appear in Hebrew. When they are printed in German they are to be designated as translations. Emphatic measures shall be taken against the abuse of German script and type; these are for the use of Germans only. The un-German spirit shall be extirpated from the public libraries.
10. We demand . . . the will and ability to overcome Jewish intellectualism and the phenomena of liberal degeneration associated therewith.

This announcement also suggested the public burning of "un-German" books on May 10, as part of the campaign of enlightenment.

The following typical newspaper accounts illustrate the manner in which expulsions and degradation of Jews were accomplished: . . .

The Commissarial Mayor of Munich stated at a Nazi meeting that in future no municipal contracts or orders would be given to any Jewish or "Marxist" firms. The newly appointed commissarial head of the Munich municipal schools declared that from the beginning of next term "No Jewish child will be allowed to attend a Christian school," and that "Jewish school doctors" will no longer be "let loose on German children."

— *The London Times,* March 27, 1933

. . .

In Hessen an order has been issued that no newspaper shall employ "non-Germans" — that is to say, Jews. In Breslau, where the Storm Troop leader and reprieved murderer, Heines, is in control as chief of the police, an order has been issued that all Jews shall be deprived of their passports so that the passports can be made invalid for foreign travel.

— *Manchester Guardian,* March 31, 1933

. . .

While the Jewish business boycott is already being forgotten, the anti-Jewish campaign in other walks of life continues in full vigor. It is estimated that the clearance of Jews from the State service and public positions has been nearly completed. Thousands of Jewish lawyers, notaries, doctors, and dentists have been dislodged. Jewish professors and lecturers at the universities are likely to be entirely eliminated before the summer term begins. In big private undertakings, for instance the A.E.G.,[3] all Jewish employees have been given notice. The Nazi *Voelkischer Beobachter* reports that "the Jewish newspaper concern of Mosse has dismissed no less than 118 Jewish employees, secretaries, and typists." The *Berliner Tageblatt,* the best-known publication of this famous Jewish house, still bears the Mosse imprint on its front page, but its contents have been largely anti-Jewish."

— *The London Times,* April 6, 1933

. . .

In future books by Jewish authors written in Germany or abroad, will not be published in Germany. This action was decided upon at a meeting of the "Boersen Verein der deutschen Buchhaendler" (Association of German Booksellers*). A resolution adopted at the meeting states that "in view of the fact that German book sellers were always in the foremost ranks of the German course, the Verein now unanimously decides to join the National front without any opposition."

— *Berliner Tageblatt,* May 12, 1933

German Government authorities today initiated a move to do away with Jewish barbers. Measures were introduced under the heading of "hygienic control" giving Nazi commissars the power to shut down "undesirable shops." The Union of tobacco retailers resolved to prohibit Jews from selling cigars and cigarettes at retail.

— *Berliner Tageblatt,* May 14, 1933

The Town Council in Coburg has adopted a law to the effect that Jews may no longer use the municipal tramcars.

— *The London Times,* June 2, 1933

The German Red Cross will be completely "Aryanized" as a result of an agreement reached today between officials of this non-sectarian relief agency and representatives of the Ministry of the Interior.

All functionaries of the Red Cross and male and female nurses will be Aryans.

— *The New York Times,* June 10, 1933

---

[3] Literally, *Allgemeine Elektrizitäts-Gesellschaft,* one of the major electrical manufacturing companies in Germany, widely known for its consumer products.
*This Association includes all book publishing and selling firms.

This regulation is particularly significant as in Germany, all nurses in hospitals and in private practice are Red Cross nurses, with the exception of those who are members of Catholic religious orders.

THE EFFECT OF THE ANTI-JEWISH MEASURES

This section illustrates some of the difficulties that contemporaries had in discerning whether the anti-Jewish actions were a temporary nightmare or the prelude to more extreme measures. Both views are represented.

No reliable statistics are available as to the exact number of people affected by the various decrees and measures. However, it is a known fact that tens of thousands of Jewish professional men have been thrown out of their careers and are utterly unable to earn a livelihood, and that innumerable Jewish businessmen have been driven out of business and ruined.

One ghastly indication of this situation is the number of people driven to suicide. Although the German authorities make every effort to suppress authentic information regarding these suicides, by listing many of these deaths as accidental, by impounding cemetery statistics, by forbidding the publication of death notices, and by withholding information on missing persons whom they know to have committed suicide, the mere list of names which has been published in the American press is shocking by its length.

Exhaustion of resources and inability to make a living are constantly leading many more Jews who have been deprived of their livelihood to take the last desperate step. . . .

The utter inability to continue in their work or to make a living has compelled a number of German Jewish writers, doctors, musicians, businessmen, etc., to leave Germany and seek refuge abroad. In most of these cases this meant not only the abandonment of the homes and surroundings to which these people had become attached emotionally and by tradition, but also substantial material sacrifices. Many of those forced into exile who were formerly in comfortable circumstances have to build up a new existence. The number of those who had to flee from Germany in order to escape their worst fate is not definitely known. . . .

The apologists for the Hitler regime in Germany have been sedulously endeavoring to assure the American public that the position of the Jews in Germany is safe.

In contrast to the reassuring voices of Nazi sympathizers and apologists in this country, we quote the following paragraphs from an appeal issued by Michael Williams, editor of the *Commonweal,* a Catholic weekly review, published in New York. This appeal was sent by Mr. Williams to the League of Nations and to other bodies about May 21st, from Vienna, after an investigation in Germany. Mr. Williams said:

Between 200,000 and 300,000 Jews have been deprived of any hope of the future. The older Jews must live out their lives deprived of all rights of citizens as long as the present appalling dictatorship dominates Germany.

The situation of the Jews in Germany is deplorable beyond words. Israel in Germany is perishing under a yoke only comparable to that under which its forefathers groaned in Babylon and Egypt.

Don't be deceived by false denials concerning the persecution of Jews under the Hitlerite regime; guard against its paid and voluntary propaganda. Pay no heed to certain journalists who seem to learn only what the dictatorship desires them to believe.

Unless the present rulers of the great German people are cast aside by the civilized Germans they now oppress, Jews and Catholic Christians will be subjected to scandalous persecution. Plans for world dominance of the Nazi system are a menace to the institutions of free men of Europe and America.

What you will decide to do is your concern. Either harden your hearts and let the worst crime of our age proceed in the deliberate extinction of nearly 1,000,000 men, women, and children, or come quickly and strongly to the rescue.

Numerous statements have appeared lately in the American press to the effect that the German Government and the Nazi Party, were about to modify their anti-Jewish policy. The Berlin correspondent of *The New York Times* reported on May 16, 1933:

Private assurances such as have been received by interested Americans that the anti-Jewish governmental attitude has undergone or is about to undergo a radical modification cannot be confirmed officially. Specifically it has been reported to have been arranged here that ousted Jewish lawyers not included in the greatly restricted quota permitted to practice might continue their office work provided Christian colleagues appeared for them publicly.

Inquiry on this point at the Reich Ministry of the Interior, which is in charge of all racial questions, brought the response:

"We know nothing about any such change. It would be contrary to our policy and would cause further disturbances. The necessary decrees laws have been adopted. Nothing new is contemplated. . . ."

As to a reported promise to cease propaganda against Jewish mercantile houses, no further propaganda is needed. The establishment of Nazi shop cells has taken care of that situation.

ACTS OF VIOLENCE AGAINST JEWS SINCE HITLER BECAME CHANCELLOR

The following section of the American Jewish Committee report was crucial. Even at this early date, skeptics and those either sympathetic to the Nazis or hostile to the Jews claimed that, much like British propaganda against the Germans in World War I, what had been reported concerning Nazi actions against the Jews was exaggerated or fabricated. *The Jews in Nazi Germany* presented official and reliable press reports as rebuttals to such insinuations. For the modern reader, it provides a vivid sense of the brutality and thoroughness of the actions taken against the Jews this early in the Nazi regime. One also can see glimmers of speculation that what was transpiring might only be the beginning.

Official Corroboration of Excesses

Much has been said and written about the so-called "atrocity story campaign" against Germany since the Nazis came into power. Repeatedly, German Government officials, organizations, private individuals, and propagandists have made general denials or minimized the occurrence of violence. It was denied in particular that any acts of violence against the Jews had taken place. However, the German Government authorities themselves have made a number of admissions, though of course these admissions are made in very reluctant and guarded form. For instance, the fact that such acts of violence did occur is indicated in the opening paragraphs of Chancellor Hitler's rescript to his followers (March 12, 1933):

Unscrupulous individuals, especially Communist stool-pigeons, are endeavoring to compromise our party through isolated actions that have no connection with the great achievement of national rising and can only burden and disparage the accomplishments of the movement.

Further corroboration can be found in the telegram dispatched by the Hon. Cordell Hull, Secretary of State of the United States, to the President of the American Jewish Committee on March 26, 1933:

You will remember that at the time of your recent call at the Department I informed you that in view of numerous press statements indicating widespread mistreatment of the Jews in Germany I would request the American Embassy at Berlin in consultation with the principal consulates in Germany to investigate the situation, and submit a report. A reply has now been received indicating that whereas there was for a short time considerable physical mistreatment of Jews this phase may be considered virtually terminated. There was also some picketing of Jewish merchandising stores and instances of professional discrimination. These manifestations are viewed with serious concern by the German Government. Hitler in his capacity as leader of the Nazi party issued an order calling upon his followers to maintain law and order to avoid molesting foreigners, disrupting trade and to avoid the creation of possible embarrassing international incidents. Later von Papen[4] delivered a speech in Breslau in which he not only reiterated Hitler's appeals for discipline but adjured the victors of the last elections not to spoil their triumph by unworthy acts of revenge and violence which could only bring discredit upon the new regime in foreign countries. . . .

Press Reports of Terrorism

In order to discredit reports of acts of violence which have appeared in the American press, Nazi propagandists in this country and abroad have charged that many stories of American newspaper correspondents were grossly exaggerated and even contained fabrications.

No better refutation of these statements can be found than an article by Mr. Mark Etheridge which appeared in the Macon *Telegraph* on May 25, 1933. Mr. Etheridge was sent to Europe on a fellowship by the Oberlaender Trust for the express purpose of having American people know the truth about Germany. In presenting his article the editor reminds the readers that Mr. Etheridge before sailing "assumed the obligation to tell the truth, if he told anything, in accepting this fellowship." Mr. Etheridge writes:

> . . . Let me reaffirm what I have said before: it is my conviction that the stories which come to you through . . . (the accredited) . . . agencies, are true. I know the correspondents here in Germany. They are educated, responsible high-type men. Two of them have won the Pulitzer prize for the best foreign correspondence in the past two years. Another framed the code of ethics for journalists which was sanctioned at Geneva. Another was formerly acting managing editor of *The New York Times*. The press corps here is, upon the whole, a body of outstanding journalists who, because what they wrote was

---

[4]Franz von Papen (1879–1969), a conservative German politician who helped to engineer Hitler's appointment as chancellor and who himself became vice-chancellor in 1933. Later, he served as a diplomat under the Hitler regime.

being watched and criticized, have not only endeavoured to verify the minutest particular of what they wrote, but have leaned backward in reporting the truth. You may bank upon what you have read from them. . . . The head of the Associated Press bureau is Louis Lochner, a Phi Beta Kappa from, I believe, the University of Wisconsin. His wife is a German. Stresemann[5] was his closest friend in Germany and Bruening[6] was another close friend. He loves Germany; he likes the German people enormously. He has lived here 12 years. He knows Germany and Germany's reactions better than he knows the United States, because the states have changed so much since he left. You know how absurd it is for anybody to pretend that a man who enjoys in the newspaper world such a reputation of Lochner's is in the employ of the Communists or Socialists or anybody else except the Associated Press. You know, too, since you know A.P. men, how ridiculous it is for the German government to pretend that what he sends out is distorted. His professional reputation is at stake; his position is at stake; the integrity of the A.P. is at stake. The same thing goes for the United Press. I need only to tell you that the former head of the bureau here, who was a Jew, asked, at the inception of the present trouble, to be relieved so that the government could have no possible ground for saying that the dispatches of the United Press were biased. It strikes me that demonstrates a pretty high sense of honor, and so, I say, you may rely upon what you read in the American press about isolated instances.

On the nights of March 9th and 10th, bands of Nazis throughout Germany carried out wholesale raids to intimidate the opposition, particularly the Jews. As hundreds have sworn in affidavits, men and women were insulted, slapped, punched in the face, hit over the heads with blackjacks, dragged out of their homes in night clothes, and otherwise molested. Large numbers of Socialists and Communists were flung into prison including Reichstag Deputies, who were deprived of their parliamentary immunity, to make certain of their non-appearance at the Reichstag session. The arrest of innocent Jews was sanctioned as "protective jailing." . . . "You are taken off to jail and put to work in a concentration camp where you may stay a year without any charge being brought against you." Never have I seen law-abiding citizens living in such unholy fear.

—Edmund Taylor in the *Chicago Tribune*

[5]Gustav Stresemann (1878–1929), a German statesman who served as chancellor in 1923 and foreign minister from 1924–29, and is credited with normalizing his country's relationship with the rest of Europe. Stresemann won the Nobel Prize for Peace in 1926.

[6]Heinrich Bruening (1885–1970), a right-wing German politician who served as chancellor and foreign minister (1930–32). Bruening exiled himself from Germany in 1934 and eventually taught political science at Harvard University.

. . .

The anti-Semitic outrages of the last few weeks are far more horrible than could reasonably have been imagined at first. Nothing like them has been known in Germany for generations. . . .

They have not arisen out of any hostility the German workman or peasant might feel for the Jews; they are the outcome of anti-Semitic propaganda carried on year after year by the Nazis, who are a party of the middle class and have the support of bankers, industrialists, and business men. This party at its meetings and in its newspapers, books, and pamphlets has made the Jew appear loathsome and sinister in the eyes of its followers. The Nazi agitation has been one continual incitement to pogroms, and the chief inciter is Adolf Hitler, the German Chancellor. It is he and, next to him, Dr. Goebbels, Captain Goering, and the other members of the present German Government who are responsible for the outrages far more than the fanatic Brown Shirts who have done the bludgeoning, stabbing, and looting.

And while the German Government, its press, and its Ambassadors abroad deny what is known to every inquirer who is not blind to all evidence, they not only refrain from discouraging anti-Semitic emotion but are continually whipping it up afresh by making the Jews appear as though they were engaged in a conspiracy of false rumor against the Nazi Government and by condoning or spreading every report that could stimulate their followers to fresh hatred. At the present moment, for example, Nazis wearing the brown uniform are selling in the streets of Berlin a pamphlet entitled "The Jews Demand the Murder of Hitler." . . .

Jewish shops have been closed and raided, Jewish homes have been searched and thrown into disorder, and hundreds of Jews have been beaten and robbed. . . .

The Brown Shirts worked in gangs of five to thirty, the whole gang often assaulting one person. Many had the brassards worn by Nazis enrolled in the auxiliary police. . . .

—*Manchester Guardian,* March 27, 1933

. . . For years Nazi newspapers and orators have hammered into the impressionable youth of Germany that the Jews were traitors, were bloodsuckers, were poison. They were taught, literally, that the Jews were disease germs that had to be destroyed to save the Teutonic people from national death.

Not even in Czarist Russia, with its "pale," have the Jews been subject to a more violent campaign of murderous agitation than in Germany since the rise of National Socialism. Hardly an issue of the Nazi newspapers appeared without more or less open incitement to pogroms.

An indeterminate number of Jews have been killed. Hundreds of Jews have been beaten or tortured.

Thousands of Jews have fled.

Thousands of Jews have been, or will be, deprived of their livelihood.

All of Germany's 600,000 Jews are in terror.

From the masters of Germany's great banks and the wealthiest men down to the poorest peddler, all the Jews in Germany today are unsure of their safety. Some of them whistle in the dark. . . .

It is impossible to ascertain how many Jews have been killed. The newspapers are suppressed, the opposition is terrorized and the families of the victims would be the last to utter a protest.

It is only possible to estimate it in the vague term "hundreds" how many Jews have been beaten, tortured, and robbed. The only means of information is through personal knowledge, by word of mouth, and in those cases where the Jews are of foreign nationality and have complained to their consulate.

The foreign Jews whose consulates have protested to the Foreign Office of maltreatment and savage torture number around 150. The Polish Embassy alone had an imposing list of affidavits to submit to Herr Neurath.[7] They comprised more than 100 instances wherein Jews had been attacked in their homes or places of business, robbed at the point of revolvers, and taken to torture chambers where "men in the uniforms of storm troopers" have beaten them with leaden balls. Nine American Jews were beaten or otherwise maltreated. Altogether, since the native Jews outnumbered the foreigners by 100 to 1, it is conservative to estimate that during the first day of the terror "hundreds" of Jews were tortured.

It is unnecessary to catalog more than a few cases to give an idea of what the anti-Semitic terror is like. Names, in some cases, cannot be divulged. All cases cited here are either confirmed by personal investigation by the *Evening Post* correspondent or are citations from affidavits filed with foreign diplomatic representatives. I have seen fifty-seven such affidavits.

I sat beside the sickbed of a young Jewish matron who told me the following incident:

On March 14 — two days after the Hitler decree against terror — four men dressed in the uniforms of the storm troops broke into her

[7]Konstantin, Baron (Freiherr) von Neurath (1873–1956), was German foreign minister from 1932 to 1938 and held other posts under Hitler during the war. He was sentenced to fifteen years at the Nuremberg Trials and served eight before being released.

home as she was on her way out. They threw her into a corner and proceeded to demolish the apartment.

She cried: "But I am not a Communist!" They answered: "You're a Jew." Then one seized a knife, grabbed her arm, and gashed again and again at her wrist. She screamed, but he kept on cutting. Then they must have become frightened, for suddenly all four fled. . . .

One of the popular Nazi songs sings of "When Jewish blood drips from our long knives."

Typical of the honorable intentions of the assailants are the following: . . .

March 9, about 8 o'clock in the evening, twelve uniformed men broke into the dwelling of a Jew in the Grenadier Strasse, beat the Jew and his wife and son until they bled, and left with 3,200 marks, the life savings of the victim. . . .

March 15, about 10 o'clock in the evening uniformed men took four Jewish guests from the Cafe Englaender in the Schoenhauser Allee to a storm troop barracks in the Schilling Strasse, where 400 marks of theirs were confiscated. Their protocol reads: "They were beaten by the uniformed men with blackjacks until they were unconscious and when they revived they were forced to lick the blood from one another and from the table."

This last item should suffice. The protocols are sworn statements.

Let there be no mistake about it. If the mass of the German population, including millions of humane and intelligent persons who voted among the 17,500,000 for National Socialism, were informed of these barbarities, the revulsion here would be great. But the German population with no free press is for the most part in utter ignorance of what has occurred. . . .

—H. R. Knickerbocker
in the *New York Evening Post,* April 15, 1933

. . . Against the Brown Shirts there is no defence, and for the torture they inflict there is no redress. The victims are altogether helpless. The German Government knows exactly what is going on. It has received abundant evidence in the form of sworn statements, medical certificates, photographs, reports from witnesses it knows to be trustworthy, but it does not take the slightest notice. This, indeed, is not surprising, for the Brown Shirts are the political executive of that Government and override the police and the judiciary with the Government's full knowledge and consent.

. . . No policeman dare interfere with the Brown Shirts, even when they torture, kill, and rob.

—*Manchester Guardian,* April 20, 1933, "Berlin"

Letters from Germany

The American Jewish Committee is in possession of copies of many original letters received by Americans from relatives and friends in Germany. Some of these letters came direct from that country, others from places outside of Germany to which the writers fled as refugees. It has been impartially established that these letters are genuine, and that the writers truthfully described occurrences which came within their personal observation. Following is the translation of extracts from one of the most significant of these letters. It was received by a German woman whose trustworthiness and credibility are established. The events described in this letter took place in a South German locality between March 17 and April 29, that is, long after such acts of violence are supposed to have ceased. For obvious reasons, names of persons and places have been omitted.

. . . MAY 1, 1933.

All the indignities which I am writing down today have happened either to ourselves or to our friends. On Friday, March 17, 1933, at 2:30 P.M., . . . walked along . . . street in order to do some shopping; a civilian grabbed him from behind and threw him violently against the door of the "Brown House," the local Nazi headquarters. When . . . made an effort to resist, the man punched him in the face with both fists. Fortunately the police station was right across the street and a policeman intervened. Both men were taken to the station house and, of course, the assailant went scot free because he used the excuse that he had mistaken . . . for the . . . manager of the department store. . . . The next day the very same brute mistreated other respectable Jewish citizens in the same manner. Everyone knows that these people are under the protection of the Nazis and the more assaults they commit the higher their reputation as "patriotic heroes."

On Sunday, March 19th, I again accompanied my husband across the street and he owes it only to my presence on that occasion that he is still alive; he would have been beaten to death because the Nazis again "mistook" him for the department store manager. This, of course, is nothing but a cheap pretext, as everybody in town knows that this particular man fled abroad before the Hitler revolution.—The night after this happened I took a shawl and managed to smuggle my husband into his sister's house. He remained there for a few weeks, but then collapsed completely physically and mentally and thereupon I brought him back to our house. To this day he does not even dare to go outside his store to examine the display in his own window.

. . . was taken from his bed at 5 o'clock one morning and kept in jail for a week without ever being informed on what grounds he was being detained. After he had been home for a few days someone called on the telephone, instructing him to go immediately to the "Brown House" — which he did. After he arrived there, he was, first of all, forced to sign a paper stating that nothing had ever happened to him and then six uniformed Nazis dragged him into the cellar. He was forced to strip completely and then the six beat him up mercilessly with steel bludgeons. The brother of . . . received the same treatment and afterwards both men were locked up in the toilet. After they got out the doctors found forty bloody welts on the body of . . . and both have been in the hospital for the last four weeks; they must lie on their stomachs all the time because their backs are so frightfully lacerated that they simply must remain in this position. . . .

All the people who have been victims of this Nazi terror are highly respectable and honest citizens and certainly better Germans and more patriotic than these hoodlums. . . .

At . . . the Nazi terroristic activities were conducted with unspeakable savagery. On Saturday morning, at the time when the Jews were about to go to the synagogue, the Nazis forced their way into their houses and into the synagogue and arrested all of them. They were taken to jail, where they were horribly mistreated. At six o'clock in the evening, the order was given: "Get out for the Jewish parade." . . . was forced to head the procession and to carry the Soviet flag. In a public square where almost the entire population was assembled, the Jews were ordered: "Kneel down; get up"; "Kneel down; get up"; "Kneel down; get up" — Then they were forced to repeat in a chorus: "We are traitors; we have cheated the people; we must disappear from the face of the earth." Then the Soviet flag was torn into strips and the strips tied around the necks of some of the Jews. Two others had to stand on each side of these unfortunate men and hold up the ends of the torn flag. The Nazis then set fire to the strips, which the Jews had to hold until their hands were burned. After this had taken place, all the Jews were loaded on open trucks and had to stand up during the four hour drive to the . . . jail. When they arrived, the warden stated that never in his career had even the worst criminals been delivered to him in such a brutal manner. . . . had six holes in his head and fifty bloody welts on his body. The men were photographed in jail and I obtained a picture only under the most tremendous difficulties.

Here is a sample of how the minds of children are being poisoned: After the gym hour at the . . . school, the children sang the Horst Wessel song[8] (Wessel has been declared a saint by the Nazis) and a thirteen-year-old boy shouted: "Let's go after the Jews!" The children

[8]Horst Wessel (1907–30), a Nazi storm trooper and rowdy who was killed in a political street brawl. He was soon made a martyr and celebrated in the most popular Nazi anthem, the "Horst Wessel Lied."

... and ... were so terribly beaten up that they cried and sobbed for hours afterwards not only from physical pains but also because they were mortified that from now on they had to regard themselves as outcasts. When ... protested to the teacher, the latter said: "Well, that's the way it goes in life; the ones who are stronger are always right."

LETTERS OF THE AMERICAN FRIENDS SERVICE COMMITTEE

Some of the most compelling American eyewitness views from within Germany came from members of the American Friends Service Committee (AFSC), who had been working in Germany since the early 1920s. These Quakers, as members of the Society of Friends are more commonly called, acted within a long-standing tradition of social action and personal commitment, most notably as advocates of peace, abolition of slavery, and racial equality. They had established themselves in Berlin, Vienna, and Paris to provide relief services after World War I. Their presence and doctrines of peace and personal witness sparked the creation of small Quaker meetings (congregations) in Germany.

With the rise of Hitler, the Quaker meetings and the AFSC Center in Berlin offered secret aid to those opposed to or hounded by the regime, including its Jewish victims. As Christians and representatives of American and British agencies, they could negotiate with Nazi officials, albeit with only small success, on behalf of Jews who wished to leave Germany. This did not prevent the harassment and even arrest of some Quaker functionaries. Of course, when war finally came, the AFSC operation closed down.

The following selections reflect the variety of ways individuals read the whirl of events around them: with terror, disbelief, disgust, or sadness. In fact, the Quakers—both German and American—more than most around them were horrified by the treatment accorded the Jews. Especially fascinating are the ways in which the letter writers attempted to find analogies, contexts, comparisons, and "good news" to temper what seemed in other ways an unprecedented campaign of terror.

CLARENCE E. PICKETT

Letter to J. S. Conning

May 5, 1932

Clarence E. Pickett was the Executive Secretary of the AFSC, and as such the leading spokesperson for the organization in the United States. In this letter to one of the leaders of the Presbyterian Board of National Missions, Pickett describes a particular incident in September 1931 that brought home to Quakers in Berlin the danger and isolation in which German Jews lived even before Hitler's accession to power. It also illustrates a typical Quaker response both in terms of direct support of the victim and the search for roads to reconciliation. Note Pickett's account of the dismal response from German clergy when the AFSC solicited ideas to promote Christian-Jewish friendship.

Dr. J. S. Conning,
Board of National Missions,
Presbyterian Church in the U.S.A.,
156 Fifth Avenue,
New York, N.Y.

My dear Dr. Conning:

Mr. Errol T. Elliott, Secretary of the American Friends Board of Missions, tells me that you are interested in knowing something of the experience which German Jews have had with regard to the German-Jewish situation.

The story to which he refers is about as follows: On the Jewish New Year, last September, as a group of Jews came out of one of the synagogues in Berlin, they were set upon by Hitlerites, who beat them up pretty generally. The following Sunday, when our little Quaker group met, someone expressed deep regret and a sense of grief that such a thing could take place in Berlin, suggesting also that the Jewish friends should be told of this feeling. A letter was drafted after the meeting, expressing regret, penitence, and sympathy that such a thing could have taken place. It so touched the Jewish community in Berlin that the next Sunday the

Clarence E. Pickett, Letter to J. S. Conning, New York, May 5, 1932, *Archives of the Holocaust: An International Collection of Selected Documents,* vol. 2, ed. Jack Sutters (New York: Garland Publishing, 1990), 3.

meeting was crowded with Jews expressing appreciation. The matter was then taken up by the International group of Friends and 300 letters sent to German clergymen, telling them of the incident and asking for their views as to what might be done to reconcile the treatment of the Jews with the Christian spirit. Only seven replied and of these only one expressed regret.

This incident has dramatized for us the tremendous problem existing in Germany today and the danger in Hitler's power. In fact, their recent accessions to increased power in Prussia will probably intensify the problem. We are taking some measures in connection with German-Americans and German-American-Jews, which we hope may bear fruit.

I am glad to know of your interest in this question.

Very sincerely,

Clarence E. Pickett

RICHARD L. CARY

Letter to Clarence E. Pickett
June 28, 1932

This excerpt from a letter by Richard L. Cary of the Berlin AFSC office to Pickett reveals other possible ways of viewing the plight of German Jews in the early 1930s. Note especially the reasoning of some Friends who were reluctant to publicize the plight of Jews. Also notice the ways in which an analogy to the racial situation in the United States is used to gauge (in this case to diminish) the perceived importance of anti-Semitism in Germany.

. . . In the Berlin Meeting there has been a slight rumpus over the Jewish question, this time involving two of our members, but it has seemed to die down without leaving us any the worse. In fact, I think some of our Friends understand the position of Friends much better now than they did before. In this point I might say that several concerned Friends have expressed doubt as to the propriety of Carolena Wood's public discussion of the posi-

Richard L. Cary, Letter to Clarence E. Pickett, Berlin, June 28, 1932, *Archives of the Holocaust: An International Collection of Selected Documents,* vol. 2, ed. Jack Sutters (New York: Garland Publishing, 1990), 4–5.

tion of Jews in Germany. They say that they are afraid that American Friends will think that the Jews are opposed by not merely a violent group of Nazis, but by a very large portion of the German people. They say that the present tension in this respect is no more characteristic of Germany than the outbreak of the Ku-Klux-Klan was characteristic of the United States, and so on. I sympathise with this point of view, for I know that some Americans have a much blacker picture of the Jewish problem in Germany than is justified by the facts, distressing though they are.

CLARENCE E. PICKETT

Letter to Gilbert L. MacMaster
March 30 (typed April 3), 1933

Here Pickett writes to Gilbert MacMaster, a Quaker agent in Switzerland, of conversations he has had with Richard Cary, who returned to the United States from Berlin just as the Nazis took power. Of note are the ways in which Pickett perceived Quaker duty regarding the Jews and what actions to take; the German Friends Meeting, which might be endangered by the International Committee's speaking out against the government; and the comparison of the situation of the Jews to other minorities in other countries. The letter's reference to the depression and the Roosevelt administration's response to it also provides a bracing sense of what was happening in the United States at this time.

Gilbert L. MacMaster
208 Inzlingerstrasse
Basle-Riehen, Switzerland

Dear Gilbert:

Dick and Mary Cary are with us and have brought us much closer to Europe and especially to Germany. It is a fortunate time to have them here. There is a great drive on to protest against the persecutions of the

Clarence E. Pickett, Letter to Gilbert L. MacMaster, Basle-Riehen, Switzerland, Mar. 30 (typed Apr. 3), 1933, *Archives of the Holocaust: An International Collection of Selected Documents,* vol. 2, ed. Jack Sutters (New York: Garland Publishing, 1990), 11–12.

Jews and other minorities together with the suppression of free speech and freedom of the press. Richard and Mary feel great doubt about the advisability of these protests and apparently from the latest steps that have been taken by the Nazis their doubts are justified. It seems to be driving the party to more drastic action. A good many Friends feel that because we have a long-standing interest in and contact with Germans especially through the childfeeding that we have a special ground on which to base a statement of concern and love for the German people and desire that they may not resort to violence. However, we are complicated in that always by the fact that there is now a German Yearly Meeting. We do not want to involve them in unnecessary disfavor with the government. A sub-committee was appointed by the Service Committee to watch the situation, to weigh carefully any steps that we might take and to especially consider the German Yearly Meeting and German Friends with regard to anything we might do.

Your letter reminds me that, after all, the persecutions which are endured by Jews in Germany are probably slight as compared with the persecutions of minorities in a good many countries that have been going on for a long time in Europe and we have made little protest. Should we definitely head more toward a vigorous and active concern with regard to those who are imprisoned and are being persecuted for conscience sake? Are we too much concerned to do the thing that is easy and that is easily approved of by governments? One puzzles and wonders. At any rate, it seems to be quite clear that the first thing we all are being compelled to learn is that peace with our own souls and our own smaller groups, family, Meeting, community, and elsewhere, and basing judgments of people on the sacredness of human personality, are perhaps the surest ground on which we can always rest.

Here in America the banking holiday has passed and the money situation seems somewhat eased. A number of banks will never open again. In some communities where large quantities of real estate mortgages were held which have now so much depreciated in value that they are almost worthless, there is very great loss of money and property. Furthermore, the business situation, from the point of view of employment, carloadings, consummation of power, etc., is worse rather than better since the holiday. The stock market has dropped back to where it was before the holiday. All predictions seem to indicate that it will be some months before there is any appreciable upturn. The longer the depression continues, the more one feels that it is going to work in our political and economic structure radical changes. Every day the American government gets deeper and deeper into the control and subsidy of business. We have not turned socialist in theory, but in practice we have made long strides in the direction of what might be called State Capitalism.

Sincerely thine,
[Clarence E. Pickett]
Executive Secretary

RICHARD L. CARY

Letter to Clarence E. Pickett

July 23, 1933

This extraordinary letter tries to assess the German situation on a multitude of levels, from the global to the most personal. Note the way in which Cary attempts to understand the fate of the Jews by analogy with other historical situations, as well as his opinion that things are getting better. Cary thus held the common view that the brutality of the early days of the regime would be supplanted by more moderate behavior. His reasons for thinking this way — sensitivity to outside views, influence of more responsible individuals, a reduction in arrests and public violence — were espoused by many people in the United States. Note his optimism concerning the growth of Quaker Student Clubs, which he saw as a sign of the waning power of the Nazis in the schools and the return of reason and morality. Even many German Jews felt that the worst was behind them by the end of 1933. Cary also indicates his belief, one held by many Germans and Americans, that the Jews themselves were partly to blame for their fate at the hands of the Nazis.

Cary's mention of concentration camps deserves special notice. He refers to those set up quickly in 1933 and 1934 to house political prisoners as well as Jews and Gypsies. Most of these camps were dismantled after a year or two, although one, Dachau, remained in operation until the end of World War II. These early camps were known for the inmates' hard labor, as well as for the Nazis' cruel and unpredictable punishment. Some inmates were killed and others eventually released, and the closing of most of the camps appeared as one more sign of a perceived moderation of Nazi policy. However, beginning in 1937, the Nazis set up an ever-widening system of camps for the dual purpose of slave labor and special punishment. This led in turn, beginning in 1942, to the organization of extermination camps in Poland, where the mass murder of Jews and Gypsies would be carried out.

Richard L. Cary, Letter to Clarence E. Pickett, Gilgen, Austria, July 23, 1933, *Archives of the Holocaust: An International Collection of Selected Documents,* vol. 2, ed. Jack Sutters (New York: Garland Publishing, 1990), 32–34.

Dear Clarence:

I am spending a week here, after visiting Friends in Prague and Vienna, and shall go from here with Mary to the German Y.M., and so back to Berlin. I now have a chance to write you without restraint, and if I make some denunciation comment, please do not refer to it in your letters to Germany!

Actually, the comment on Germany must now be milder. I have heard no accounts or even rumors of brutality during the past month or six weeks. There was much of it during March and April. A serious exception, of which you have read, is the series of several murders which followed the killing of an S.A. man in Kopinick, a suburb of Berlin, by a young Socialist during a search of his house. The young man and his father and mother are all dead (his father perhaps a suicide) and Dr. Schilling, Socialist leader in that district, was also murdered. The affair was analogous to our lynchings after a crime of violence, designed to intimidate the Socialists. Of the same type—this time official—is the arrest of five of Scheidemann's[1] relatives to prevent him from writing hostile articles abroad.

But this mixture of violence and barbarism is not so evident as it was, and the general trend of events is toward good order. There will never be peace while Hitler holds to his obsession that no one must criticise his policies or the Nazi behavior, for even in Italy, long organized on the same program, there is hidden apprehension, and Hitler, like Mussolini, lacks Roosevelt's ability to engage in radical action without suppressing his opponents. Roosevelt's success in converting the country and carrying it with him is regrettably unique.

Well that is the background against which things are happening. The treatment of the Jews is in complete accord with it and is, in fact, almost exactly the same as the treatment of German civilians in the United States and England during the war. We beat some of them, we put them in concentration camps, we boycotted their shops, we eliminated them from teaching and, partly, the professions, we requestrated their possessions. The status of the Jews will improve slowly but they will never obtain justice, just as Germans who suffered in 1914–18 have never obtained justice.

What to do? I suppose we must persevere and not lose heart. The economic crisis has aroused fears and hatreds more oppressive than those of the war. We had to stop fighting before we could regain our senses. Now we must regain economic peace to the same end. While the crisis endures,

[1]Phillipp Scheidemann (1865–1939), a founder and first chancellor of the Weimar Republic. A Social Democrat, he fled Germany upon Hitler's assumption of power in 1933.

I feel somewhat as a Chinese might have felt in the United States during the war, if he had tried to appeal to the finer instincts of Americans in order to reconcile them with the German civilians. Such is our detachment from the struggling forces, our vague knowledge of the emotions at work!

But we have, of course, been busy. Visitors come in, foreigners as well as Germans. I have had chances to speak and shall have more. Corder has had several talks with Lord Noel Buxton, who wants Friends to visit the Concentration Camps. This seems to me most unlikely of fulfillment, but, of course, I have only a vague notion of what Buxton really found out. More interesting in this connection is the general movement toward milder treatment. The camps are becoming better organized, a chief difficulty being that the inmates have nothing to do. Prisoners are being kept for shorter and shorter periods.

The tendency of the government, too, seems toward the Right, at least for the present. Just after I left Berlin, a general board of control for industrial activity was appointed and its membership is almost entirely from Big Business—Bosch, Thyssen, Krupp, and Simens are typical members. This means that the government recognizes the point of view of the industrialists, and they know how much Germany needs a better reputation abroad. To gain this reputation, the Jews must be treated more fairly and the Concentration Camps must be abolished. —German exports during the first six months of this year were shockingly low. —This is one part of the story. The other part is that the unemployed are bitter. Whether they approve of putting Big Business in command is a question which may become important next winter when people are hungry and cold. Do not forget that taxes are falling off and the government is almost bankrupt, so that unemployment relief will be inadequate.

Just how to describe the German Friends in this situation, I don't know. They are all bearing the all-important testimony [that] the hatreds and the fears of today are groundless and evil, and are to be remembered abroad as among the most sincere of our membership in the world. I think particularly of Manfred Pollatz and Gerhard Ockel (the latter most a member). Manfred has done a good deal to help people in his neighborhood by inquiring of the police why arrests have been made and has defended the Jews in season and often out. Mary has doubtless written of her visit to his home in Guben, and I found during mine how he is conducting a campaign within the medical society of his neighborhood (he is an M.D.) to restore equal rights to Jewish physicians. (He has won no great victories, but the effort is fine.) Gerhard and Olga Halle in Berlin are fine, too. Gerhard wanted to protest on his genealogical report (all officials and quasi-officials must declare themselves Aryan or non-Aryan!) that he, although Aryan, could not approve the elimination of the Jews. But we talked it all over with him and he refrained. He will not dodge his duty as he sees it and has told his chief and his associates how he feels. A noble soul. Poor Hans Albrecht's wife is almost distracted with anxiety and Hans has a most unhappy time of it. Fortunately, Etta is made of fine stuff and supports her father bravely. —One of the most helpful events was Barrow Cadbury's gift, a few weeks ago, of £500 for the Pyrmont Meeting House. They now need only a thousand dollars more to put everything in fine shape, including the cemetery. The money that the English Friends have sent is a convincing proof of their affection and concern, and has been valuable beyond its financial significance. —Wilhelm Hubben has his visa, or rather the assurance from Consul Davis in London (whom I know) that he will get it. He too has been true blue. —Herta Kraus is in good shape according to last reports. She will go to New York in September, I believe. She fights against it, but she has a streak of intolerance which warps her judgment of the Nazi movement. In fact, the only Jew I know who manages to be fair is Martin Fuchs, whom Carolena M. Wood knows. Of course the Jews are not to be blamed for their resentment, but neither can they be approved. They are helping to perpetuate the hostility from which they suffer.

A sign of the times is the growth of our Student Clubs in Berlin. The membership of all three has about doubled, presumably because of what Friends represent. Politics as such is mentioned only occasionally, but there is also an absence of the stereotyped propaganda from which most gatherings now suffer. A chief reason for the interest of the students, perhaps 150 altogether, is Doris Handley's fine spirit. She has fought hard for constructive tolerance, no, she hasn't fought, but has kept her peace. Just now the future is uncertain for, as you may have heard, she fell ill with pneumonia a few weeks ago and I learned yesterday that she must spend some three or four months fighting T.B. All this, I feel sure, is a direct result of her unremitting devotion during the past six months, during the worst of which she was practically alone. She is now in a good sanitarium and about two weeks from now we shall review her case to see whether she is making satisfactory progress.

I expect more sanity from now on. Dodd[2] is said to be a good man, willing to come to Germany only because he was assured that the Jewish problem is not to grow worse, but will be handled more mildly. I have a letter from Douglas Waples about him and shall get in touch with him on my return. I do not mean that we shall all be happier as we become saner, for the economic situation is frightful; but Germany seems to be looking facts in the face and abandoning its attempt to cure itself by emotional outbursts.

Needless to say, we do not consist of bad Nazis and good "others." The Nazis are as diverse and deserve as much sympathy as the rest. It will be

[2]William E. Dodd (1869–1940), American ambassador to Germany from 1933 to 1938.

a bad winter, perhaps, but not merely for Germany. All Europe is affected, as the London Conference[3] and its callous statesmen showed. So the Friendly ideal of friendliness still remains as necessary as it is untried. There's where we try to come in.

Richard L. Cary

THE ANTI-NAZI BOYCOTT

One option open to Americans horrified by events in Germany was to boycott German goods, and a small number of organizations participated in such a campaign in 1933. The boycott intensified in the late 1930s, as anti-Jewish policy in Germany stiffened and World War II approached. In both Britain and the United States, however, a debate ensued as to the wisdom of a boycott. Those in favor, including such major organizations as the American Jewish Congress and the Jewish Labor Committee, saw the boycott of German goods as a way to have a direct impact on German affairs as well as to keep the plight of German Jews on the minds of most Americans. Those opposed, which included the American Jewish Committee and the B'nai B'rith, a Jewish fraternal organization, argued that quiet diplomacy would be far more effective in curbing Nazi zeal than actions that might, so they thought, inspire even more brutal measures and coalesce German public opinion against the Jews. Even reports from German Jews were mixed, at least in the beginning. Many thought a boycott would blunt the perceived trend toward moderation detected in Nazi Jewish policy in 1934.

The following documents illustrate the nature of the boycott and the tone of advocacy.

---

[3]Meetings held in 1930 to work out limitations on the construction of warships and the rules of submarine warfare.

G. E. HARRIMAN

Anti-Nazi Boycott Circular Letter

1933

THE BOYCOTT IS THE MORAL SUBSTITUTE FOR WAR

NON-SECTARIAN ANTI-NAZI LEAGUE
TO CHAMPION HUMAN RIGHTS, Inc.
20 WEST 47th STREET, NEW YORK

Dear Student:

BELIEVE IT OR NOT—All German instruments and supplies can be replaced, in most instances with American products!

In making your purchases, beware of importations from NAZI GERMANY.

If your college or university supply house cannot furnish you with NON-GERMAN merchandise which will meet your requirement, get in touch immediately with this organization. Watch out particularly for the following categories:

DRAWING INSTRUMENTS AND SUPPLIES:
Compasses, thumbtacks, T-square, drawing boards, paper, and pencils
ARTISTS MATERIALS AND SUPPLIES:
Paints, brushes, pencils, easels, crockery, etc.
SCIENTIFIC & CALCULATING INSTRUMENTS:
Scales, slide rules, thermometers, surveying and engineers' instruments, electrical measuring instruments, etc.
CHEMICALS & LABORATORY SUPPLIES:
Chemicals and colors; glassware; steel, rubber, and porcelain instruments
NOVELTIES: Souvenirs, Party goods, etc.

MEDICINAL, SURGICAL, AND DENTAL SUPPLIES:
Drugs; steel, glass, and rubber instruments of all kinds
MUSICAL SUPPLIES:
Harmonicas, string instruments, wind instruments, strings, reeds, mutes, rosin, etc.
SPORTING GOODS:
Cameras, pistols, rifles, fencing equipment, fishing tackle
WEARING APPAREL:
Fabric gloves, etc.

Should you have any reason for suspecting the origin of specific items which are offered, or if you desire further information, we shall be glad to assist you.

Very truly yours,

G. E. Harriman
Executive Secretary

NAZI GERMANY IS THE ENEMY OF CIVILIZATION   REFUSE TO TRADE WITH THE ENEMY

G. E. Harriman, Circular Letter of the Non-Sectarian Anti-Nazi League to Champion Human Rights, New York, 1933, in *Archives of the Holocaust, An International Collection of Selected Documents: Columbia University Library, New York, The Non-Sectarian League to Champion Human Rights Papers; The Non-Sectarian Anti-Nazi League Pamphlet Collection,* Volume 6, ed. Karen J. Greenberg (New York: Garland Publishing, 1990), 4.

JEWISH LABOR COMMITTEE

Anti-Nazi Poster

1934

Despite efforts of the Jewish Labor Committee and other labor, Jewish, and Christian organizations, a strong boycott of German goods never materialized in the 1930s.

Robert F. Wagner Labor Archives, New York University.

MAINSTREAM VIEWS

In the 1930s and 1940s, the *Christian Century* was at the time the most important and influential nondenominational Protestant journal in America, reaching thousands of lay readers each month. It focused on religious issues within the broadest context of church, national, and world affairs. In 1933 and thereafter, it periodically concerned itself with Hitler's rise and the persecution of the Jews. The following two selections reflect both shock at events in Germany and attempts to understand Nazi policy in relation to American culture and to other contemporary events. Knowing in retrospect that the early persecutions led inexorably to the gas chambers at Auschwitz, we can read such articles as naive and almost apologetic. Nonetheless, they amply illustrate a number of common American understandings of the Nazi campaign against the Jews.

ROBERT E. ASHER

A Jew Protests against Protesters
Christian Century, April 12, 1933

On April 1, 1933, the Nazi government and its extralegal, brown-shirted storm troopers boycotted Jewish businesses, attacked Jews in the street, and painted anti-Semitic slogans on walls and streets all over Germany. The following article appeared almost immediately after these actions. Robert E. Asher, self-identified as "a German-American Jew" and later in life a distinguished social scientist, analyzed the causes of German anti-Semitism, the course of the Nazi revolution, and similar discrimination in the United States. His article echoes views commonly held by Americans during the turbulent first years of Hitler's rule.

Note especially his comparison between German anti-Semitism and

Robert E. Asher, "A Jew Protests against Protesters," *Christian Century,* Apr. 12, 1933, 492–94.

American treatment of blacks and Asians, as well as his disdain for those who decried discrimination selectively. From what we now know about both the Holocaust as it developed and the history of racism in America, how well does his argument stand up?

I am a German-American Jew. I have countless relatives and many Jewish friends living in Germany today. Two years ago, as a student at the University of Berlin, I was hooted at by boisterous Nazis, and had I been more foolhardy might have come off with a hiding instead of a hooting. At a café in Weimar a friendly headwaiter once advised me to leave immediately, if I wished to avoid trouble with the mustard shirts. I have as much reason to oppose Hitler and everything for which he stands as any American.

And yet I am convinced that Americans protesting present conditions in Germany are working up a great deal of well intended, but irrational, misdirected and too long delayed resentment. As usual in times of great social distress, clear thinking is impossible; emotions guide our actions. Suddenly we are shocked and sickened. Why? Because, after loading an intolerable burden upon backs that were already broken, after failing to give wholehearted support to any of the real statesmen which post-war Germany produced, we are amazed to see the people turn in desperation to a transparent demagogue who promises them a Germany which will dominate instead of being dominated. We listen complacently for two and a half years to the demagogue's party as it threatens drastic measures. How can we be outraged when those threats are systematically carried out?

We have allowed, nay helped, the clock to be set back, not to 1914, but to 1830 or 1848. A tremendous revolution has taken place—incidentally with less violence and less loss of life than almost any other similar revolution. Now, when it is over, we begin trying excitedly to prevent it. Unfortunately it is too late.

The whole world is to blame. Innocent and guilty alike must suffer now. Moreover, the innocent are not 100 per cent blameless, either. Many of the German Jews themselves helped appreciably to prepare the way for the revolution. The well-to-do Jews, of whom there were a great many in Germany, were so capitalistically inclined that they lent their support to reactionary parties, parties which depended for their success upon distinctions between classes. Perhaps these people were merely trying to prove that they were German. But in so doing, they deserted the only groups that were striving for a classless society. The comparatively well-to-do Jews never fully recognized that their hope in post-war Germany lay in supporting the social democratic party. Now they are suffering for it, out of all proportion to their sin, it is true, but not entirely unallied to it. The poor Jews never had anything anyhow and will therefore suffer no more than before. Their misery will be due to the tribulations of poverty rather than to those of prejudice.

Both groups failed to concern themselves sufficiently with an anti-Semitism that has been growing ever since the war, Hitler or no Hitler. It has been due in part to the increasing percentage of prominent Jews; whenever a particular group grows disproportionately conspicuous, suspicion and envy are aroused. More especially, it has been due to the huge influx of Russian and Polish orthodox Jews, who by insisting upon particular foods, easily-recognized costumes, and Saturday as a holiday, do set themselves off as aliens.

Governmental Precedents

As a readily distinguishable alien group, they are unique in Germany. In America there are people who look more foreign than the Jew. There are Negroes, Japanese, and Chinese. In Germany there are not. The Nazi government has drastically restricted the participation of this alien group. It has in effect reverted to the pre-war days of a "staatsreligion" and made Christianity a condition of citizenship. However, we in this land also recognize the right of a government to limit the privileges of specific groups. We have anti-Japanese legislation, severe penalties for those who refuse to bear arms for their country, and Jim Crow laws. Who shall say that Jews in Germany must be given full freedom while Negroes, Japanese, and pacifists are discriminated against in America?

In Germany, which lacks our traditions of democracy, civil rights are more generally recognized as something bestowed by and in the hands of the government. In America we refer to these rights as "inalienable." Throughout our history we have made more of civil liberties—theoretically at least—than the Germans. Actually, we use some of the same restrictions the Nazis are using. Hitler's policies of limiting Jewish participation in national life to the percentage of the total population which the Jews represent will not become written law. As unwritten law, it is also practiced by American finishing schools and eastern universities. Total exclusion of Jews from certain hotels, societies, and business concerns, from fraternities and clubs, is generally known. We limit not merely the freedom of the Jews, but still more obviously the freedom of the Negro. And, since the problem is a human one, cultural differences are irrelevant, and the German can claim just as much right to his conduct as we do (which is indeed, no ethical right at all).

Civil Rights

In Germany Jewish doctors are being excluded from responsible positions in hospitals. Here we have practically the same situation, but unofficial and in existence for so long that Jews have gone ahead and established their own hospitals. Jewish school teachers have always been rare in Germany. Now, however, they are officially excluded, while over here, on the other hand, they are gradually breaking through. Jews in Germany are at present excluded from political office. In the United States politics has never had the same honorable standing and high-class Jews have seldom gone into it.

Hitler is completely eliminating communists, socialists, and Jews from positions of any influence whatsoever. Although American liberals and idealists refuse to grant that when a revolution, or even a significant political change, takes place, it is sound tactics to clean out all opposition; nevertheless history proves too well the necessity for this type of political realism, whether morally right or wrong. If the socialist government in Germany had not left so many of the old regime in responsible positions, they might still be in office.

Let us take a very mild example from American history. In 1824 President John Quincy Adams, against the advice of Clay and his followers, failed to clean house completely. He left political opponents in office and during his entire term they were conniving against him. He was defeated for reelection by hard-boiled Andrew Jackson who introduced the notion of "to the victor belong the spoils," with the result that he served eight years and named his successor, Van Buren. Which, you can argue, may have been worse for America. But as far as political tactics are concerned, it was certainly the more expedient move. Hitler, we know, is a politician, not a humanitarian.

Both American Jews and Gentiles misunderstand a part of the entire question. The Americans take it to be a question purely of religion, of mere freedom of worship. They do not doubt that the American Jew is an American. But to the Nazis it is a problem of race. They consider the Jews a foreign group who persist in maintaining their foreign-ness. They have no objection, for example, to Catholics, because they still regard the Catholic as a German, but they do point, with considerable evidence to substantiate their contention, to the orthodox Jew as an alien.

What Jews Have the Right to Protest?

Much of the worldwide protest, then, has been unreasoning emotion. The 60,000 "liberty-loving" Jews who gathered at a monster mass-meeting in New York because they were Jews and their brethren in Germany have been terrorized did not ipso facto have the right to protest. All Zionists among them, of course, had a clear right. For the Zionists recognize the racial as well as the religious identity of the Jews. But those Jews in this country who have tolerated the treaty of Versailles, stood for the collection of reparations, and advocated a high protective tariff are partially responsible for the conditions leading to the very crisis against which they are protesting. Neither can those Jews who countenance our reign of terror in the mine area (which is as real as any Nazi terror), whose blood does not boil at news of every lynching, who fail to protest against the hideous brutality of the American police, who are loud in support of what are essentially fascist measures — neither can they demand that their voices now be heard.

Furthermore, to be consistent even today, those Jews must do what they have not yet done: protest with equal vigor against the Nazi oppression of socialists and communists. Twenty centuries should be enough to prove the utter futility of Jewish persecution, which only cements the solidarity of the irrationally oppressed. Hitler's hatred of Marxism is just as great as his hatred of Judaism and his determination to exterminate it just as unshaken. From the point of view of further world progress, it may even prove to be the more significant and more tragic aspect of his program. Yet in America we are ignoring Hitler's persecution of the Marxists, neglecting to give it publicity because we ourselves have so little sympathy for them.

Legitimate Protest

Legitimate protests must embrace all of the Hitler injustices. They should be on a really broad humanitarian and historic basis. We may and must protest vehemently, here and abroad, against the "stifling of culturally valuable groups," against dictatorship (even this dictatorship of the majority), reversions to medieval barbarity, cold and systematic cruelty, and restrictions of religion and occupation. There is reason enough for protest. But in voicing our condemnation, we must have clearly in mind the grounds on which we are protesting and must not allow sensational news dispatches to blind us to equally great injustices much closer to home, or to the dangers of strengthening the forces of reaction by hysterical deeds.

Our cry must be a cry not alone against Hitler, but against the world that produces a Hitler. Against human folly and stupidity, against the ostrich mentality which prevents us from foreseeing a disaster until it has overwhelmed us, against the inertia which so invariably hinders collective action until it is too late for that action to be effective — against these, must we direct our protests.

Mass Meeting Protests Hitler's Anti-Jewish Program
Christian Century, April 26, 1933

In a short note, the editors of the *Christian Century* reported on a meeting at New York's Carnegie Hall jointly sponsored by Christian and Jewish organizations, one in which rabbis and ministers decried Hitler's actions against the Jews. Such public meetings were common in this era of economic and social crises. More noteworthy was the response of the *Christian Century*'s editors, who endorsed the spirit of the meeting but felt certain that Hitler must have had some reason beyond prejudice for instituting his anti-Semitic policies. This view was a common anti-Semitic distortion.

Carnegie hall could not contain half the people who sought to attend the protest meeting. Hundreds, maybe thousands, stood out in the plaza and shouted as the loud-speakers brought to them the speeches from inside the hall. Rabbi Goldenson made an effective address and Col. Harden Church evoked much applause by his remarks. May we ask if Hitler's attitude may be somewhat governed by the fact that too many Jews, at least in Germany, are radical, too many are communists? May that have any bearing on the situation? There must be some reason other than race or creed—just what is that reason? It is always well to try to understand.

"Mass Meeting Protests Hitler's Anti-Jewish Program," *Christian Century,* Apr. 26, 1933, 574.

WALTER LIPPMANN

Hitler's Speech

Los Angeles Times, May 19, 1933

The famous and influential columnist Walter Lippmann brought to the chaos of 1933 his own Olympian view of things. Reacting favorably to an eloquent address by Hitler that seemed to pave the way for moderation inside Germany and peace with its neighbors, Lippmann counseled moderation and understanding as Americans considered the events in Germany. Note his manner of dealing with the anti-Jewish actions of the Nazis, both in assigning blame and comparing these atrocities to those in other countries. He makes somewhat of the same argument as Robert Asher (see pages 36–40), though with considerably less passion. Note that, like Asher, Lippmann was a German-Jewish American. Unlike Asher, however, Lippmann's ambivalence about that identity led him to hide it in his public persona and reject it in his private life.

It was evident from the first impression of Herr Hitler's speech that he had chosen the path opened to him by President Roosevelt, and that the immediate crisis had, therefore, been surmounted. A close reading of the full English text of the address is even more reassuring. In so far as words can bind the actions of a people, the Chancellor went further than anyone had dared to hope in offering specific guarantees that he did not wish to disturb the peace. Not only was he definitely reassuring on those very points which are at the root of the European political disorder, but in the manner which he employed to present the German case. No fair-minded person can fail to recognize that the bitter truculence of the Nazi propaganda was singularly lacking and that Herr Hitler remained strictly within the limits of honest indignation at the injustices and humiliation to which Germany has been subjected.

The specific assurances are to be found in his discussion of the problem of the frontiers. Thus, after saying that Versailles had failed to find a solution of the eastern boundaries which "met Poland's understandable claims just the same as Germany's natural rights," the Chancellor stated that "nevertheless no German government will of its own volition break

Walter Lippmann, "Hitler's Speech," *Los Angeles Times,* May 19, 1933.

an agreement that cannot be abrogated except by substituting a better one. However, this acknowledgment of the legal character of such a treaty can only be a general one. Not only the victor has claims to the rights granted therein, but also the vanquished. The right to demand revision of this treaty, however, is founded on the treaty itself. As the motif and measure of its demand, Germany desires nothing but the experiences thus far attained, and the undeniable findings of logical, critical reason." Unless I am greatly mistaken this is the most definite pledge that has yet been given by any German government that it would pursue its claim for revision within the framework of the Covenant of the League of Nations. For it is in the Covenant, most particularly in Article XIX, that the right of the "vanquished" to appeal to the "findings of logical, critical reason" is stipulated.

This pledge as to the territorial ambitions of Germany was supplemented by a specific offer, which is certainly of the utmost importance. This was in the Chancellor's emphasis on that part of the MacDonald plan, which is also a fundamental requirement of the French plan, that armaments should be subjected to international supervision. What is important here is that he offered, provided other nations took a similar position, to submit not only the German army to international supervision, but all the semimilitary and semiofficial organizations, such as the Nazi storm troops and the steel helmets. That such supervision of all kinds of actual and potential military force is fundamental to any kind of disarmament by treaty has long been evident to those who have worked on the problem. The Chancellor's willingness to submit the whole German military power to international inspection is, therefore, as definite an evidence of good faith as it was in his power to offer the world.

For the address itself, both as to its substance and its manner, there must be a very high degree of general approval. The difficulty, which will cause the world to be reserved in its judgment, will come from trying to reconcile it with the Nazi propaganda, with Herr Hitler's own speeches in the past, with the recent speeches of some of his own ministers, with the ruthless injustice of the treatment meted out to the German Jews, with the violence of the attack, as symbolized by the burning of the books, upon the spirit of peace and international comity. How does one reconcile this genuinely statesmanlike address with official words and official actions that have caused consternation throughout the civilized world?

There will be some who will say that the address is merely a shrewd maneuver and that it must be rejected as insincere. I do not take this view. The truer explanation, I believe, is that we have heard once more through the fog and the din, the hysteria and the animal passions of a great revolution the authentic voice of a genuinely civilized people. I am not only willing to believe that, but it seems to me that all historical experience compels one to believe it. The idea that any people is intrinsically outcast has no foundation except in ignorance and cupidity. It was an intolerable idea when it was applied to the German nation and written into the Treaty of Versailles, and it is an intolerable idea when it is applied now by the Germans themselves to an integral part of their own nation. To deny today that Germany can speak as a civilized power because uncivilized things are being said and done in Germany, is in itself a deep form of intolerance: Like all intolerance it betrays a lack of moral wisdom, in this case the moral wisdom of religious insight into the dual nature of man.

Those who have that wisdom will pass judgment upon the actions of men, but never upon their whole natures. Who that has studied history, and cares for the truth would judge the French people by what went on during the terror? Or the British people by what happened in Ireland? Or the American people by the hideous record of lynchings? Or the Catholic church by the Catholic church of the Spanish Inquisition? Or Protestantism by the Ku Klux Klan or the Jews by their parvenus? Who then shall judge finally the Germans by the frightfulness of war times and of the present revolution? If a people is to be judged solely by its crimes and its sins all the peoples of this planet are utterly damned. Such judgments can produce only the deepest kind of anarchy. The civilized judgment on which depends all the possibilities of a decent human life, requires that men, while condemning and resisting evil deeds, should be unfaltering in their faith in and their response to the healing impulses of their fellowmen.

So the outer world will do well to accept the evidence of German good will, and seek by all possible means to meet it and to justify it. Herr Hitler has said that "the generation of this young Germany, which in its life hitherto came to know only the distress, misery, and woe of its own people, has suffered too tremendously under the madness of our time to intend to inflict the same upon others."

It is the intention of the young Germany, which Adolf Hitler leads, that has troubled mankind as the German Chancellor must know from the reports of every honest German diplomat and emissary in the outer world. He will find that the further he can go to prove that it is not the intention of young Germany to inflict upon others the misery and humiliation it has suffered, the greater will be Germany's dignity and power in the council of nations. For the world, and most certainly the American part of it, desires neither that Germany should be morally isolated or politically encircled or economically destroyed, and every interest of the American nation is to prevent that from happening. This is not 1914. As world power is now distributed Germany can become isolated or encircled only in so far as she rejects the common standards of civilized men and by deliberate injustice or calculated violence cuts herself off from the confidence of mankind.

PERSONAL AMERICAN PRESS REPORTS FROM HITLER'S GERMANY

The following articles indicate the ambiguities inherent in day-to-day reporting out of Germany. These reports aptly reflect splits in the Nazi party itself over policy concerning the Jews and confused assessments of the future.

Editor Holds Riots Inspired by Nazis
New York Times, July 26, 1935

The *New York Times* interviewed Varian Fry, a critic and editor of the literary magazine *Living Age,* upon his return from a tour of Hitler's Germany. To get the inside story on an anti-Jewish riot in Berlin, Fry had called upon a German American Harvard classmate, Ernst "Putzi" Hanfstaengl, who was Hitler's press adviser. The chat with Hanfstaengl revealed not only the Nazis' tactics to win support for their anti-Semitic policies but also various splits in the Nazi movement. Try to imagine how a reader in 1935 might have assessed the information in this article, only further complicated by a personal denial of the story by Hanfstaengl that appeared in the *Times* on July 28, 1935.

The anti-Jewish rioting in Berlin's fashionable Kurfuerstendamm early last week was thoroughly planned by the Nazi party, according to Varian Fry, editor of *Living Age,* who returned yesterday from the scene of the rioting on the North German Lloyd liner Bremen.

Mr. Fry, who went to Germany to study the people and get a firsthand knowledge of what was going on, declared that he received from Dr. Ernst Franz Sedgwick Hanfstaengl, Reichsfuehrer Adolf Hitler's press adviser, an admission that the supposed Jewish patrons who hissed a Swedish film — the hissing on which the subsequent events were officially blamed — were not Jews at all but Storm Troopers.

"Editor Holds Riots Inspired by Nazis," *New York Times,* July 26, 1935.

"Dr. Hanfstaengl told me many things and asked me not to mention some of them, but he did not give me this information in confidence, and I see no reason why I should not tell you," said Mr. Fry. "The original hissing took place on Friday, three days before the Monday rioting, which I witnessed. Dr. Hanfstaengl said he had reliable information that those who did the hissing were Storm Troopers."

Mr. Fry explained that in the 4 P.M. edition of the Angriff on the Monday of the riot attention was called to the "behavior of the Jews," and the German people were urged to "show the Jews a hard hand." Three hours later the rioters, who later dragged patrons out of cafés and beat them, began to gather before the theatre.

Mr. Fry said he was finishing dinner at 9 P.M. when he heard of the rioting, and he immediately went to the scene. He said there were at least 500 youths, each wearing a white shirt, and there were several hundred Brown Shirts who directed the activities. These men, unmistakable in their uniforms, would come together in a huddle, he added, and, after a whispered conference, would separate, crying, "When Jewish blood spurts around the knife, then everything will be fine in Germany." By-standers, including many fashionably gowned women, aided the white-shirted attackers by pointing out any one who appeared to be a Jew.

"There were literally hundreds of policemen standing around," he continued, "but I did not see them do anything but protect certain cafés which I was told were owned by Nazis. And once I saw two of them lead a man with a spurting wound in the back of his head around the corner to a small station. They made no attempt to halt the rioting. With all the policemen on hand and the Storm Troopers and the organized youths who did the work, there is no question that it was all planned deliberately."

On the day after the rioting, said Mr. Fry, he strolled along the street and saw many stickers pasted on walls, posts, and lampposts, depicting a caricatured Jew with captions. He pulled two of them off, and two policemen who saw him took him into custody and questioned him in the lobby of the theatre around which the trouble revolved. They asked him why he took down the posters and Mr. Fry said he wanted them for souvenirs. The policemen, he said, patiently explained that the stickers were "party propaganda" and that in removing one he was frustrating the program.

He replied that he thought the stickers were circulated by the newspaper Stuermer and inquired if "the rioting last night" had also been a party affair. The policemen replied in the affirmative, he asserted.

Mr. Fry said that in his talk with Mr. Hanfstaengl he was told that there were two anti-Semitic groups, one the radical section that desired to solve the Jewish question with bloodshed and the other a moderate group that wished to segregate the Jews by law into a specified area.

Mr. Hanfstaengl also told him, he added, that Reichsfuehrer Hitler was suffering considerable embarrassment and trouble because of certain men in his party who had helped him rise to power but who now were not only useless but were hindering the party's progress.

Mr. Fry, who lives in New York, said he talked with many Germans during the weeks he toured Germany and found "an amazing amount of outspoken criticism."

REVEREND L. M. BIRKHEAD

Nazis Ask World to Combat Jews

New York Times, July 28, 1935

The *New York Times* picked up this striking story from the Associated Press, which meant that it was available to virtually all newspapers in America. Reverend L. M. Birkhead, an American Unitarian minister, sought out the Nazi Jew-baiter Julius Streicher while on a fact-finding visit to Germany, Italy, and the Soviet Union. He was struck by the reach and extremism of the Nazi anti-Semitic program, even encountering a British fascist and anti-Semite visitor while he was in Streicher's office. Most of all, note Streicher's revelation to Birkhead that a secret network of anti-Jewish groups and publishers existed in America. As we shall see in later selections, anti-Jewish feeling in America existed across society and expressed itself in various forms.

The Nazi anti-Semites, under the leadership of Julius Streicher, now in the midst of a violent campaign to eliminate Jews from Germany's cultural and political life, have started plans to anti-Semitize the world and spread the poison of hatred against Jews everywhere.

I made this discovery while visiting Nuremberg, where I sought an interview with Streicher. After insisting for several hours that I should see him and question him regarding the anti-Jewish campaign, I was sent to the "secret

Reverend L. M. Birkhead, "Nazis Ask World to Combat Jews," *New York Times,* July 28, 1935.

office" maintained by Streicher and his violently anti-Jewish newspaper, *Der Stuermer,* where foreigners with proper anti-Semitic credentials are received.

I found this office about three blocks from the Stuermer's quarters. Over the entrance was the legend "Fencing School." I was greeted with the question: "How did you get into this secret office to which only properly credentialed persons are admitted?"

Why Streicher should maintain a secret office is a mystery to me, for he had been one of the boldest and most uncompromising leaders. After explaining I wanted to know the whys and wherefores of Streicher's anti-Jewish drive, I was informed this so-called secret office of Streicher's was operated by Paul Wurm and that he was in touch with anti-Semitism throughout the world. His concern is not the German-Jewish situation, which is only incidental.

This office, I learned, is maintained to promote anti-Jewish hatred in every land.

I asked numerous questions about Streicher's life, character, and further plans. Then the files, which hitherto curtains had concealed, were exposed. I was shown books, papers, pamphlets, cartoons, and clippings from anti-Jewish agitators in all major countries.

In other words, the office was an anti-Semite clearing house to which they have sent fulminations which Streicher has filed handily for his own use and where they also display them to foreigners with the idea of encouraging them to engage in anti-Jewish activities. There seems to be frequent and regular correspondence between Streicher and anti-Semites everywhere.

A representative of the English Imperial Fascist League, which represents the British "racial Fascists," seems to be on the friendliest terms with Streicher and is frequently in counsel with him.

"Wurm," said Streicher's English friend, "hand this man our circular entitled 'Britons Awake and Oppose the Jewish Stranglehold.' "

A circular was immediately produced from the files which line the walls. Furthermore, I learned more about anti-Semitism in the secret office than I had learned through a careful study through newspapers, magazines, books, and interviews in the United States.

I had come to Nuremberg to discover there were anti-Jewish groups and leaders in America about whom the American public does not know and American anti-Semites who hope through Streicher's help and inspiration to duplicate his plans and technique in the United States.

I received the address of a publishing company in Chicago, where I was told copies of "The Protocols of the Elders of Zion" could be procured. I was shown copies of such American publications as "The Cause of Anti-Judaism in the United States," "Secret World Government," "The Red Network," and "Jews Must Live."

As an example of Streicher's connections, I discovered he had anti-Jewish papers and pamphlets from as far distant as Wichita, Kan.

Streicher's representative informed me that, as an American, I should know "President Roosevelt's government is completely Jewish." To establish this dominant Jewish character of the Roosevelt government, an American pamphlet was brought from the files purporting to list the Jews and Jewish-dominated Gentiles connected with the administration.

The terror which has been practiced against German Jews should be carried throughout the world, Streicher insists. Moreover, evidence indicates Streicher is providing the anti-Semites of other countries with German anti-Jewish technique.

I protested to Streicher's representative:

"But if you drive the Jews from every country, including Palestine, where shall the Jews go to find peace?"

"That isn't our problem," Wurm replied. "That's the Jews' problem."

PART TWO

Exclusion, Emigration, and War, 1935–1941

The Nazis' shocking treatment of German Jews continued to mount as the 1930s progressed. Mocking the hopes of those who imagined the early outbreaks of violence to be an aberration, the Nazis became even more violent as the decade proceeded. Americans, of course, anxiously monitored the entire range of developments in Europe, of which the fate of German Jews was but one aspect. Germany's territorial designs, political repression in the Soviet Union, Italy's invasion of Ethiopia, the Spanish civil war, and political instability in France all threatened peace and, depending on one's political outlook, argued for a more active American role in foreign affairs or a more extreme version of isolationism.

Most Americans, however, looked upon Nazism as a misfortune for Germany and the world. Whether as a brutal dictatorship or a threat to peace in Europe, it hardly fit basic American notions of government or society. Even so, the fact that the world remained in the midst of a dire economic depression made some features of the Nazi revolution attractive. Just as some Americans on the political left admired the perceived accomplishments of Stalin's brutal rule in the Soviet Union, some conservative Americans marveled at Hitler's ability to galvanize German society, to revive its economy, and to renew its sense of national pride. And some excused Hitler's rearmament plans as necessary for self-defense. They also looked upon Nazi Germany as a bulwark against the Soviet

Union and international communism. For these Americans, the treatment of German Jews seemed an explainable, if unfortunate, side effect.

In any case, a majority of Americans in the 1930s perceived Jews in their midst with varying degrees of fear and mistrust. They were "different" and a potential threat to what most assumed was an intrinsically Christian nation. Traditional themes of anti-Semitism—the Jew as Christ killer, stiff-necked resister to Christian conversion, ruthless businessman, or worse—inevitably tainted the culture. Such a mood became especially prevalent in the aftermath of the great immigrations of the 1890s and early 1900s. Millions of Eastern and Central European Jews, among millions of others from those same areas in Europe, entered the country and soon began to have an impact on every aspect of American life. Anti-immigrant sentiment combined with traditional anti-Semitism and modern racial forms of anti-Jewish ideology (theories based on genetic differences) to produce virulent strains of anti-Semitism during periods of social and economic stress such as World War I, the 1920s, and the Great Depression.

One paradoxical goad to seeing Jews as a problem was that these new immigrant Jews rapidly achieved prominence in highly visible areas, whether as merchants, writers, or leaders in the music and movie industry. Others became leaders in the new union movements and in such radical organizations as the Communist party. The discomfort that many Christian Americans felt concerning the new, mainly urban and cosmopolitan environment of the early twentieth century often found an apt symbol in "the Jew." Extreme and widely circulated anti-Semitic tracts solidified these fears. Worried that the very essence of Western civilization would be destroyed by a worldwide Jewish conspiracy, the auto manufacturer Henry Ford wrote *The International Jew* and used his own prodigious financial resources to distribute his and other anti-Semitic tracts. By the 1930s, demagogues, including the popular radio priest Father Coughlin (see pages 77–82), as well as the German-American Bund and other fascist organizations, fanned the flames of anti-Semitism. Some of these groups had direct ties with Nazi Germany and mixed imported propaganda with homegrown hate sheets. Outbreaks of violence against individual Jews, as well as desecration of synagogues and Jewish places of business, occurred across the nation.

Anti-Semitism infected more than the margins of American society. In the 1920s, Harvard and other academic institutions placed quotas on

Jewish admissions. Job discrimination and exclusion existed at all levels of the economy, as did discrimination in housing and public accommodations. Cultural tensions in the 1920s and the crisis of the Great Depression in the 1930s created an atmosphere in which Jews as a group were blamed for a variety of social and economic problems and Jews as individuals were caricatured with an array of unflattering images. Thus, in the cultural mainstream, whether in popular books and magazines or in politics, a "question" arose concerning the place of Jews in America.

This controversial place of Jews (as well as the legalized segregation of African Americans) inevitably informed reactions to the fate of German Jews in the middle to late 1930s. American views of the so-called Nuremberg Laws of 1935, which drastically circumscribed the limits of Jewish participation in German society, were relatively mild because of the common use of racial categorization and suspicion of Jews in the United States. The Nuremberg Laws defined the status of Jews racially rather than religiously, a full Jew being someone with at least three "racially" Jewish grandparents. So-called mixed Jews, or *mischlinge,* had at least one Jewish grandparent. That anyone fitting these categories had converted to Christianity or rejected his or her Jewish identity did not matter. Legally, these individuals were Jews. This meant that they could not marry or have sexual intercourse with non-Jews and they could not hire non-Jewish women under the age of forty-five as household servants. Other parts of the laws stripped Jews of most rights of German citizenship and strengthened earlier restrictions on education and employment opportunities. These codes proved to be a quantum leap toward the destruction of German Jewry. Yet many Americans saw them instead as a step toward stabilizing the legal status of Jews and a "solution" to the "Jewish problem," much as many white Americans saw Jim Crow laws in the United States as a solution to the "Negro problem."

This view found additional support when, in 1936, Germany hosted the Olympics in Berlin. The site had been selected before the Nazi takeover, and anti-Nazi groups all over Europe protested the Olympic Committee's plans to allow the games to go on under the Nazis. As part of a propaganda barrage to counter such protests, the Nazis removed anti-Semitic propaganda and other signs of the anti-Jewish campaign from Berlin just before the Olympics. They also allowed Jewish athletes from outside Germany to compete and cynically announced the possibility of German Jewish participation, even though the Nazis had excluded Jews from using the athletic clubs necessary for Olympic training.

A number of American newspapers, organizations, and individuals (Jews and Christians alike) forthrightly called for an Olympic boycott. They argued that Nazi racial ideology mocked the international spirit of the games. Interestingly, African American leaders were largely in favor of going to Berlin. They argued that the extraordinary array of black talent on the American team would be the best reply to Hitler's racial notions and that bringing back medals would aid the cause of civil rights at home. Most Americans simply wanted the games to proceed. Many thought that politics should be kept out of athletics or chose to see the Olympic pause in overt Nazi anti-Semitism as a sign of the future.

Such optimism turned out to be unwarranted. The anti-Jewish campaigns resumed after the Olympics and reached another peak in 1938. On the evening of November 9–10, 1938, *Kristallnacht* (literally, "night of crystal," more meaningfully translated as "night of broken glass"), whatever illusions Americans retained as to the fate of Germany's Jews were shattered. In a coordinated campaign of violence, Nazi thugs in and out of party uniform raped, maimed, and killed Jews; set fire to synagogues and places of business; and humiliated Jews in every way possible. Between *Kristallnacht* and the end of the year, the Nazis sent thirty thousand Jewish men to concentration camps, confiscated masses of Jewish property, and totally banned Jewish participation in the German economy.

Kristallnacht also convinced German Jews that no hope remained. Most now attempted to emigrate. This in turn created a refugee crisis of unprecedented proportions. At a moment when most countries in Europe and the Americas were still suffering from high unemployment rates, hundreds of thousands of German Jews hoped to gain admission as immigrants. Between 1933 and 1938, thousands had left Germany for the United States, France, Britain, Palestine, and various countries in Latin America and Africa. The sudden and massive demand for visas made immigration and resettlement an issue in the West in the years 1938 and 1939. Virtually every country, including the United States, enforced strict limits on numbers of immigrants. During this period, thousands emigrated, but thousands more could not escape for lack of entry visas to other countries. The onset of World War II in early September 1939 effectively sealed the fate of the German (and Austrian) Jews who remained.

Although the Roosevelt administration was sympathetic to the plight of the émigrés, it saw much political danger in opening the immigration door very wide given the depression and rising anti-Semitism. Roosevelt did convene a conference at Evian, France, to discuss the refugee crisis, but the attending countries, including the United States, budged little on their immigration quotas. The failure of American policy in this regard was dramatized by the fate of the refugee ship *St. Louis,* which was refused entry into U.S. ports after having been turned away in Havana, Cuba.

The outbreak of World War II in 1939 brought renewed attention to American Jews. It amplified suspicions and outright anti-Semitism. Those who wished to keep America out of the war joined with blatant anti-Semites in spreading charges of "Jewish influence" to enter the fight against Hitler. Yet the period also witnessed widespread calls for tolerance from Christian America. Those of a more pluralistic bent and those who had been increasingly alerted to the Nazi threat defended Jews in the name of American democracy. Between September 1, 1939, and the attack on Pearl Harbor on December 7, 1941, the issues of Nazi anti-Semitism and the Jewish presence in America became increasingly intertwined.

The following selections illustrate some of the ways Americans viewed the events of the 1930s and early 1940s. They provide a broad cross section of ideas, opinions, and factual knowledge available to Americans as the United States moved toward war and the Nazis began the annihilation of Jews across Europe.

Germany: Hitler Decrees Swastika Reich Flag; Bars Intermarriage; Relegates Jews to Dark Ages

Newsweek, September 21, 1935

The passage of the Nuremberg Laws in September 1935 marked a major turning point in the Nazi campaign against German Jews by decreeing their legal exclusion from citizenship, which later led to their expulsion and extermination. Yet many American reports underestimated the significance of what was transpiring or emphasized more colorful developments at the Nuremberg rally and meetings that promulgated the laws.

"Germany: Hitler Decrees Swastika Reich Flag; Bars Intermarriage; Relegates Jews to Dark Ages," *Newsweek,* Sept. 21, 1935, 12–13.

In the fall of 1935, the big story from Europe was Mussolini's threatened (and later successfully executed) war to conquer Ethiopia.

Newsweek's coverage of the Nuremberg Laws and the annual Nazi meeting there illustrates the texture of much American reportage. In the September 21, 1935, issue, Ethiopia headlined the news, while the following article functioned more as a feature story. Note the placement of the sections on the anti-Jewish laws. Note also the tone of humorous contempt that dominates the article.

If P. T. Barnum could have seen the show he probably would have called himself a piker. The Nazi political circus played to a visible audience of 700,000 and broadcast its acts to a nation of 66,000,000.

Party leaders billed their third annual convention last week as the "Congress of Freedom," signifying Germany's freedom to rearm by conscription. Advance agents had worked out every detail of the seven-day stand.

Acres of red Swastika flags brightened Nuremberg's musty old buildings. Tents covered surrounding fields. In the great Luitpold arena, rows of pegs marked positions for Nazi units in review.

Parade

Some 500,000 people marched in the parade to Luitpold Hall. Nazi officials accounted for 150,000 of the total. The city's streets swarmed with brown-shirted Storm Troops, black-uniformed Hitler Guards, bare-kneed, khaki-clad Hitler Youth. White poles along the route flaunted the varicolored medieval banners of every city in the Reich. Ancient embroidered heralds and lions looked down on the mighty demonstration of Germany's resurgence.

Its Leader, in plain brown uniform and Sam Browne belt, rode in his 250-horsepower Mercedes, saluting the cheering thousands. Shortly before 6 P.M. he arrived before the huge green bulk of Luitpold Hall.

Big Top

He walked into a glass-roofed auditorium adorned with red bunting and silver and gold eagles. He took his place on the platform beneath a 50-foot Swastika. Thirty thousand of his followers crowded into the oblong building. The rest milled around loudspeakers outside.

In accordance with Nazi custom, Hitler delegated Adolf Wagner, husky Interior Minister of Bavaria, to read his proclamation. Nazis waited tensely for the pronouncement on party policy.

Extremists heard opinions that pleased them. Hitler catalogued enemies of the Nazi State under three classifications: "Jewish Marxism and its related parliamentary democracy; the politically and morally corrupt Catholic Centrists (a party he dissolved); and certain incorrigibly and stupidly reactionary bourgeois elements."

Eight times he assailed Jews, invariably linking them with Communists. Pointedly he rebuked Dr. Hjalmar Schacht, Economics Minister, who wants to soft-pedal Jew-baiting. "Certain circles . . . may entertain the thought that just as former States with their normal apparatus were unable to cope with Jewish problems so also the present State should capitulate before them. . . . That is the gravest mistake."

He warned Catholics to keep out of politics. He cautioned businessmen against trying to raise prices. At the same time he announced bluntly that low-paid German workers could expect no immediate raises.

His most triumphant passages concerned the new army. "Our nation tasted for fifteen years the experience of being at the mercy of every one of good will or ill will. Where are Wilson's fourteen points? . . . We see in our army a shield that protects our peace and labor."

Sideshows

The star of the big top also stole most of the sideshows. At the city hall, decorated by Albrecht Duerer,[1] Hitler received a 4-foot gold-hilted sword, copy of a 17th century heirloom. He reviewed gray-uniformed troops who presented arms, and green-clad labor service members who presented glistening spades. He told 50,000 women their place was in the home—and made them like it. He alarmed his bodyguards by walking into crowds and shaking hands with admirers.

In a speech to 50,000 Hitler Youth representatives he flung a warning to foreign nations. "We will not cross anybody's path, but let others leave us alone." The noise of 150 small, swift tanks clanking over the city's cobblestones emphasized his point.

Only one Nazi performer ventured to present a sideshow of his own. Julius Streicher, editor of *Der Stuermer* (The Stormer) opened a "chamber of horrors" ridiculing Jewish art and culture, and got out a special edition filled with lurid accounts of murders charged to Jews. The bald Jew-baiter, apparently in high favor, delivered the opening address of welcome. Germans wondered whether he had anything to do with Education Minister Bernhard Rust's order the day before. Rust decreed segregation in special schools for Jewish children between 6 and 14. The ruling becomes effective next Easter.

---

[1]Duerer (1471–1528) is generally considered to be the greatest German artist of the Renaissance.

Added Attraction

The day after Hitler issued his proclamation he ordered the Reichstag to meet in Nuremberg on Sunday to hear another.

Nazi press headquarters announced he would call on Britain, France, Italy, and Japan to enforce the Memel statute. Lithuania tore Memel's 943 square miles out of Germany's side in 1923. The big powers permitted her to keep it, but in 1924 they forced Lithuanians to grant the German population local autonomy. Since then, Germans maintain, Lithuanians have persistently evaded the agreement. The bitter row threatens to flare into a Baltic war.

A few hours after the press headquarters announcement, Hitler changed his mind—no mention of Nazi foreign policy. Instead some spokesmen predicted he would designate the Swastika banner Germany's official flag. This would constitute his answer to Communist desecration of the liner Bremen's Swastika in New York last July and to Magistrate Louis Brodsky's denunciation of Nazis Sept. 6.

Diplomats didn't wait for him to change his mind again. Britain, France, and Italy promptly warned Lithuania to respect her pledges. They demanded assurance Germans would have full liberty to vote in the Memel general elections Sept. 29. Two days later Antanas Smetona, Lithuania's scholarly President, promised a fair ballot.

Meanwhile Cordell Hull, American Secretary of State, also beat Hitler to it. In reply to a Nazi protest against Brodsky's remarks he told Dr. Rudolf Leitner, German Embassy counselor, that they did not appear "a relevant or legitimate part of (Brodsky's) judicial decision." He expressed regret for the incident.

Ringmaster

Sunday, the Reichstag convened. The Dictator addressed his 600 puppet legislators in a voice weakened by the strain of convention oratory. He emphasized Germany's "great unshakable love for peace."

At Lithuania, however, he looked with "uneasiness." Memel, he announced flatly, was "stolen . . . and the robbery legalized by the League of Nations."

Then he announced three new laws. The first established the Swastika flag as Germany's official emblem, abolishing the old imperial black, white, and red. The second restricts Reich citizenship to those of German or racially related blood who earn the right to the honor. The last forbids marriages or extra-marital relations between Jews and German citizens on pain of imprisonment. Jews may not display the German flag or engage "Aryan" feminine domestics under 45 years of age.

The brown-shirted Reichstag members leaped to their feet to approve all three unanimously.

German Jews, reduced to the status of disfranchised "State members," faced a medieval future. Only after centuries of oppression did they achieve full-fledged citizenship in 1869. But most feudal barons, who persecuted their religion rather than their race, winked at marriages between Christians and baptized Jews.

Germany: Jews Begin to Feel a Soft Spot in the Iron Heel

Newsweek, September 28, 1935

The follow-up piece in the September 28, 1935, issue of *Newsweek* further puts into doubt the significance of the laws by highlighting countervailing sentiment among the Nazis themselves. Note that *Newsweek*'s editors chose to emphasize the "soft spot" of the story in the headline despite the fact that the report itself had at least as much bad news as good for Germany's Jews.

Flags fluttering on German ships throughout the world last week symbolized a Dictator's latest move to unify a nation. Masts flaunted the new national flag—a black swastika against a white circle on a field of red, instead of the striped Imperial banner.

In German cities Jews brooded about other edicts passed at the Nazi party convention a week earlier. What future could they expect as disfranchised "State members" forbidden to marry or consort with "Aryans"?

The Black Corps, journal of the Black Shirt Special Guards, spoke sharply.

It may be expected that now the Jewish boycott propaganda against German goods will be increased. An attempt to bring about modification (of anti-Semitic laws) through economic pressure failed once.

The Fuehrer left no doubt in his speech before the Reichstag that in case the new law should provoke dissatisfaction there would be no recourse but to resort to additional far-reaching and drastic measures. The Jews had better take these words as a warning.

Nazi labor leaders in Berlin department stores started a movement to ease Jews out. They informed owners that workers were passing the hat to buy the establishments.

Yet the Nazi organization for trade and industry appealed to members to patronize Jewish shops. It begged Jews to resume commercial dealings with citizens. The peace move appeared inspired by Dr. Hjalmar Schacht, economic dictator, who constantly warns that Jew-baiting hurts business.

Jews also took hope from an order issued by Dietrich von Jason, Storm Troop commander in Berlin. "I forbid every violence against Jews . . . and in general every unauthorized action whatsoever."

PARTICIPATION IN THE 1936 BERLIN OLYMPICS: JEWS, AFRICAN AMERICANS, AND OTHERS

The Nazis passed the Nuremberg Laws just as the world was preparing for the 1936 Olympics. The International Olympic Committee (IOC), in 1931 having honored the new democratic Germany by choosing Berlin for the 1936 games, now found itself facing the embarrassment of a Nazi Olympics with racial restrictions on Jewish athletes and similar harassment of African American and other nonwhite competitors. As early as 1933, questions were raised in a variety of quarters as to whether the invitation should be reconsidered. In 1934, the IOC sought assurances from the Nazis that Jewish and other "non-Aryan" athletes both in Germany and from other nations would be allowed to train and compete on equal terms with others. They received official promises that this would be the case, but reports of discrimination against Jewish athletes and the general deterioration of the status of Jews in German society led some Americans and Europeans to advocate an Olympic cancellation or boycott.

The debate in America heated up in 1934. In September, the American Olympic Association (AOA) voted to accept the German invitation. In December, however, the Amateur Athletic Union (AAU), the link between the AOA and the athletes themselves, delayed accepting the invitation until charges of German discrimination against Jewish athletes could be investigated. Meanwhile, a number of Jewish and Catholic organizations as well as labor unions, supported by the *New York Times* and other newspapers, called for a boycott.

Avery Brundage and General Charles Sherrill, two of the three American members of the IOC, led the offensive for participation. Both were concerned that the issue of Jewish athletes would prevent an American presence in Berlin, and each pressed the Germans for assurances of equal treatment. Sherrill closely questioned the Germans on this point at meetings of the IOC. Brundage, as president of the AOA, had made a fact-finding trip to Germany that had led the AOA to accept the German invitation. In their minds, by the fall of 1935 they had removed the major stumbling block to American participation in the games.

A number of significant individuals and groups, both inside and outside the Olympic community, disagreed. Various Jewish and Catholic organizations (the Nazis had closed down Catholic sports organizations and in other ways limited the power of the church), labor unions, the *New York Times* and other newspapers, and several Protestant organizations, including the National Council of the Methodist Church, advocated a boycott. They did so in large part because of general opposition to the Nazi regime, and they saw American nonparticipation as a way of condemning Germany's policies of religious and political repression. In fact, according to a Gallup poll taken in March 1935, 43 percent of Americans favored a boycott.

Brundage became unhinged by such opposition, demanding that "Radicals and Communists must keep their hands off American sport" and characterizing criticism as "obviously written by a Jew or someone who has succumbed to the Jewish propaganda." A Christian colleague on the AOA accused him of being "a Jew hater and Jew baiter."[1] Sherrill reacted to the opposition with similar recklessness.

[1] Brundage quoted in Allen Guttmann, *The Games Must Go On: Avery Brundage and the Olympic Movement* (New York: Columbia University Press, 1984), 72–73.

Statement of Non-Jewish Advocates of Boycott
New York Times, October 25, 1935

Such was the emphasis on Jewish opposition on the part of those in favor of going to Berlin that a group of distinguished non-Jews issued a public statement arguing that the boycott was not a "Jewish question" but an "American question."

———

The statement over their signatures was as follows:

> . . . The impression has been created that only Jews are interested in the question of the American refusal to participate in the Olympic

"Statement of Non-Jewish Advocates of Boycott," *New York Times,* Oct. 25, 1935.

Games under Nazi auspices. We who are not Jews desire to make it as clear as possible that we do not regard this as a Jewish question.

It is an American question. It involves the principle of fair play in sports. We know that in Nazi Germany, which has by decree robbed all non-Aryans, Jewish or Christian, of citizenship rights, there can be no fair play in the arrangements of the Olympics. We who exercise our right as American citizens in the interest of clean and honorable sport, oppose American participation and hope that there shall be such widespread declination that it will be clear to the German people that the Nazi treatment of non-Aryans is repugnant to the conscience of mankind.

The statement was circulated over the signatures of Dr. Henry A. Atkinson, secretary of the Church Peace Union; Dr. S. Parkes Cadman; Dr. Samuel McCrea Cavert, general secretary of the Federal Council of Churches of Christ in America; Dr. Henry S. Leiper; Dr. Fred B. Smith, chairman of the American section of the World Alliance for International Friendship Through the Churches; and Michael Williams, editor of *The Commonweal*.

Among others who signed the statement were the Rev. Hugh Elmer Brown, pastor of the First Congregational Church of Evanston, Ill.; Mrs. Carrie Chapman Catt; Dean E. W. Chubb of Ohio University; Dr. Henry Sloane Coffin, president, Union Theological Seminary; Dr. Tyler Dennett, president, Williams College; Dr. John H. Finley; Dr. Harry Emerson Fosdick, pastor, Riverside Church; Dr. John C. Futrall, president, University of Arkansas; Dr. L. Hamilton Garner; James W. Gerard, former Ambassador to Germany; William Green, president of the American Federation of Labor; the Rev. Herman J. Hahn, pastor, Salem Church of Buffalo; John Haynes Holmes of the Community Church; Dr. Hamilton Holt, president, Rollins College; Paul Hutchinson, editor, Christian Century; Dr. R. A. Kent, president, University of Louisville; Dr. Frank Kingdon, president, Dana College; Mayor F. H. La Guardia; the Rev. Dr. Charles S. MacFarland, secretary emeritus, Federal Council of Churches; Theodore Marburg of Baltimore; Dr. Daniel L. Marsh, president, Boston University; the Rev. Dr. Reinhold Niebuhr, Professor of Christian Ethics, Union Theological Seminary; the Rev. Dr. Albert W. Palmer, president, Chicago Theological Seminary; Amos Pinchot; E. Merrill Root of Earlham College; John A. Ryder, track coach at Boston College; William J. Schieffelin, chairman, Citizens Union; Dr. Charles G. Selecman, president, Southern Methodist University; Jack Shea, former Olympic champion; George Shuster, managing editor, *The Commonweal;* the Rev. E. F. Stanford, president, Villanova College; Ernest Fremont Tittle; Dr. Luther A. Weigle, dean, Yale University School of Divinity; Dr. Ernest H. Wilkins, president, Oberlin College; and Dr. Mary E. Woolley, president, Mount Holyoke College.

ERNEST LEE JAHNCKE

Letter to Count Henri Baillet-Latour

November 25, 1935

Despite the stated opposition of scores of Olympic hopefuls, sportswriters, and sports officials, Brundage and Sherrill pretended that the debate over the Olympics was one between all true sportsmen and Jews and radicals. However, they could not ignore the voice of Ernest Lee Jahncke, a German American and former assistant secretary of the Navy in the Hoover administration. The third American member of the IOC and a powerful voice in amateur sports, Jahncke forthrightly recommended nonparticipation or a change of venue for the 1936 games. The man to whom he wrote, Count Henri Baillet-Latour, was president of the IOC.

Jahncke did not expect his sentiments to be greeted warmly. Baillet-Latour immediately asked him for his resignation from the IOC and, when Jahncke refused, had him expelled.

Letter to Baillet-Latour

My dear Colleague:

I have your recent letter in which you express your confidence that my devotion to the Olympic idea and my realization of my duty as a member of the International Olympic Committee will lead me to do all that I can to bring about American participation in the 1936 Olympic games, and in which you are also good enough to supply me with "arguments" which I can use for that purpose.

I am sorry that I must disappoint you. As you know, I am of German descent and I am very proud of that origin. In fact, I am the only one of the three American members who is so definitely of the Teutonic race.

It is precisely my devotion to the Olympic idea and my sense of my obligation as a member of the body charged with preserving and protecting it that will cause me to do just the opposite of what you so confidently ask of me. I shall do all that I can to persuade my fellow Americans that they ought not take part in the games if they are held in Nazi Germany.

No one has more clearly understood or better expressed the Olympic idea than your noble compatriot de Coubertin, the father of the modern Olympics.

"Jahncke Asks Ban on Olympic Games," *New York Times,* Nov. 27, 1935.

The Olympic idea, he said, is the conception of physical strength united with the spirit of fair play and chivalry. And the International Olympic Committee, of which both of us have the honor to be members, has said that without fair play there is no beauty in sport and that chivalry is its ennobling feature.

I shall urge upon my countrymen that they should not participate in the games in Nazi Germany because it is my opinion that under the domination of the Nazi government the German sports authorities have violated and are continuing to violate every requirement of fair play in the conduct of sports in Germany and in the selection of the German team, and are exploiting the games for the political and financial profit of the Nazi régime. Neither Americans nor the representatives of other countries can take part in the games in Nazi Germany without at least acquiescing in the contempt of the Nazis for fair play and their sordid exploitation of the games.

I am convinced, moreover, that to hold the games in Nazi Germany will be to deal a severe blow to the Olympic idea. And, tragically enough, it will have been damaged by the International Olympic Committee, which is its custodian and to which it was given in sacred trust more than a generation ago by those fine sportsmen who revived the Olympics. If our committee permits the games to be held in Nazi Germany, the Olympic idea will cease to be the conception of physical strength and fair play in unison, and there will be nothing left to distinguish it from the Nazi ideal of physical power. It will take many years to re-establish the prestige of the games and the confidence of the peoples of the world. Sport will lose its beauty and its nobility and become, as it has already become in Nazi Germany, an ugly, ignoble affair.

Our committee was true to its trust in June 1933, when it demanded and received from the Nazi sports authorities, as the condition of permitting Germany to retain the games, guarantees that the Nazis would observe the Olympic Code and would not discriminate against German athletes on religious grounds. In spite of all your alleged proofs, the nature of which you do not disclose, the plain and undeniable fact is that the Nazis have consistently and persistently violated their pledges. Of this they have been convicted out of their own mouths and by the testimony of impartial and experienced American and English newspaper correspondents. If our committee were still true to its trust it would long since have taken the games away from Germany and have arranged for them to be held in some country in which the spirit of fair play and chivalry is alive.

You remind me of my duty as a member of the International Olympic Committee. Therefore I feel sure that you will not consider me presumptuous in reminding you of your duty as president of the International Olympic Committee. It is plainly your duty to hold the Nazi sports authorities accountable for the violation of their pledges. I simply cannot understand why, instead of doing that, you are engaged in formulating and in spreading "arguments" to show why those of us who still believe in the Olympic idea should take part in the games in Nazi Germany.

My good friend Dr. Lewald and the Nazi sports authorities and General Sherrill and the American Olympic Committee have already made us familiar with these arguments, which are either, in my opinion, irrelevant or without adequate foundation in fact.

I do not doubt that you have received all sorts of assurances from the Nazi sports authorities. Ever since they gave us their pledges in June 1933, they have been lavish with their promises. The difficulty is that they have been stingy with their performance of them.

However much you would like us to believe that the Germans have kept their pledges, the fact is that the Nazi sports authorities have dissolved Catholic sports clubs and have denied Germany's Jewish athletes adequate opportunity to condition themselves for competition in the Olympic elimination contests, and this, of course, is equivalent to excluding them as a group from the German team.

However much you would like us to believe the contrary, the fact is that Jewish athletes, as a group, have been denied adequate opportunity for training and competition. Indeed, the Nazi sports authorities have themselves admitted that to be so. And The Associated Press, an impartial news service, has reported: "In only a few German cities may Jews use public athletic fields. To build and maintain their own grounds is almost impossible because of the cost. Consequently, many Jewish sportsmen have been forced to play in country fields and pastures where no facilities are available for many contests such as track events. Swimming also is impossible because nearly every municipality has adopted regulations banning the use of pools and beaches by Jews."

Does it surprise you that under these conditions few non-Aryan athletes have been able to attain Olympic form? Or that under these conditions the Reichssportfuehrer is willing to assure you that such athletes who hold "sufficient records" will be admitted to the elimination contests?

No one pretends that the games should be taken away from Germany merely because Jews are not admitted to the Nazi sports clubs. The point, my dear Count, is that by excluding them from those clubs the Nazis have, at the same time, excluded them from the use of training facilities and opportunity for competition.

You quote an argument used by propagandists for holding the games in Nazi Germany—the fact that Negroes are excluded from many private clubs in America, as if what some Americans do in their own private social relations, however unfortunate it may be, were at all comparable to the treatment of the German Jews by the Nazi Government and party. It may interest you to know that American Negroes themselves see how false this analogy is. Only recently the National American Association for the Advancement of the Colored People adopted a resolution calling upon American Negro athletes not to take part in the games in Nazi Germany.

You suggest that the German sports authorities have done all that they could under the circumstances to keep their pledges. Of course, the circumstances are that they are mere puppets without any power whatever and can do only what they are directed to do by the Nazi government and party. I am more than willing to credit my good friend, Dr. Lewald, with the best intentions, but that does not seem to me to be a very good reason for holding the games in Germany.

The argument that the opposition to holding the games in Germany is politically inspired is a favorite argument of propagandists for American participation. Sports, they say, as you say, are not to be mixed with politics, and sportsmen are not concerned with Nazi persecution of Jews and Catholics even when it occurs in sport itself.

Was our committee actuated by political motives in 1933 when it demanded the German pledges or was it on the contrary actuated by the desire to safeguard the Olympic idea? Were we mixing sports with politics in 1933 when we demanded that Germany should treat her non-Aryan athletes fairly or were we on the contrary trying to keep Nazi politics out of the Olympics, which was our sacred duty?

Let me, in conclusion, my dear Count, make an earnest appeal to you. It is still not too late to save the Olympic idea and to maintain the Olympics as "a school of moral nobility and purity," as de Coubertin intended them to be. There is still time to arrange for holding the games elsewhere than in Germany. Let me urge upon you that you place your great talents and influence in the service of the spirit of fair play and of chivalry instead of the service of brutality, force, and power. Let me beseech you to seize your opportunity to take your rightful place in the history of the Olympics alongside of de Coubertin instead of Hitler. De Coubertin rescued the Olympic idea from the remote past. You have the opportunity to rescue it from the immediate present and safeguard it for posterity.

Very sincerely yours,
ERNEST LEE JAHNCKE.

Count Henri Baillet-Latour,
Comité International Olympique,
Lausanne, Switzerland.

NAACP Asks AAU to Abandon Olympics

Pittsburgh Courier, December 14, 1935

Jahncke's letter to Baillet-Latour dealt with a question that hovered over the debate concerning the Olympic boycott—the analogy between Nazi laws limiting Jewish life and America's legal and de facto segregation of the races. Olympic advocates argued that the German situation was no different from that in America. Only the identities of those excluded were different. Most boycott advocates forthrightly rejected racial laws in both countries but noted that, unlike German Jews, African Americans had not been systematically excluded from Olympic training and tryouts. Indeed, many of the most promising members of the American team were black.

The African American community itself was divided on the question of participation. Few had any illusions about the Nazis, who placed black people below Jews in their hierarchy of race. Some worried that African American athletes might be taunted or worse if they went to the Olympics. At the same time, in an era when few other routes to success were open in America, the black community generally recognized sports as an arena in which to prove emphatically the equality and even superiority of black talent. Probable African American members of the 1936 team constituted a particularly strong group. Blacks thus faced a dilemma. If they boycotted an Olympics held in a nation that despised them, they would miss the opportunity to strike a blow for equality in the United States by garnering fame and Olympic medals in the lion's den. Nonetheless, in December 1935 Walter White, head of the National Association for the Advancement of Colored People (NAACP), the leading civil rights organization of the 1930s, requested that the Amateur Athletic Union (AAU) vote against participation. Note not only the text of the statement but also the sentiments expressed in the final paragraph of the article, which appeared in one of the leading African American newspapers of the era, the *Pittsburgh Courier.*

"N.A.A.C.P. Asks A.A.U. to Abandon Olympics," *Pittsburgh Courier,* Dec. 14, 1935.

At the opening of the convention of the Amateur Athletic Union here today a request was received from the National Association for the Advancement of Colored People that the A.A.U. vote against participation in the 1936 Olympics in Berlin. The N.A.A.C.P. telegram, signed by Walter White, reads as follows:

> Will you convey to the Amateur Union the very sincere request of the National Association for the Advancement of Colored People that it vote decisively against American participation in the 1936 Olympic games if they are held in Germany. This is asked in no spirit of racial selfishness nor in any holier than thou attitude. The United States has much to answer for in the matter of racial discrimination especially against Negro athletes in the South. Instead we ask the A.A.U. to vote against participation on the ground that Germany has violated her pledges against racial discrimination and for American athletes to participate would be to negate every principle upon which the Olympic games are based. Refusal to participate will, we believe, do untold good in helping Germany and the world to realize that racial bigotry must be opposed in its every manifestation. To participate would be to place approval upon the German government's deplorable persecution of racial and religious groups and would stultify the Amateur Athletic Union and all athletes who participate.

A further outline of the N.A.A.C.P.'s opposition on the Olympic games was made in a speech by Mr. White at Mecca Temple, New York City, December 3rd, at a mass meeting of the Committee on Fair Play in Sports, in which he said: "But in opposing for these reasons American participation in the 1936 Olympics, I would be a craven did I not express Fair Play in Sports, and all others opposed, quite rightly, to participation in the 1936 Olympics do some needed work in our own United States."

In the end, of course, the American team went to the Olympics. Brundage, Sherrill, and their allies won all the major votes in the AOA and the AAU, though sometimes through questionable parliamentary means. Olympic momentum picked up, and, for the most part, athletes made individual choices to participate. Some boycotted, including some of the most talented Jewish American athletes. Most participated, even a handful of Jews. Assured of fair treatment, black athletes leaped at the opportunity to prove themselves in the international arena. The editorial cartoon from the *Pittsburgh Courier* on page 69 expresses the expectation and pride that the African American community showed in so heavily representing the United States at Berlin.

The Black Eagles

Pittsburgh Courier, July 11, 1936

"The Black Eagles," Political Cartoon, *Pittsburgh Courier,* July 11, 1936.

The performance of African American athletes at Berlin astounded the world. Jesse Owens garnered four gold medals and was easily the most acclaimed participant at the games. His black teammates Ralph Metcalf, Matthew Robinson, Archie Williams, James Lu Valle, John Woodruff, Cornelius Johnson, David Albritton, and Frederick Pollard also won medals. These men became heroes in the black community and helped to create a public atmosphere in the United States that was more conducive to the movement toward equal rights for African Americans. As for the Nazis, they handled such victories awkwardly but ultimately won a great propaganda victory in hosting an Olympics filled with superb athletic performances and grand public spectacle. Soon after the games, however, the realities of German racial policies returned with increasing force.

REFUGEES, *KRISTALLNACHT,* AND COUGHLIN

President Roosevelt convened a meeting of countries in Europe and the Americas that in the past had welcomed Jewish refugees and might have some wisdom on how best to proceed now that the demand for visas had skyrocketed. Held at Evian, France, in July 1938, the conference produced little in the way of new initiatives and expanded opportunities for emigration. This *Time* report conveys the various positions held by nations at the conference and the general feeling of stalemate that pervaded negotiations. Note the specific practical problems and political realities against which the search for a solution to the refugee problem took place and the recognition even on the part of a contemporary newsmagazine that the conference was doomed to failure. A major issue, unmentioned because it was assumed, was the continuing plague of unemployment and fear of labor competition from refugees.

Refugees

Time, July 18, 1938

By 1938, both political pressures and public opinion in England and the United States called for a solution to the "refugee question" — in short to find places for German Jews to start a new life. Cries for action grew louder with the Nazi annexation of Austria on March 12–13, 1938. More than 180,000 Jews lived in Austria, the vast majority in Vienna. Nazi forces began roundups, beatings, confiscations, and other harassment almost immediately.

Around the shores of blue Lake Léman, dividing France and Switzerland, lie historic international conference cities, Geneva, Lausanne, Montreux, Nyon. Last week, the gay French resort of Evian-les-Bains was added to the list as delegates from 32 nations, including three world powers (U.S., France, Britain), four British Dominions (Australia, New Zealand, Canada, Eire), most of the Latin American nations, and several smaller European powers, there set up headquarters in the luxurious Hotel Royal. They came in answer to President Roosevelt's invitation, issued soon after Germany annexed Austria, to see what could be done to provide new homes for racial and political refugees. Germany was not invited; Italy, out of sympathy for the Reich, declined to attend.

Evian is the home of a famous spring of still and unexciting table water. After a week of many warm words of idealism, few practical suggestions, the Intergovernmental Committee on Political Refugees took on some of the same characteristics. Two days of stalling went on before a president was elected. No delegate wanted the post, each fearing that his nation would then be responsible for the conference's all-too-probable failure. Finally stocky, publicity-hating Myron C. Taylor, onetime Chairman of U.S. Steel Corp. and chief U.S. delegate, agreed to accept.

All nations present expressed sympathy for the refugees but few offered to allow them within their boundaries. Britain, France, Belgium pleaded that they had already absorbed their capacity, Australia turned in a flat "No" to Jews, and the U.S. announced that she would combine her former annual Austrian immigration quota with her German to admit 27,370 persons (who can support themselves) from Greater Germany next year. Almost sole note of encouragement came from eight Latin

---

"Refugees," *Time,* July 18, 1938, 16.

American nations: Argentina, Colombia, Ecuador, Uruguay, Peru, Venezuela, Mexico, and the Dominican Republic (which nine months ago massacred 1,000 neighboring Haitians because they moved into her territory) offered to accept a limited number of refugees if they came as agricultural workers.

As each nation presented its views, it became clear that there were two fundamental splits to be bridged before a plan could be put into effect:

1   Britain and France want any plan for transplanting refugees to be carried out by existing League of Nations bodies. The U.S., backed by non-League Latin American nations, feels that since the conference's first move will have to be negotiation with League-hating Germany for removal of her Jewish and anti-Nazi population, a body completely removed from League influence would have more chance of success.

2   Britain and France want to limit proposals to the handling of refugees from Germany alone. The U.S. insists that the conference constitute a permanent body to handle not only the German problem but any other refugee question that may arise, from such potential refugee producers as Italy, Poland, and Rumania.

LOUIS LOCHNER

Letter to Betty and Bobby

November 28, 1938

Louis Lochner, bureau chief for the Associated Press in Berlin and central Europe from 1928 to 1940, wrote regularly to his children concerning his experiences in the German capital (see page 18). He was fluent in German and at ease in the company of Nazis and anti-Nazis, which made his reports home especially intimate and vivid and often more complete than his official reports, which were molded by Nazi censorship and informal pressure. The following letter reported his feelings and experiences in the wake of *Kristallnacht* with a candor and depth of feeling missing from even the most graphic press reports of these events. Note that

---

Louis Lochner, "Letter to Betty and Bobby," Berlin, Nov. 28, 1938, as reprinted in *Wisconsin Magazine of History,* Summer 1967, 324.

Lochner and other foreigners risked expulsion or even imprisonment by opening their homes to Jews seeking protection from the Nazis. Look also for his mention of increased applications for immigration visas to the United States. Finally, Lochner notes the shock of many Germans to Nazi excesses during *Kristallnacht,* a fact confirmed by secret Nazi reports.

[To Betty and Bobby]

To think that I haven't written you a Round Robin letter since October 10th! I never dreamed such a long pause would ensue. But just about the time I was getting down to the monthly letter, the most terrible experience in all my life came to us—the anti-Semitic orgy of November 10 and days following. I never dreamed that human nature could descend to such depravity and sadism and cruelty as I was witness to these last weeks. We have all become much older, and we sometimes wonder when we shall ever be able to really laugh again.

Our home has been a refuge harbor, as have the houses of hundreds of foreigners here. Haunted and hunted creatures pitifully begged for a night's lodging, and no Christian that I knew said no; we left it to the heathens to take upon themselves the odium of perpetrating crimes that will some day cost the country dearly. I cannot go into detail here. I can only tell you that for once all the foreign correspondents lied—lied in the sense that they understated many times rather than even approach the truth, for fear that their authentic sources might be led to new tortures if they were revealed.

Putz has been helping out at the U.S. Consulate for the past two weeks because the personnel simply couldn't cope with the situation. When she started, she had the daily task of perusing, classifying, and registering a daily mail of about 600 letters. Now the number has risen to one thousand, with prospects of this number increasing. Pitiful letters they are, of persons whose fathers or brothers are in concentration camps for the sole "crime" of having been born as Jews; of families whose modest little shops have been smashed to smithereens by a blind mob; of highly cultured, wealthy "first families" who have become penniless overnight. All, all want to emigrate to the U.S.A.! And when they tell about the 520 synagogues that have been burned, and about the 1,300,000,000 Reichsmarks worth of damage that, according to insurance experts was done and about the harmless men and women who were wantonly killed or, sadder still, who committed suicide in despair, can you wonder that we are down and out? . . .

What this situation has cost us also in the way of nerves as far as my journalistic work is concerned, you can only imagine. By the most devious ways I had to assemble my material. One of our men who had been present at a wrecking scene went into a public phone booth to telephone me what he had seen. He was nearly mobbed on the grounds that he was spreading false reports! They've done everything to gag us, but I am determined to tell the truth honestly, though with understatement. On the other hand we have also seen how thoroughly disgusted the German people themselves are. Don't think for a moment that the rank and file approved! They feel ashamed, thoroughly ashamed. . . .

HENRY MORGENTHAU

Diary Entry
November 16, 1938

The horrors of *Kristallnacht* reverberated in the White House as well. This entry from the diary of Secretary of the Treasury Henry Morgenthau, a Jew and one of the few champions of Jewish refugees in the cabinet, reveals Roosevelt's continuing thought on the question. He was also one of the president's closest friends. To understand the seriousness of the conversation concerning Jewish resettlement in Africa, one must conjure up the period before World War II, when what we now call the third world was largely "owned" or administered by European powers. In the late nineteenth century, European nations had claimed parts of Africa for themselves through economic influence and military might and had carved out areas of colonial rule. Europeans thus gained natural resources and strategic advantages crucial to their economic growth. They justified this "scramble for Africa" as part of Europe's mission to bring Christianity and civilization to what they saw as backward peoples.

Plans to resettle Jews in Africa were, of course, kindled by the resistance of countries in Europe and the Americas to expand their intake of refugees. It was also sparked by British reluctance to increase the quota for Jewish emigration to Palestine in the wake of Arab protests. Yet European settlements in the colonies were hardly novel, and in the context of

---

"Concerning Placing Jewish Refugees," Morgenthau Diaries, Nov. 16, 1938, in *America and the Holocaust: Responsibility for America's Failure,* vol. 13, ed. David S. Wyman (New York: Garland Publishing, 1991), 7.

the times only the size and specificity of the project, as well as the pressures of time, seemed extraordinary.

It is hard to imagine in our postcolonial world, with its emphasis on self-determination, that statesmen of the great powers would ponder moving populations as if playing a board game with the land of others. However, note the serious tone of the conversation. In 1938, such ideas seemed reasonable.

I said, "I have got the first concrete suggestion to make for the Jewish refugees." He said, "Well, for Heaven's sake, what is it?" I said, "Constantine Maguire has sent me a letter suggesting that we make a settlement with Great Britain and France on their war debts for British Guinea and French Guinea, and then somehow or other raise enough money to buy off Holland for Dutch Guinea."

He said, "It's no good." He said, "It would take the Jews from 25 to 50 years to overcome the fever and," he said, "it's just no good." He said, "What's the matter with the idea I have been talking to you about for a long time and," he said, "that's the Cameroons." He said, "The Cameroons was a former German colony and now belongs to France and," he said, "the same suggestion that you have of giving these countries a credit on their debt to us would apply there and," he said, "I know from explorations that have been made in the Cameroons that they have some very wonderful high land, table land. . . ."

Exchange between Raymond Geist
and George Messersmith
December 5 and 20, 1938

In the wake of the failed Evian Conference and *Kristallnacht,* the desperate state of German Jews provided a harsh contrast to the unwillingness of the rest of the world to act on their behalf. The following exchange between Raymond Geist, the U.S. consul in Berlin, and George Messersmith, assistant secretary of state and former U.S. consul general in Berlin, reveals some of the more principled concerns of the U.S. State

---

Richard Breitman and Alan M. Kraut, *American Refugee Policy and European Jewry, 1933–1945* (Bloomington: Indiana University Press, 1987), 67.

Department as it failed to respond to the pleas of Jews in Germany and Austria as well as a realistic assessment of the situation.

Geist, as in this excerpt from a letter to Messersmith on December 5, 1938, was perhaps the only member of the State Department strongly to voice the need for action:

The Jews in Germany are being condemned to death and their sentence will be slowly carried out; but probably too fast for the world to save them. . . . After we have saved these refugees, and the Catholics and Protestants have not become new victims of the wrath here, we could break off relations and prepare to join in a war against them [the Germans]. We shall have to do so sooner or later; as France and England will be steadily pushed to the wall and eventually to save ourselves we shall have to save them. The European situation was lost to the democracies at Munich and the final situation is slowly being prepared. The age lying before us will witness great struggles and the outcome when it comes will determine the fate of civilization for a century or more.

Messersmith, no less gloomy about the prospects, asserts the need to withstand any special dealing with Germany but admits the costs of such firmness.

Fundamental issues are at stake. These issues are greater than any individual or any individual suffering. . . . What we must do is maintain our principle in every field and one cannot maintain principle of so fundamental character by making concessions in individual cases or by soft-pedalling our adhesion to these principles. . . . Human ingenuity and the capacity of governments for action are not up to taking care of a refugee movement such as that which is being created by the German government and which may only be in its beginnings if the present movement continues.

FATHER COUGHLIN

From *Am I an Anti-Semite?*

December 11, 1938

One of the reasons for Roosevelt's timidity in suggesting significant increases in the immigration quotas to rescue German Jews was the virulent strain of anti-Semitism that infected America in the 1930s. In those years, Father Charles E. Coughlin (1891–1979) was one of the principal disseminators of anti-Semitic propaganda in mainstream American culture. Ordained a Catholic priest in 1923 and made pastor of the Shrine of the Little Flower in Royal Oak, Michigan, in 1926, Coughlin embraced the new medium of radio in 1930 and soon broadcast sermons nationally. As the economic crisis worsened, he began mixing politics into his preaching and at first championed Franklin D. Roosevelt and the New Deal. He soon soured on the New Deal, however, and formed his own organization, the National Union for Social Justice. In radio broadcasts and in his new magazine, *Social Justice,* he hammered away on the theme of justice for the common people and drew pictures of a vast conspiracy of government and bankers working to preserve the status quo. He combined these with a defense of Christianity against modern indifference and communism. Significantly, he increasingly identified hostile banking interests and world communism with Jews and "Jewry."

By 1938, he had become the most powerful and popular purveyor of anti-Jewish propaganda in the nation. Soon he became informally associated with the Christian Front, an organization that featured as one of its slogans "Buy Christian" and that published the *Christian Index,* a guide to non-Jewish merchants in New York City. Young Christian Front members threatened Jews in the streets and defaced synagogues with swastikas. Coughlin split the American Catholic community with his political demagoguery and anti-Semitism. Although some moderate and liberal Catholic leaders publicly criticized him for his inflammatory rhetoric and especially his anti-Semitic diatribes, most were either silent or openly supported him.

Charles E. Coughlin, *Am I an Anti-Semite?* (Detroit: Condon Printing, 1939), 94–95, 104–6.

Figure 1. Father Charles C. Coughlin, radio priest and anti-Semite. In the 1930s and early 1940s, his broadcasts and magazine, *Social Justice,* mixed sympathy for the poor with diatribes against Roosevelt and the Jews. Before Pearl Harbor, he campaigned against U.S. entry into the war against Hitler.

Despite his obvious predilections, Coughlin claimed he was not an anti-Semite but an anticommunist. The following excerpt comes from a sermon he published in a collection titled *Am I an Anti-Semite?*

———————

My friends, it is appropriate for me to re-express the thoughts which were woven in bold colors throughout the last three discourses. They are these: I hold no animosity towards the Jews. I distinguish most carefully between good Jews and bad Jews as well as I do between the good gentiles and bad gentiles.

I sincerely sympathize with the millions of humble, religious Jews both in America and elsewhere who have been persecuted by a thoughtless world — a world which does not always distinguish between the good Jews and the bad Jews; a world which lashes at the pillar of persecution the innocent Jews for the misdemeanors of the guilty Jews.

Openly and fearlessly do I admit that my main contention is with the atheistic Jew and gentile; the communistic Jew and gentile who have been responsible and will continue to be responsible, in great part, both for the discriminations and the persecutions inflicted upon the Jews as a body.

To prevent happening in America what has happened elsewhere, and to end once and for all the hostility of German Naziism towards Jews, I asked my fellow citizens not only to oppose Naziism, an effect of Communism, but to fight manfully against Communism itself.

I further appealed to them to apply the basic principle of science in their common effort to destroy persecution — the basic principle which teaches us that, in order to remove effects permanently, the causes which produce them must be removed first.

And finally, I reminded both Jew and gentile that ours is not a problem of anti-Semitism; ours is a problem of anti-Communism.

Thus, the issue is clear. The Jews of America cannot afford to be identified with Communism or with communistic activities. They are asked to disassociate themselves from the atheistic Jews who espouse Communism.

Therefore, every person worthy of the name of Christian stands prepared to oppose the excesses of Naziism; stands prepared to extend the right hand of sympathy towards the persecuted Jews in Germany.

But every intelligent American Christian whose heart bleeds for his 20 million fellow Christians who were butchered by the Trotskys and the Bela Kuns, the Bronsteins and the Cohns, in Soviet Russia, in the Ukraine, in Hungary, and elsewhere — these American Christians appeal to the Jews of America to join with them in removing Communism, the cause of Naziism. They appeal particularly to the eminent sons of Jewry who have risen so high in government, in journalism, in banking, in broadcasting, and in motion pictures, to launch an effective, determined campaign against the Red menace which has baptized the hillsides and valleys of Europe with the blood of 20 million Christian martyrs.

The best answer that Jewry can give me or America is not a passionate denial that Jews, far beyond their proportion of population, are not interested in furthering Communism. Official action will speak more eloquently than ten thousand denials.

In asking the gentiles of America to oppose the gentiles of the Nazi party in Germany, Jews are not seeking anything that is unreasonable.

On the other hand, when the gentiles of America ask the Jews in this country to oppose the Jews in Russia, in Spain, and elsewhere, who are supporting Communism to our detriment and to the detriment of the Christians living abroad, we are asking nothing unreasonable.

There comes a time in the life of every individual as well as in the life of every nation when righteousness and justice must take precedence over the bonds of race and blood.

Tolerance, then, becomes a heinous vice when it tolerates the theology of atheism, the patriotism of internationalism, and the justice of religious persecution. No matter, then, what ties of blood and common parentage bind the God-fearing Jews in New York with the atheistic Jews in Moscow, those ties must be severed for God, for country, and for the preservation of the teeming masses of Jews in America who have been victimized by the silence of their leaders and the propaganda of the press.

Everyone recognizes that Soviet Russia has made anti-Semitism a crime.

The entire world recognizes that Soviet Russia has made pro-Christianity, pro-theism, and pro-religion likewise crimes.

Everyone recognizes the predominance of atheistic Jews in the pattern of Russian Communism. Evidence is so overwhelming to substantiate this statement that it is idle for any informed person to attempt disputing it. . . .

Oh, how can the General Jewish Council and the Jewish Community Councils who are about to answer me today through the lips of a fellow religionist, and with the voice of a fellow descendant of that same Irish race which suffered death and persecution—how can they be so unkind to us with their admitted preeminence in banking, in press, in cinema, and in radio, and with the law on their side—to protest against the innocent practices of Christmas and Eastertide?

The banking institutions can rob our Christian citizenry through the practice of usury.

A controlled press can veil the eyes of a nation against the Christian blood which has run ankle-deep in Barcelona.

Members of your race can devise reasons to exclude a voice from the airways which seeks to tell America the truth.

And pitiless propaganda can exhibit itself upon the silver screens of our nation to deceive us. These things are not worthy of protest. They are negligible. But when, constitutionally and legally, you tell us in your official publication of instituting a successful program—to use your own words—of "persuading the public school officials to stop Easter and Christmas practices which have been embarrassing to the Jewish children . . ." then, silence on my part were criminal if I did not point out to you that you are injuring yourselves; that you are piercing the very heart of America; yes, driving in the lance to let the last drop of blood flow from the godless, lifeless corpse of our once glorious civilization.

My fellow Jews, please understand our Christian attitude towards all this: You are a minority—a small but powerful minority. We are a majority—an easy-going, patient majority—but a majority always conscious of our latent power.

Sometimes we are a careless majority. The saintly Pope Pius X, referring to our apathy, spoke of the heroism of Blessed Joan, and contrasted it with the timidity of so many, particularly in our day: "In our time more than ever before, the chief strength of the wicked lies in the cowardice and weakness of good men. . . . All the strength of Satan's reign is due to the easy-going weakness of Catholics."

We are a democratic people. In our conception of democracy Christmas and Easter were accepted as axiomatic truths by most of those who framed our Constitution—as axiomatic as the law of gravitation which these founders troubled not to write into the document which safeguards our rights and our liberties. But that was unfortunate for us.

The acceptance of these truths, I confess, is not so general today amongst all our Christians and citizens. However, in the hearts of those who have ceased practising religion, or who regard it as a non-essential for the well-being of our national life—in their hearts there is a resentment towards any organized group which, either directly or indirectly, assails the ideals cherished by their mothers.

My friends, when I quote for you the evidence of a program injudiciously but constitutionally designed by a minority group to cooperate with those who are aiming to complete the de-Christianization of America, I am presenting no novel program recently conceived either by the General Jewish Council or the Jewish Community Councils themselves. That program has been in our midst long before the General Jewish Councils were organized.

However, I ask the religious Jews of America—and I believe they are in the majority—Jews who, perhaps, are not aware of this policy and program—I ask them to be kindly towards us.

Russian Communism was motivated by a man who swore he would drag God from His false heaven.

Communism over the world is identified with this godlessness, this extinction of Christ and of God from the lives of men.

Whether you are aware of it or not, this regrettable policy of godlessness is indelibly stamped with the hallmark of world Communism.

The words which I have spoken today are reaching Cleveland and Bridgeport and practically every other city in this nation where Christmas and Easter practices have been excluded from the public schools through the self-admitted agency of cooperative, constitutional Jewish activity. I feel that the fine, intelligent, religious Jews of America will not persist, in this instance, in their constitutional rights.

With no rancor or resentment am I unveiling these thoughts today. I am simply protesting in the name of the inarticulate millions—protesting against those Jews and gentiles who seek—through intolerance?—to withhold from the children of this land the tender story of the Christ Child and His glorious resurrection from the dead. Jews are not intolerant. No, I cannot believe that.

My friends—Christians and religious Jews—I am motivated by a desire to strike courageously at all persecution. Let us, therefore, join together hand in hand to strike at the cause of all persecutions, irreligiousness, godlessness, Christlessness.

Jews of America, look back down the ages to the great traditions that are yours. Sounding high from the tops of Sinai spoke your God and my God to Moses. Down its slopes to the wanderers in the desert came Moses with the Commandments which both of us revere. God is your God. God is my God. Why, therefore, shall you persist in your constitutional rights when we Christians revere our Christ as the Second Person of the Most Blessed Trinity? Why shall you persist? I know you will not. I know you will desist!

Thus, when the spirit of Christmas is about to descend upon the entire world, I regret that I found occasion to remind this audience that the General Jewish Council—responsible for disbarring not the Christian religion, not the preaching of the Bible, not the recitation of prayers, but the last vestiges of Christmas practices from many of our schools—that the General Jewish Council has engaged the services of a fellow Catholic to discuss my recent challenge. It was a challenge occasioned by a 400-million-dollar fine levied against 600 thousand Jews—a challenge for Christians to protest against this and other Nazi persecutions of a minority people—.

But it is likewise the occasion for Christians to remind the Jews of their Trotskys,[1] their Bela Kuns,[2] their Lunacharskys,[3] and their commissars who, since 1917 until this present hour, have been engaged not in levying fines against Christians but in destroying them from the face of the earth. . . .

---

[1]Leon Trotsky (1879–1940), one of the great Communist theorists and leaders of the Russian Revolution of 1917, who lost a struggle for power with Stalin after Lenin's death and who was assassinated by Stalin's agents in Mexico.

[2]Bela Kun (1886–1939), a Hungarian Communist revolutionary who ruled that nation for four months in 1919 in the wake of World War I.

[3]Anatoly Lunacharsky (1875–1933), a Russian playwright and Communist revolutionary eventually purged as a "Trotskyite" by Stalin.

Topics of the Times: Refugee Ship

New York Times, June 8, 1939

One of the most dramatic events of the immediate prewar period in the Western hemisphere was the ill-fated voyage of the Hamburg-America Line's passenger ship *St. Louis*. The *St. Louis* left Europe on May 13, 1939, and returned on June 21. This short piece tells the basic story but also comments on the intense frustration of the experience. Note especially whom the piece blames for the fate of the ship and its passengers. Does it offer a solution to the more general problem the ship seemed to pose?

The saddest ship afloat today, the Hamburg-America liner St. Louis, with 900 Jewish refugees aboard, is steaming back toward Germany after a tragic week of frustration at Havana and off the coast of Florida. She is steaming back despite an offer made to Havana yesterday to give a guarantee through the Chase National Bank of $500 apiece for every one of her passengers, men, women, and children, who might land there. President Laredo Bru still has an opportunity to practice those humanitarian sentiments so eloquently expressed in his belated offer of asylum after the refugee ship had been driven from Havana Harbor. His cash terms have been met. But the St. Louis still keeps her course for Hamburg.

No plague ship ever received a sorrier welcome. Yet those aboard her had sailed with high hopes. About fifty of them, according to our Berlin dispatch, had consular visas. The others all had landing permits for which they had paid; they were unaware that these permits had been declared void in a decree dated May 5. Only a score of the hundreds were admitted. At Havana the St. Louis's decks became a stage for human misery. Relatives and friends clamored to get aboard but were held back. Weeping refugees clamoring to get ashore were halted at guarded gangways. For days the St. Louis lingered within the shadow of Morro Castle, but there was no relaxation of the new regulations. Every appeal was rejected. One man reached land. He was pulled from the water with slashed wrists and rushed to a hospital. A second suicide attempt led the captain to warn the authorities that a wave of self-destruction might follow. The forlorn refugees themselves organized a patrol committee. Yet out of Havana Harbor the St. Louis had to go, trailing pitiful cries of "Auf Wiedersehen." Off our shores she was attended

"Topics of the Times: Refugee Ship," *New York Times,* June 8, 1939.

Figure 2. Two young Jewish refugees on the SS *St. Louis.* The ship's fruitless attempts in May 1939 to disembark its passengers, virtually all of them German Jews looking for a new home, has become symbolic of the strict immigration quotas that frustrated refugees as they sought escape from Hitler's Germany and Austria in the late 1930s.

by a helpful Coast Guard vessel alert to pick up any passengers who plunged overboard and thrust them back on the St. Louis again. The refugees could even see the shimmering towers of Miami rising from the sea, but for them they were only the battlements of another forbidden city.

It is useless now to discuss what might have been done. The case is disposed of. Germany, with all the hospitality of its concentration camps, will welcome these unfortunates home. Perhaps Cuba, as her spokesmen say, has already taken too many German refugees. Yet all these 900 asked was a temporary haven. Before they sailed virtually all of them had registered under the quota provisions of various nations, including our own. Time would have made them eligible to enter. But there seems to be no help for them now. The St. Louis will soon be home with her cargo of despair.

Her next trip is already scheduled. It will be a gay cruise for carefree tourists.

When the *St. Louis* returned to Europe, most of the passengers were able to find haven in France and other European countries. This happy ending was short-lived, however, since within a few years the Nazis had conquered these countries of refuge and had deported most of the refugees to Auschwitz and other killing centers.

AN *ATLANTIC MONTHLY* SYMPOSIUM ON JEWS

On September 1, 1939, the Nazis invaded Poland, thus igniting World War II. A few days later, Britain and France declared war on Germany, but the United States remained neutral. Germany conquered Poland in three weeks. After an uneasy peace, in May 1940 the Germans moved against Western Europe and within little more than two months had occupied France, Holland, Belgium, Denmark, Norway, and Luxembourg. In the summer of 1940, the German *Luftwaffe* began bombing English cities. By early 1941, Hitler had added Yugoslavia, Bulgaria, and Crete to his conquests. Germany began to challenge British strongholds in the Mediterranean and North Africa as well. Only Britain and the Soviet Union stood in the way of Hitler's total domination of Europe. In June 1941, Hitler broke a nonaggression pact he had signed with Stalin in 1939 and invaded the vast territories of the Soviet Union. German armies swept across the Russian plains and were at the gates of Moscow by late 1941.

The Roosevelt administration moved steadily toward entering the conflict, fearing the risk to America if Hitler were to conquer the Soviet Union and Britain. Fear of war provided a fertile environment for American anti-Semites. Father Coughlin raged against "interventionist" Jewish influence in Washington. The America First Committee and other isolationist voices angrily charged that Roosevelt was manipulating the nation into war and often added that "the Jews" were among those most in favor of war with Hitler. Such concerns even inspired a coercive congressional investigation of highly visible Jewish studio owners, writers, and performers in Hollywood to see if they were producing "interventionist" propaganda.

In this volatile atmosphere, the *Atlantic Monthly,* one of the nation's most respected journals of cultural and political commentary, launched a five-month series on the status and reputation of Jews in America. The editors asked Albert Jay Nock (1870–1945), a prominent, idiosyncratic essayist, biographer, philosopher, and social critic, to write an article titled "The Jewish Problem in America." Nock's libertarianism, which put him at odds with Roosevelt's New Deal, along with his elitist nostalgia for America before big government and massive immigration, informed a two-part piece that caused enormous controversy. It prompted the magazine to print responses through October 1941.

ALBERT JAY NOCK

From *The Jewish Problem in America*
Atlantic Monthly, June and July 1941

Note the way that Nock differentiates Jews from "Americans," as well as his sense of the threat of powerful states and mass movements. Where does he place the blame for anti-Semitism? What kinds of arguments and evidence does he use to make his case, and in what tone does he cast his

Albert Jay Nock, "The Jewish Problem in America," *Atlantic Monthly,* June 1941, 699–700, 703; July 1941, 68–73, 75–76.

argument? Pay special attention to the ways in which the Nock articles, and the responses to it, address the nature of American democracy and the questions of "racial" distinctiveness and acculturation that are still alive, in somewhat different forms in today's cultural dialogues.

I

Up to two years ago I had no idea that such a problem existed. Never having given a moment's thought to the matter, and having lived for many years abroad, I would have said that the highly satisfactory *modus vivendi*[1] of my early days was still in force. When I was a boy in a Mid-Western town the few Jews there were regarded as other people equally respectable and personable were regarded. Since their standard of character and manners happened to be uncommonly high, they were much looked up to. As for social discrimination against the Jew *qua* Jew, there was none even among us children. My own special cronies, for example, were seined out of two large families of Jews and an equally abundant run of French Canadians. As my thoughts turn back to old man M. and his numerous family, the stiffest kind of orthodox Sephardic Jews and the finest kind of people, I so well recall how diligently all our girls used to fish for dances with his grown-up sons Nate and Mose, charming young men, delightfully well-bred, and the best dancers we had. Again in my later youth I saw much the same state of things in another Mid-Western town. One or two Jews there were unpopular because they were swindlers in a petty way, but this did not affect the esteem in which the rest of the town's small Jewry was held. . . .

Much as any well-disposed citizen must dislike to say so, there can be no doubt that if even only the destructive force now latent were released by the circumstances we are postulating, the consequences would be as appalling in their extent and magnitude as anything seen since the Middle Ages. The American mob's grim reputation for sheer anthropoid savagery is equaled only by that of the revolutionary mobs of Paris. At the outset of the German Government's movement against the Jews, an American visitor asked Herr Hitler why he was making it so ruthless. The Reichskanzler replied that he had got the idea from us. Americans, he said, are the great rope and lamppost artists of the world, known of all men as such. He was using the same methods against the Jews that we used against the loyalists of '76, the Indians, the Chinese on our Western Coast, the Negroes, the Mexicans, the Filipinos—every helpless people, in fact, whom we had ever chanced to find underfoot. This may be a rank exaggeration, but the

[1] Literally, "way of living," but more the manner in which society and persons handle particular issues and situations.

barb in it sticks. I recall another incident which anyone who knows our history will recognize at once as symptomatic. To get the force of it one must bear in mind that its hero was utterly humorless, utterly incapable of expressing himself in a deliberately humorous exaggeration. He was speaking the language of dull, serious, workaday matter-of-fact. Passing through a Missouri village two or three years ago, one of my friends stopped for a chat with a citizen, evidently a man of local mark, who was in a state of mind over the commercial practices of certain Jews who had settled there. "I tell you, we are going after those people some day," he said, "and when we do, we ain't going to be gentlemanly about it, like Hitler."

II

My former paper began by stating the problem thus: It is the problem of "maintaining a *modus vivendi* between the American Jew and his fellow-citizens which is strong enough to stand any shocks of an economic dislocation such as may occur in the years ahead." I went on to give reasons why this must be done if we are to avoid extremely damaging consequences; and I then proposed to show in this present paper the specific difficulties and complications which lie in the way of doing it.

First and foremost in point of difficulty, we must guard against becoming victims of a misnomer. The problem is not essentially Jewish, not essentially Semitic; it is an Oriental problem, Jewish only in so far as the Oriental people concerned in it happen to be Jews rather than Syrians, East Indians, Persians, or some other. The moment this is understood, one perceives the degree to which it differentiates this particular problem of population from others which are superficially similar. For example, in the period following the Civil War great hordes of poverty-stricken Irish arrived on our shores, and the economic effect of their presence, coupled with their extraordinary genius for petty politics, set up a terrific commotion which raged from coast to coast. "No Irish need apply" was a phrase so common that it degenerated into irrelevant slang as a mere expression of strong feeling directed at anything or nothing. The reader will find what is perhaps the classic example of this usage if he looks up Mark Twain's account of Buck Fanshaw's funeral, in *Roughing It*. We had a full-sized Irish problem in those days, but it was Irish, pure and simple; it was an Occidental problem. Therefore when in course of time, perhaps twenty years or so, the economic aggravations got themselves ironed out in one way or another, the Irish promptly became acceptable as an Occidental people living among Occidentals, and they have remained so ever since.

The conditions of our problem become clearer when we fix in our minds the fact that the Jews are the only Oriental people who ever settled in an Occidental civilization in any large numbers and took any active part in Occidental life. The common saying that Jews are strangers everywhere is not quite correct. As a refugee people they were everywhere strangers in a sense, but not everywhere in the same sense. They were strangers among other Oriental peoples only in the sense that the refugee Irish and Huguenots were, and British, Scandinavian, or French refugees might be, strangers among us....

That the problem of establishing a satisfactory *modus vivendi* is Oriental rather than Jewish may be easily shown by imagining the appearance here of another Oriental people in equal numbers and in the same circumstances. We have a small implantation of Armenians, excellent people who have done well, mostly as urban dwellers and in small businesses, and are well thought of. They do not mix much, keeping largely to a social life of their own, and they do not put themselves forward in our public life. The Armenian's trading instinct is said to be much keener than the Jew's; we have all heard the saying current in the Levant, "Two Jews, one Greek; two Greeks, one Persian; two Persians, one Armenian." Their position among us is thus roughly comparable to that of the Jews, say, seventy years ago.

Now suppose that instead of this small implantation we had nearly five million Armenians in this country, and that New York was the centre of the whole Armenian world, culturally, commercially, financially. Suppose that in the period 1881–1929 there had arrived here 2,314,668 Armenians (in the one year 1906 more than 150,000), virtually all of them refugees from a most hideous oppression and persecution; hunted and driven; poor, desperate, degraded by having been for years condemned to modes of life to which no decent person would subject a worthless dog; ready with a blood-thirsty eagerness to face any conditions, to compete with anyone and everyone on any terms, in order to get a living. Suppose that where fifty years ago you saw one Armenian you now see twenty, and most of them, by force of circumstances, not very personable specimens. Suppose you saw a steady infiltration of Armenians into positions of the highest prominence in our public life. Would the ensuing problem be essentially Armenian or Oriental? Would the general instinctive reaction between the two peoples be the same as it would be if the Armenians were an Occidental people? Would the resultant mixture be chemical? The parallel case of the Irish gives pretty substantial evidence that it would not; and, to a significant extent, so does the case of the Chinese....

The first Jewish immigration to America was a small one of Spanish and Portuguese Jews, known as Sephardim and speaking Ladino. The Russian and Polish Jews, known as Ashkenazim and speaking *jüdisch-deutsch,* or Yiddish, came later and in enormous numbers. It is interesting to observe the rather deep social cleavage between these two branches of the same people. Coming comparatively lately out of a civilization so largely their own, in which they had figured with such high distinction, the Sephardic Jews in Europe have a benevolent but prideful feeling of superiority towards the more unfortunate Ashkenazim, regarding them somewhat, though not precisely, as the cultivated Southerner of earlier days might regard poor-white trash. The Ashkenazim, especially those who have become prosperous, repay this disfavor with interest, even to the extent that marriages between the two groups are discouraged on both sides, and by both are termed "mixed marriages." Descendants of the original Sephardic families still exist in this country, but are vastly outnumbered by the Ashkenazim.

Thus it appears that in virtue of his special position in Occidental society the Jew is under a disability whereby the Occidental has never been, and is not, able to meet him except on special terms of acceptability. This does not make him an *Untermensch*,[2] however, as is sometimes asserted, because the Occidental is under a disability precisely similar, whereby the Jew has never been, and is not, able to meet him on the same terms as those accorded to one who is *"von unsere Leute."*[3] The existence of this reciprocal disability is the fundamental thing that any effort to arrange a durable *modus vivendi* between the two peoples must take into account. Failure to do this is mainly responsible for the very puny results attained by such efforts hitherto — efforts like those of Mr. Asch, of the National Conference, of Mr. White's Council Against Intolerance. They overlook the fact that Jew and Occidental are each the product of a distinct and special history. They fail to heed the austere saying of Ernest Renan, that "man does not improvise himself." Not being a Jew, I have not presumed to analyze the Jew's disability, but as an Occidental I am on safe ground in analyzing the disability which I share in common with my kind.

In discussing these matters with one of my friends not long ago, a very learned rabbi finally said, "You are right. What it comes to is that you are a fine man and I like you, but I don't trust you, and you don't trust me." My friend thought this over for a moment, and said, "That is so." Now, this did not imply that their word was not good, or that their pocketbooks were not safe; it carried no ethical implications whatever. It meant that in each there were great areas of consciousness which the other could not possibly enter upon, let alone explore; therefore no satisfactory presumptions could be made upon the content of those areas or upon the reactions which the motion of that content might set up. My friend, speaking of the Jews, put the whole matter admirably in a single sentence: "They have got something which they don't need to tell one another, and they can't tell us." In all probability (though on this I must speak provisionally and under correction) the Jew finds this as true of us as we of him. . . .

When I was a young man of twenty-five or so, I was once marooned for eight days on one of society's most arid islands, in company with a Jewish girl of twenty-three. There being virtually no one else to talk with, we were

---

[2]An inferior being, often used in contrast to *Ubermensch,* a superior being or superman. The term was used by the Nazis to describe Jews, Slavs, Africans, and others they considered racially inferior to "Aryans."

[3]Literally, "of our people," but in this usage it conveys a deep sense of affinity or connection among members of a particular people.

pretty strictly limited to each other's society, and became very intimate. She was the only girl I ever saw who seemed to me the acme of everything desirable, with no offset that I could discover—everything in nature and disposition, education, beauty and charm, cosmopolitan culture and manners. Such I have always imagined Fanny Mendelssohn must have been or perhaps rather Henriette Herz, at the time when the mighty Schleiermacher was making up to her and the great Wilhelm von Humboldt was writing her his charming and whimsical love letters. What especially interested me was my complete certainty that with the best will in the world on both sides I should know her no better at the end of a hundred years of close companionship than I did at the end of those eight days. I never saw or heard of her afterwards, nor tried to do either. I have often thought, however, of what would happen if some rash and personable young Occidental fell in love with her—no one could help doing that—and married her. If he were sensitive, how distressed and dissatisfied he would be as he became aware of the vast areas of her consciousness from which he was perforce shut out forever; and on the other hand, if he were too insensitive to feel that he was shut out from them, how intolerable her life with him would be. . . .

Then there is the matter of immigration for our social engineers to think of. Today as I write this I read a disclosure from the State Department that 4,000 refugees a month are coming here, that 600,000 more have applied for visas, half of them, "including many Jews," in Germany and German-occupied countries. I also read that "thousands of Viennese Jews are cabling relatives here to deposit the cost of their passage over." However the intelligent Occidental may regard this prospect, the Occidental mass-man does not regard it as he would that of a similar irruption of Occidental refugees. In the latter case it would be only the economic side of the matter that would concern him, while in the former it would be more than that, as it would be in the case of any other Oriental people. Furthermore, he has collateral beliefs which operate as an aggravation. He believes that every Jew in the world who can find his way here will do so by hook or by crook; also that Jews have better-organized facilities for getting here than other refugees have; also that in this direction, despite the letter of our immigration laws, our government is distinctly and specially and reprehensibly squeezable. Whether or not he is right in believing all this is not to the point. The point is that he believes it firmly, and that our architects must take due notice of his belief.

I have no observations to make on the purely economic features of our problem, because I see nothing peculiar or special about them, except, of course, that the Occidental mass-man's view of the Jew's economic successes and economic practices is liable to the special coloration which it would have in the case of another Oriental in the same circumstances. He is inclined to be more resentful of the Oriental as a competitor than of another Occidental, and his resentment has a qualitative difference marked by a vague sense of cosmic injustice, a sense of being unduly and intolerably "put upon." He is also more inclined to bring an indictment against a whole Oriental people on the strength of the occasional roguery or swinery which he has encountered in individuals. Where the Oriental is concerned he is quicker to generalize, to take *omne ignotum pro magnifico,*[4] as on our Western coast when he evolved the maxim that "for ways that are dark and for tricks that are vain the heathen Chinee is peculiar." All this may be deplored as unjust and indefensible, but there it is for our social architects and engineers to deal with as best they may. The civilized Occidental knows that an Oriental people, like any other, must be granted its fair proportion of rogues and swine, and he makes his general estimate accordingly; but here again it is not the view of the civilized Occidental which counts, but the view of the Occidental mass-man.

As my space is running out, I shall mention only one more complication which is seriously disabling; it arises from the peculiar and suspicious sensitiveness which the Jew has developed, whereby he is prone to see enmity where there is none, and even more regularly to attribute dislike or distrust to a cause which does not exist. As a Jewish writer says of his people, "They tend to nurse the obsession that the only reason for the slightest rebuff from which they may suffer in business, social life, or any other activity, is a causeless anti-Jewish prejudice, quite unjustified by anything in their personal behavior as individuals." Or as an acquaintance once put it to me in more colloquial terms, "A Jew always thinks you dislike him because he is a Jew. It never seems to occur to him that you might possibly dislike him because he's offensive." . . .

---

[4]Everything unknown seems magnificent.

JAMES MARSHALL

From *The Anti-Semitic Problem in America*
Atlantic Monthly, August 1941

James Marshall was a well-known legal scholar and writer. Note Marshall's direct response to the premises of Nock's argument, especially as they relate to the mystification of race and specific facts concerning Jews. Also notice Marshall's optimistic, democratic solution to what he thinks is really the "anti-Semitic problem."

James Marshall, "The Anti-Semitic Problem in America," *Atlantic Monthly,* Aug. 1941, 144–45, 147–49.

... The problem discussed by Mr. Nock is not a "Jewish problem in America" at all. It is the problem of American democracy. In part Mr. Nock would agree with me, only he says: "The problem is not essentially Jewish, not essentially Semitic; it is an Oriental problem." Let us now pursue this Oriental bogeyman.

Mr. Nock tells a charming little story of the Jewish girl of twenty-three with whom, when he was a young man, he "was once marooned for eight days on one of society's most arid islands." No one could help falling in love with her. She was, says he, "the only girl I ever saw who seemed to me the acme of everything desirable." There follows a passage redolent with her charms and the names of German philosophers. He never saw or heard of her again— but she became the mother of his bogeyman. He was certain that, with the best will in the world on both sides, a hundred years in her sight would bring him no better knowledge of her than those eight days, for she was "Oriental."

Here we have a bad case of Oriental mysticism confused with the normal mystery which women possess for all young men. (He evidently let her go her way in silence, and the mystery grew.) What more natural than that, the Jewish people having hailed from the East, the mystery and the Jews became irretrievably bound to the Orient?

The Jews lived over a thousand years in Germany, but to Mr. Nock they remain Oriental. One would have thought that, in view of the Oriental origin of the German tribes, under the Nock formula the Jewish people and the German people would have worked things out better. . . .

I have written at considerable length about Mr. Nock's bogey, the mysterious Oriental with whom he identifies the Jew, not merely to show the absurdity of Mr. Nock's premise, but because the mystery-creating pattern is a deep psychological pattern, deep in the whole human race, and is the basis for many misunderstandings between groups of people. This investing with mystery and power, and the resultant reactions in feelings of dispossession and fear, stem, as the psychiatrists tell us, from the nursery itself. They arise out of the struggle of brothers and sisters and the fascinated fear of siblings of the other sex. The process of growing up is the process of realizing that one does not have to be all things to all men and women, and from this that one does not have to feel dispossessed because one does not share the same ancestry, or fearful because one has not identical knowledge or capacity or cultural background.

Just as Mr. Nock makes the mistake of talking about Ashkenazic Jews as being all from the ghetto and the Pale (for the Jews of the Rhine Valley, of France and England, were never of the Pale and have been out of the ghetto for centuries), so too in his relegation of the Jew to the rôle of "Oriental" he is inaccurate. It is true that he says he is not "venturing on any stark anthropological doctrine of 'race,' first because I know nothing about such matters, and second, because they appear not to be particularly concerned in the circumstances which I am discussing." But though he does not discuss race doctrines, of which he says he knows nothing, his Oriental theory has all the indicia of a race theory, so warming to the heart of the Nazis. It would not require much compromise by Goebbels to accept the "Oriental" doctrine in place of the "Aryan."

As a matter of fact, as anthropologists have shown time and again, there is no pure Jewish race. The Jews are a people containing the blood of all peoples with whom they have dwelt for any substantial time. The variations of physical structure, pigmentation, and the color of their eyes and hair bear this out to the most casual observer. And culturally there is as much difference between a Jew of New York City and a Yemenite Jew of the Southern Arabian Peninsula as there is between a member of the University Club and a Bedouin. There is as much difference between a member of a Reformed Jewish congregation in Cincinnati and a Chasidic Jew of Warsaw as between an Episcopal bishop of Boston or New York and a parish priest in Central Siberia. Unfortunately, today religious devotion is not even a bond among all Jews any more than it is among all non-Jews. The term "Jew" is a catchall for those whose ancestors were of the Jewish faith, just as in the United States the word "Protestant" has become a catchall for those whose ancestors were Christian but not of the Catholic Church. It is a part of our passion for labels, which, if they are sufficiently vivid and enticing, will sell the patent medicine no matter what is in the bottle.

This variation among the Jews cannot be too strongly emphasized, because it results in antipathetical approaches to life, to politics, to business, and to cultural values among Jews themselves. It is well illustrated in the Jewish saying that when two Jews get together they immediately become three parties. . . .

I believe that the *modus vivendi* for which Mr. Nock sought, and which he failed to find between the American Jew and his fellow-citizens, is the identical *modus vivendi* which the entire American people must find to assure survival of democratic processes and democratic approaches to life. If with our varying interests, capacities, and backgrounds we cannot have a common faith in democratic aims and make common cause of those ends through democratic procedures and mechanisms, then our American institutions will fall. Then the programless defeatism of our Junkers[5] will leave us nothing but the totalitarian alternative.

Nothing can be so destructive of these values, nothing can play so well into the hands of the totalitarians, as a defeatism which finds it impossible to discover a *modus vivendi* and escapes into juvenile mysticism, rationalized into terms of "We cannot understand each other; we cannot escape the history of five thousand years; we cannot find a bridge between our

---

[5]The landowning aristocrats of Prussia, who continued to wield significant power through the period of the Weimar Republic.

variations." It is not history that repeats itself, but human patterns. We know now that we can conquer starvation and epidemic; we know now that the ways of democracy can work. It is the patterns of human behavior that must be our next conquest. Men of good will, men of courage, have made possible the conquests of the past. I for one am confident that we can triumph in the future.

FRANCES STRAUSS

The Intermarriage

Atlantic Monthly, September 1941

The editors of the *Atlantic Monthly* continued the symposium with a sense of urgency as the Nock and Marshall articles "brought into the open the hopes and fears of many conscientious Americans who feel that this issue must be faced without flinching or prejudice in the present emergency." They responded by printing a set of three shorter essays under the title "Americans: Jew and Christian." The first, by Congressman Emmanuel Celler, refuted with statistics Nock's argument that Jews were overly prominent in government employment. The last, by Dr. Louis Finkelstein, president of the Jewish Theological Seminary of America, was titled "For a Complete Democracy." Finkelstein argued much along the same lines that Marshall did, stressing the success of the American experiment in religious and cultural freedom and diversity. Significantly, he emphasized the positive effect of anti-Semitism in that it brought together liberal-minded Americans in a common cause: "The totalitarian attempt to divide Americans has evoked a deeper consciousness of national unity and a firm determination to achieve even more through understanding and integration. This amazing resurgence suggests that the present ideational struggle, vast and comprehensive as it is, and associated with unprecedented military operations, may be the last gasp of a dying paganism."

Frances Strauss, "The Intermarriage," *Atlantic Monthly,* Sept. 1941, 289–92.

The middle essay, reproduced here in full, uses intimate experience to refute the backbone of Nock's argument—the essential and unbridgeable differences between Christians and Jews. It is less easily summarized and brings to the discussion the immediacy of personal life too easily lost in a broad debate about social ideals.

Strauss, a non-Jew but married to a Jew, responds to Nock's assertion that Jews and Christians in the United States possessed irreconcilably different values and consciousnesses. She uses her own experience with her Jewish husband and his family to discuss the apparent differences but essential similarities between American Christians and Jews.

Yesterday I saw two portraits of my Jewish husband's great-grandfather and great-grandmother. They had been painted in Bavaria, where they lived. I looked at their open, their Nordically open, faces; I looked at their straight noses and their richly shaped, kind mouths. I thought of my husband's grandmother, who came to this country in a sailing vessel. I thought of how she brought up her family in a little Iowa town, forcing her children to stay at home on Saturday, because it was the Jewish Sabbath, and how she kept all seven of them at home on Sunday because that was the Sabbath of their neighbors and must be respected. I thought of how she worked at the needlework guild of one Christian church and sewed in the circle of another, to be impartial.

Lastly I thought of the circle of myth and speculation which non-Jews have placed around Jews. It is a hard circle to break through.

I broke through it with marriage, and not at once, either. Like any non-Jew, I thought there were special attributes of Jewishness. I thought—oh, I thought a hundred things that all non-Jews think. After ten years of a marriage requiring no more adjustment than any other, I know Jews, and I should like to try to dissolve that circle of myth for others. I remember the assumptions well, for I had all of them. Let me discuss a few of the more familiar ones in the light of my own experience.

One of the most often heard—that Jews are clannish—is, of course, true. Perhaps this is no more so than with the Irish or the Italians who live in this country, but, since Jews are more recognizable, their clannishness is the more noticeable. They have their separate fraternities, clubs, camps, summer resorts. Their social life is largely a Jewish one.

Assume for a moment that you have been born a Jew. You begin to learn early, as my children will shortly begin to learn: you learn when you are perhaps six or seven, when the neighborhood children refuse to play with you because you are Jewish. And early your mother says to you (and who can measure the heartbreak?), "It's hard to explain. There really isn't any reason, but that's the way the world is. Now let's have your cousin over; you can play with him and forget about Alice." You begin to play with your cousin and other Jews. You can share your hurt. You can, for a brief time, forget it.

As to the next assumption, that Jews are shrewd and tricky, I can only say that I am sure many of them are. I have heard, too, of shrewd Yankees, of Gentile robber barons and of Jewish ones. However, there have been many Jews like Haym Salomon, who helped finance the new American Republic and of whom James Madison later wrote, "I have for some time past been a pensioner on the favor of Haym Salomon, a Jew broker." The future President wrote, "The kindness of our little friend . . . is a fund which will preserve me from extremities, but I never resort to it without great mortification as he obstinately rejects all recompense."

I myself have had little to do with shrewd Jews. In my husband's family we have often had to put our minds to the problem of this or that unshrewd member: the doctor who could never bring himself to send bills; the trusting business man who again and again took notes which were no good, from shrewd Gentiles; the other who assumed that a verbal agreement between gentlemen was enough. A little traditional Jewish shrewdness would have increased our peace of mind.

It is often said that Jews are more emotional, and my first impulse would be to say yes, for I fall back into my old, non-Jewish judgments now and then, and I remember my emotional father-in-law. Yet there is my mother-in-law, who is as silent about her emotions as the little Spartan boy with the fox.

When I had my children in a Jewish hospital, I listened to a good deal of wailing at the wall (and did a little myself, I am told). As I lay in bed I thought, "Of course, this is a Jewish hospital." When I progressed to the wheel-chair stage and went calling on my neighbors, I discovered that some of those wails had been Jewish, it is true, but as many had been Catholic and Lutheran.

Psychologically, I was a Gentile for twenty-six years. Now I am a Jew. I have learned, for instance, to see a J on a printed page long before my eye has read the intervening words. I prefer not to discuss winters in Florida with non-Jews. Jews themselves comment unhappily on the kind of Jews in Florida.

For a Jew is born with many additional burdens. He is his brother's keeper as no non-Jew can ever be. Since many Jews are easily identified, what bad manners one exhibits are attributed to all. The bad manners of a non-Jew are his alone.

I have walked up and down suburban and downtown streets, collecting money both for the Community Fund and for the Jewish Welfare Drive. I have been turned down again and again for the Community Fund — and with justification. I have never been turned down for the Jewish Welfare Drive, although the justification was as great. "But that's for their own," you say. Yes, but so is the Community Fund for our own.

"Yet," one hears over and over, "when all is said and done, Jews are different — Oriental, not to be assimilated."

I have been entertained in an Orthodox or Kosher home, which presumably is as far as one can go in "differentness" and "Orientalism." I have not been passed butter at table in that house, or eaten any form of pork. The furniture was of an elaborate design; the colors were too gaudy for my taste. I have been in non-Jewish homes which were too elaborate and gaudy for my taste, and I have been in Catholic homes where no meat was served on Friday.

Below this surface difference? The usual run of faults and virtues, with kindness, hospitality, and love of children predominating. Are these qualities different, or Oriental?

Orthodox Jews have maintained, in their synagogues and their homes, certain traditions and pageantry which reformed Jews no longer practise. Look for Orientalism, even of this surface kind, in the reformed Jew's life, and you will find none. I shall never forget the surprise and disappointment I felt at my first Jewish temple service of the reformed kind: except that certain responses were read in Hebrew, I might have been in the Congregational church I had attended all my life!

There is my husband's cousin, who read Mr. Nock's article on the way back from her college reunion and hurried to meet me for lunch. Her merry Nordic face crinkled up as she said to me, "Do you find depths of Orientalism in me which you cannot fathom? Do you in your husband?" We both laughed.

One reason often given for this feeling of "difference" is that Jews are urban people, and cannot work with their hands. When I hear this said I think of this same cousin and her husband, of their enormous vegetable garden, their eighty apple trees, all the product of their four Jewish hands. I think of another pair of Jewish friends who have a chicken farm which they largely work themselves. I think of the agricultural miracles which have been accomplished in Palestine by Jewish hands.

Lastly there is the statement that intermarriage between Jew and Gentile can never work. Because of it I looked for differences between us which I could put down to race, and for years I braced myself to detect those differences and to meet them with courage and, I hoped, with wisdom.

But with complete honesty I can say that I have never found what I could label by my own old standards, or the world's standards, as Jewish. I do not feel ill at ease or out of place in the home of my husband's parents or relatives, or in any Jewish home I have entered. Nor, conversely, does my husband feel ill at ease in the home of my parents or that of a non-Jewish friend. I have never had to call upon either courage or wisdom to meet a "Jewish difference." However, both courage and wisdom will certainly be called upon in years to come in helping our half-Jewish children to meet the world—but that is a different story.

In short, my own experience has made me conclude that Jews have the same virtues and vices as other people, and that, could Jews live in real security, without constant fear of the next persecution, you, the non-Jew, could find no more trace of racial difference than I have found.

THE LINDBERGH CONTROVERSY

Isolationism and the question of Jewish influence on the Roosevelt administration came together in the unlikely figure of Charles A. Lindbergh, who had in 1927 made the first solo flight across the Atlantic. Among the most famous and revered public figures of the era, the "Lone Eagle" gambled and lost what might have been a chance to become president of the United States as he fought Roosevelt's move toward war. Sympathetic to aspects of the Nazi revolution in the 1930s, and in any case preferring Germany to the Soviet Union, Lindbergh steadfastly campaigned for nonintervention. By September 1941, he was accusing Roosevelt of manufacturing hostile incidents in the Atlantic to force America's entry into the war. These encounters occurred as the U.S. Navy and Coast Guard protected convoys destined for Britain and the Soviet Union.

F.D.R. Creating War Incidents, Lindbergh Says
Chicago Daily Tribune, September 11, 1941

On September 11, Roosevelt finally ordered American vessels to "shoot on sight" any German or Italian warships or airplanes encountered in these "defensive" operations. That evening, Lindbergh made a major address to eight thousand supporters at an America First rally in Des Moines, Iowa. The speech reviewed what Lindbergh saw as an organized campaign toward intervention that had begun soon after the outbreak of war in Europe. He saw the principal pro-war conspirators as "the British, the Jewish, and the Roosevelt administration." What follows is most of that speech and two reactions to it in major opinion magazines.

———

It is now two years since this latest European war began. From that day in September 1939 until the present moment, there has been an ever-increasing effort to force the United States into the conflict. That effort has been carried on by foreign interests and by a small minority of our own people, but it has been so successful that, today, our country stands on the verge of war.

At this time, as the war is about to enter its third winter, it seems appro-

Figure 3. Charles A. Lindbergh addressing an America First Rally, October 10, 1941. Lucky Lindy, who made the first solo flight across the Atlantic and instantly became one of the great heroes of the age, lent his prestige to America First efforts to keep the United States out of World War II.

priate to review the circumstances that have led us to our present position. Why are we on the verge of war? Was it necessary for us to become so deeply involved? Who is responsible for changing our national policy from one of neutrality and independence to one of entanglement in European affairs?

Personally, I believe there is no better argument against our intervention than a study of the causes and developments of the present war. I have often said that if the true facts and issues were placed before the American people, there would be no danger of our involvement.

Here, I would like to point out to you a fundamental difference between the groups who advocate foreign war and those who believe in an independent destiny for America. If you will look back over the record you will find that those of us who oppose intervention have constantly tried to clarify facts and issues, while the interventionists have tried to hide facts and confuse issues.

We ask you to read what we said last month, last year, and even before the war began. Our record is open and clear, and we are proud of it. We have not led you on by subterfuge and propaganda. We have not resorted to "steps short of" anything in order to take the American people where they did not want to go. What we said before the elections we say "again, and again, and again" today. And we will not tell you tomorrow that it was "just campaign oratory."

Have you ever heard an interventionist, or a British agent, or a member of the administration in Washington, ask you to go back and study a record of what they have said since the war started? Are these self-styled defenders of democracy willing to put the issue of war to a vote of our people? Do you find these crusaders for foreign freedoms advocating the freedom of speech, or the removal of censorship here in our own country?

The subterfuge and propaganda that exists in our country is obvious on every side. Tonight I shall try to pierce thru a portion of it to the naked facts which lie beneath.

When this war started in Europe, it was clear that the American people were solidly opposed to entering it. Why shouldn't we be? We had the best defensive position in the world; we had a tradition of independence from Europe; and the one time we did take part in a European war left European problems unsolved, and debts to America unpaid.

National polls showed that when England and France declared war on Germany in 1939, less than 10 per cent of our population favored a similar course for America.

But there were various groups of people here and abroad whose interests and beliefs necessitated the involvement of the United States in the war. I shall point out some of these groups tonight, and outline their methods of procedure. In doing this, I must speak with utmost frankness, for in order to counteract their efforts, we must know exactly who they are.

The three most important groups who have been pressing this country toward war are the British, the Jewish, and the Roosevelt administration. Behind these groups, but of lesser importance, are a number of capitalists, Anglophiles, and intellectuals who believe that their future, and the future of mankind, depends upon the domination of the British empire.

Add to these the communistic groups who were opposed to intervention until a few weeks ago, and I believe I have named the major war agitators, not of those sincere but misguided men and women who, confused by misinformation and frightened by propaganda, follow the lead of the war agitators.

As I have said, these war agitators comprise only a small minority of our people; but they control a tremendous influence.

Against the determination of the American people to stay out of war, they have marshaled the power of their propaganda, their money, and their patronage.

Let us consider these groups, one at a time. First, the British. It is obvious and perfectly understandable that Great Britain wants the United States in the war on her side. England is now in a desperate position. Her population is not large enough, and her armies are not strong enough to invade the continent of Europe and win the war she declared against Germany. Her geographical position is such that she cannot win the war by the use of aviation alone, regardless of how many planes we send her. Even if America entered the war, it is improbable that the allied armies could invade Europe and overcome the axis powers.

But one thing is certain. If England can draw this country into the war she can shift to our shoulders a large portion of the responsibility for waging it, and for paying its cost. As you all know we were left with the debts of the last European war and unless we are more cautious in the future than we have been in the past we will be left with the debts of the present one....

The second major group mentioned is the Jewish. It is not difficult to understand why Jewish people desire the overthrow of Nazi Germany. The persecution they suffered in Germany would be sufficient to make bitter enemies of any race. No person with a sense of the dignity of mankind can condone the persecution the Jewish race suffered in Germany. But no person of honesty and vision can look on their pro-war policy here today without seeing the dangers involved in such a policy, both for us and for them.

Instead of agitating for war the Jewish groups in this country should be opposing it in every possible way, for they will be among the first to feel its consequences. Tolerance is a virtue that depends upon peace and strength. History shows that it cannot survive war and devastation. A few farsighted Jewish people realize this and stand opposed to intervention. But the majority still do not. Their greatest danger to this country lies in their large ownership and influence in our motion pictures, our press, our radio, and our government.

The Roosevelt administration is the third powerful group which has been carrying this country toward war. Its members have used the war emergency to obtain a third presidential term for the first time in American history. They have used the war to add unlimited billions to a debt which was already the highest we had ever known. And they have used the war to justify the restrictions of congressional power, and the assumption of dictatorial procedures on the part of the President and his appointees.

The power of the Roosevelt administration depends upon the maintenance of a wartime emergency. The prestige of the Roosevelt administration depends upon the success of Great Britain to whom the President attached his political future at a time when most people thought that England and France would easily win the war. The danger of the Roosevelt administration lies in its subterfuge. While its members have promised us peace they have led us to war heedless of the platform upon which they were elected.

In selecting these three groups as the major agitators for war, I have included only those whose support is essential to the war party. If any one of these groups—the British, the Jewish, or the administration—stops agitating for war, I believe there will be little danger of our involvement. I do not believe that any two of them are powerful enough to carry this country to war without the support of the third. And to these three, as I have said, all other war groups are of secondary importance.

When hostilities commenced in Europe, in 1939, it was realized by these groups that the American people had no intention of entering the war. They knew it would be worse than useless to ask us for a declaration of war at that time. But they believed that this country could be enticed into the war in very much the same way we were enticed into the last one. They planned, first, to prepare the United States for foreign war under the guise of American defense; second, to involve us in the war, step by step, without our realization; third, to create a series of incidents which would force us into the actual conflict. These plans were, of course, to be covered and assisted by the full power of their propaganda.

Lindbergh's Nazi Pattern
New Republic, September 22, 1941

The liberal journal *New Republic* endorsed Roosevelt's "shoot on sight" order as a historic and welcome defiance of Hitler and the first step toward his defeat. It blasted Lindbergh's speech, noting parallels between his arguments and those of the Nazis. Note the way in which the article characterizes the growth and nature of the American public's attitudes toward the Nazis.

"Lindbergh's Nazi Pattern," *New Republic,* Sept. 22, 1941, 360–61.

To get at the real meaning of Charles A. Lindbergh's anti-Semitic speech at Des Moines, one must begin not in Des Moines in 1941 but in Germany before 1933. We agree with Michael Straight's report from Washington, in this issue of *The New Republic,* that the various recent attacks on the Jews are not merely a coincidence. Just as the sinking of an American ship by a Nazi raider is not an isolated "incident," so Lindbergh's threat to the American Jews, stark as it is, must not be viewed by itself. Those who had studied the history of the Nazi movement knew it was coming, as they also knew the attack on Hollywood was coming. Anti-Semitism has been implicit in the whole record of the America First Committee and its satellites among the isolationist Senators. Now it has become explicit. Lindbergh's speech, like the Nye-Clark-Wheeler campaign against the film industry, is best seen as part of a pattern, and that pattern is Nazi.

For the Nazi pattern has always been to use anti-Semitism as the most powerful ingredient in the crucible of hatreds. The recipe is simple: you appeal to as many discontented groups as possible; there will be clashes of interest and attitude among them, however, and so, to get past these difficulties and fuse the disparate elements in your movement, you invoke the powerful force of unreason formed in religious hatred. You may start with the best of intentions; you may at the beginning prefer to avoid intolerance. But ultimately, if you are in a movement which is indifferent to Hitlerism or seeking to appease it or apologize for it or cooperate with it, the temptation to use the force of anti-Semitism is too great, and you succumb to it.

Consider Lindbergh as an instance. Up to now he has played the part of the detached and non-political patriot. Not for him to stir hatreds, or soil himself in the mud of politics. He recognized, of course, even when he was talking loftily of the inevitable triumph of the Nazis, that Hitler had committed ghastly cruelties. But in the phrase popularized by his wife, he saw Hitlerism as "the scum on the wave of the future." The idea was that we could skim off the scum, and have the clear waves wash our American shores.

Now he is neck-deep in the scum itself. There are three groups, he told us in his Des Moines speech, who are trying to get America into the war: the British, the Jews, and the administration. With a sickening hypocrisy he admits that the Nazi persecutions "would be sufficient to make bitter enemies of any race." But, he goes on to warn, the Jews are "agitating for war." They own and control "our motion pictures, our press, our radio, and our government." And if they continue agitating for war, "they will be among the first to feel its consequences."

This is at once slick and crude. Goebbels could not have done better. For this is the precise language of the Nazi yahoos. One of the earliest of the Nazi slogans, even before Hitler came to power, was that the Jews owned and controlled the press, the radio, the government. Actually it was not true in Germany as it is not true in America, but since when has the

Nazi mentality cared for the facts? The Nazis used the "stab in the back" *(Dolchenstoss)* slogan: the Jews, they said, had stabbed Germany in the back and lost the war for the Germans. Lindbergh's variation is that the Jews are getting us into the war. But the pattern is the same. Lindbergh knows that there is a deeply rooted hatred of the British in America. He knows that there is still a die-hard minority that hates the administration as it hates little else in the world. He knows what fighting words are "Communists," "capitalists," "intellectuals" in the vocabulary of American ignorance and prejudice. All of these, in his speech, he makes part of his indictment of the warmongers. But he finishes and fuses the pattern by his appeal to religious hatred. And in doing so he is, in effect, inviting all the separate hate-groups to combine in a common hatred of the Jews.

The Forbidden Theme
Christian Century, September 24, 1941

The conservative *Christian Century* took a different view of the Lindbergh address. Significantly, the article preceding this one blasted Roosevelt's "shoot on sight" policy as part of a series of actions calculated to bring America into the war and urged Congress to resist. Still, the editorial board approached Lindbergh's speech with grave misgivings as to its effects. Essentially endorsing his view of the situation but criticizing his raising of the "Jewish question" as ill-timed, the article reprinted here launches into its own views of that very topic. Note the tightrope the editors attempt to walk as they outline their own sense of the place of Jews in American society and in the realm of national discourse.

Colonel Lindbergh's genius for rushing in where angels fear to tread does not classify him with those to whom Alexander Pope originally attributed this propensity, but his latest adventure does put an editorial commentator in a tight place either to criticize or defend him. Defense of his reference to the Jews as one of the sources of war agitation in the United States could conceivably be made if the literal text of his remarks could be calmly

"The Forbidden Theme," *Christian Century,* Sept. 24, 1941, 1167–69.

kept in mind. But the issue which he touched is so superheated with prejudice and fear that any articulation of it opens up an abyss of social possibility before which all but the stoutest or most callous will shrink.

The subject had been thrust upon public attention, however, before Mr. Lindbergh spoke. It had been our hope that the Senate's investigation of the motion picture monopoly might proceed without raising the racial question. This hope, held precariously and with grave anxiety, was rudely dispelled when Wendell Willkie charged that the investigators were motivated by anti-Semitism. Denials by the leaders of the investigation, accompanied by their forthright asseverations of racial, religious, and democratic tolerance, only served to rivet the nation's attention upon the fact that the movie industry of the United States is virtually in the control of Jewish magnates.

The fat was in the fire. Mr. Willkie's charge made explicit a situation which has long been recognized privately but kept from open discussion in press and forum by considerations of discretion and public policy. To widen the scope of the issue beyond that of a particular industry, it remained only for someone to point out that American Jewry, allowing for some notable exceptions, has stood actively and almost solidly, if not for this country's actual participation in the war, at any rate for those policies of the administration which inevitably spelled war. It was Mr. Lindbergh's fate to give public voice to this fact.

Though he spoke with fine feeling and sympathy for a people who have suffered as no others have suffered at the hands of the Nazi regime, the grave psychological effects which will flow from his candor are not lessened thereby. He pleaded with his Jewish fellow Americans to rise above their racial sense of solidarity with their brothers in Europe and determine their attitude toward America's participation solely by the fact that they are Americans. But this will be forgotten in the dust of pro-war and anti-war passion with which his plea was associated. Whether or not he envisaged the exacerbation of race animosity in this country as the result of his calling attention to Jewish aggressiveness in war propaganda, his remarks are bound to be regarded as a threat if not a condoning of anti-Semitic activity.

We believe that both Mr. Willkie and Mr. Lindbergh were gravely ill-advised in lending themselves as the instruments by which the Jewish problem has been brought to the front of the national consciousness at this time. That the problem exists, no one will deny. We have taken numerous occasions to discuss it in these pages, striving to probe deeper into its reality and its roots than those are accustomed to go whose efforts are confined to the generating of good will by appeal to the sentiment of tolerance. But such discussions were long before the war. The Jewish problem can be fairly faced with any prospect of making progress toward its solution, only in periods of peace and relative national calmness. That it should be opened up in a time when passion runs high, and that it should be associated with other issues concerning which men's hearts are on fire, opens the way for the most disastrous and diabolical "solution" conceivable.

Did Mr. Lindbergh and Mr. Willkie envisage such an outcome, or were they actuated merely by an impulsive candor? Did Mr. Willkie, on his part, assume that the spirit of tolerance had become so widespread and so deeply rooted in American life that, by branding certain leaders as anti-Semitic, he would effectually discredit the anti-war movement? If so, we believe he was grievously mistaken.

Despite all the attempts to gloss over and to conceal the tension between Jew and gentile in this land of freedom, the simple truth is that the spirit of tolerance is hardly more than skin deep. It is mixed with pretension and insincerity, with politics and commercial prudence. The ideology of tolerance is a façade behind which there exists an uneradicated dislike, resentment, and intolerance. Our claim of tolerance is all too clearly intended for public consumption, while private feeling and sheltered conversation deny our public pretension. Had Mr. Willkie's charge of anti-Semitism been left to follow its own course, he would have been profoundly disillusioned with respect to the rallying of popular sympathy for the Jews in support of his position.

But it was not left to follow its own course. Within a few days Mr. Lindbergh, coming in from the opposite side, interjected the racial issue more daringly by charging the Jewish population with concerted war propaganda. Did Mr. Lindbergh, on his part, act on impulse, or did he deliberately count upon rallying support for the anti-war cause by arousing the suppressed animosities which ferment in the private soul of large masses of our non-Jewish population? If so, we believe he, too, was sadly misadvised.

There will be no rallying on behalf of either intervention or non-intervention because of racial feeling against the Jews. The reason is that anti-Semitism is not logical; it is an irrational passion which, when once released from the inhibitions of public convention, is as likely to flame out in one direction as in another. It cannot be controlled in the interest of any rational public policy. Once let the prejudices and animosities which are nursed in private break through the amenities of public tolerance and you have unleashed a force which will attach itself to any cause or any public policy which promises drastic action against the Jew.

That this force is latent but alive in American society, only sentimentalists will deny. In the years when the problem could have been approached with some degree of calmness, neither Jew nor gentile attacked it with realistic candor and objectivity. In the political approach, the formula, "Make America safe for differences," has succeeded only in erecting a political front behind which the age-old racial acerbities have been both hidden and exploited. The whole range of social contacts has been virtually unaffected by this political ideology. On the contrary, with the mounting Jewish population, especially in the great cities, the social rule of segregation is being applied with increasing rigor. A hundred clubs and hotel foyers rang with denunciation of Lindbergh on the morning after his Des Moines speech—clubs and hotels which bar their doors to Jews.

With the conspicuous emergence of an increasing number of successful

Jews in big business, the professions, and government, the latent racial prejudice of the gentile community easily passes into irrational jealousy coupled with suspicion and credulity, giving rise to all sorts of weird tales about the Jews "taking the country" and "running the world." The problem remains with us, despite the political illusions by which we seek to conceal and evade it.

The churches and synagogues have followed essentially the same method as the politicians and publicists. They have sought to hold the racial and social tension in a quiescent equilibrium by translating the issue into terms of religion and pleading for religious tolerance as both a Christian and a democratic principle. This procedure is fallacious and has proved ineffective as a way of getting at the essential problem. True, a flourishing interfaith organization of Protestants, Catholics, and Jews has done much to create sentiments of good will. In the past half century a distinct change has been wrought in the area of mutual religious appreciation. But the movement has lacked realism. It has developed amenities, but has scarcely touched realities.

We say it is fallacious. Religious intolerance in the United States is no menace to our peace. The Jewish problem is not primarily a religious problem. It is a racial or social problem. It cannot be stated in terms of Jew and Christian, but can be stated realistically only in terms of Jew and gentile. Its explosive possibilities do not inhere in any conflict of religious forms or creeds, but in a tragic social unassimilibility. Political cooperation on the basis of democracy leaves the essential problem untouched. Likewise, religious amiability under the banner of mutual tolerance leaves the problem untouched. The churches and synagogues have never come to grips with the real issue.

Yet these conventional amenities of politics and religion, reinforced by the self-imposed restraint which has characterized the nation's press, have successfully kept the issue from becoming publicly acute. We may wish that there had been more candid efforts to probe the issue and bring it into the light of objective consideration while the nation was in a more rational mood. But having defaulted in that duty, we may now be thankful for the existence of a convention which makes this a forbidden theme, and inhibits any attempt to make controversial capital out of the Jewish-gentile problem.

Today, emphatically, is no time to face this issue or to raise it. The thesis of this writing is that it ought not be discussed now at all, and the foregoing has been written to say why. By injecting the racial question into the bitter controversy over the war, we believe that both Mr. Willkie and Mr. Lindbergh did a distinct disservice to American democracy.

It should be the profound aspiration and prayer of every American citizen, be he gentile or Jew, that the amenities and conventions by which our political, publicity, and religious agencies have repressed this problem in the past may continue to check realistic discussion until quieter times return, when reason—at best a precarious and uncertain judge in a matter so charged with passion and unreason—resumes again her now vacant throne.

PART THREE

Imagining the Unimaginable, 1942–1945

On December 7, 1941, carrier-based Japanese warplanes attacked the American naval base at Pearl Harbor, Hawaii. The United States declared war on Japan the next day. Three days later, Japan's ally Germany declared war on America. The United States' involvement in the war — pressure for which had been increasing but still remained a matter of angry controversy as late as December 6 — instantly became a reality that mobilized the nation into a fighting machine. Events in Europe now had a direct impact on the lives of Americans, and the Nazis' war on the Jews was the act of a declared enemy of the United States.

THE NAZI WAR AGAINST THE JEWS

American entry into the war roughly coincided with a developing Nazi policy and plan to systematically annihilate the Jews of Europe. As Germany's expansionist plans (most recently demonstrated in Austria and Czechoslovakia) created increasing opposition and talk of war in England, France, and America, Hitler blamed "International Jewry" for fomenting such opposition. On January 30, 1939, Hitler declared in a dramatic speech that Europe's Jews would not survive a new war. The invasion and occupation of Poland in September 1939, which put 3.3 million Jews directly under German control, were the first loosely organized steps to make good on that threat. As the Nazis moved into Poland, German soldiers and storm trooper (SS) units harassed, humiliated, imprisoned and often killed Polish Jews. By 1940, the Nazis had begun a highly organized campaign of concentration, one in which the Jewish inhabitants of towns all over Poland were sealed into urban ghettos in Warsaw, Cracow, Lodz, and other cities. They lived in terribly overcrowded quarters, were given too little to eat and little or no medicine, and were forced to work in factories and at hard labor in support of the war. Hundreds of thousands eventually died in the ghettos as starvation and disease took their toll.

Having succeeded in Poland, Hitler turned his armies west against Norway, Denmark, the Netherlands, Luxembourg, Belgium, and France, as well as south against Greece, emerging victorious against all. Thousands more Jews came under German control. In each of these nations, the Nazis almost immediately began to limit the freedom of Jews and to plan for more serious actions against them.

In 1941, the Germans again turned east and implemented a new strategy of destruction as part of their invasion of the Soviet Union in June 1941. Hitler declared a *Vernichtungskrieg* (war of annihilation) against the Soviet Union, in part because he considered communism to be Germany's mortal enemy and in part because he considered the Soviet people inferior to the Germans and fit only for slavery. The Nazis also created *Einsatzgruppen* (special units) to follow the victorious German army as it swept toward Moscow in the summer and fall of 1941. The sole mission of these units was to round up and kill Jews, Gypsies, and community leaders and partisans. By December 1941, they had murdered at least half a million persons in Estonia, Latvia, Lithuania, Ukraine, and other parts of the Soviet Union.

The success of the Nazis' ghettoization policy in Poland and the killing squads in the Soviet Union spurred them to consider more efficient means of killing Jews and others in these areas, as well as strategies to murder Jews in Western Europe without disrupting the German occupation of those countries. The idea of extermination centers, to which Jews from all over Europe could be transported, came as a logical if ghastly extension of the Nazi commitment to an *Endlösung,* or Final Solution, to the "Jewish problem."

In the fall of 1941, the Nazis began to experiment with new extermination methods and technologies at Polish sites. On September 23, 1941, they used gas to kill six hundred Soviet prisoners and two hundred Poles at a prisoner of war and labor camp called Auschwitz. On December 8, the day after Pearl Harbor, they set up a killing center at Chelmno, cramming mostly Polish Jews into sealed vans and piping in carbon monoxide exhaust. At Belzec, in the winter of 1941–42, Nazi technicians constructed airtight chambers within wooden huts and killed Jews using poison gas. Larger and more sophisticated gassing facilities were soon set up at Auschwitz, Majdanek, Treblinka, and Sobibor, where gassing Jews became a sometimes round-the-clock industry. In these camps alone, approximately 3.2 million people, mostly Jews, perished. The names of these centers for mass murder have become almost synonymous with the Holocaust itself.

These killings continued even as, beginning in 1942, the German army experienced reverses on all fronts. Only with the approach of the Soviet army from the east did the Nazis abandon the Polish extermination camps and march surviving prisoners to Germany. Those prisoners who did not die from starvation, exposure, or disease on the marches were crowded into existing concentration camps and left to die. By April and May 1945, these camps—Dachau, Buchenwald, Nordhausen, Mauthausen, and many others—had become overcrowded with the dead and dying, in short the very images of hell on earth.

AMERICAN KNOWLEDGE AND COMPREHENSION

It was, in fact, the reports, pictures, and newsreels taken by Allied journalists, Signal Corps photographers, and liberating soldiers that brought home the reality of Nazi brutality and mass murder. Some who suspected that prior reports had been exaggerated or were simply propaganda felt compelled to admit, "So it was true!" Others simply exclaimed, "We didn't know!"

What did Americans know about Nazi genocide as it developed in the years 1941 through 1945? This much is painfully clear: Beginning virtually from the time of Hitler's invasion of the Soviet Union, Allied intelligence sources were aware of instances of mass murder and the creation of killing centers remarkably soon after such actions and projects were accomplished. Stories appeared in the press but public knowledge of Nazi atrocities was piecemeal and hampered by government secrecy.

Americans received such news fragments alongside what were understandably far more important stories to them—those that chronicled the progress of American and other Allied forces against Japan and Germany. Yet the public had access to some significant coverage of Nazi murder and, furthermore, to passionate and insightful commentary about its meaning and consequences.

Historians have spent much time debating what could and should have been done by the government and private organizations in America and Britain in response to this knowledge. By nature of its brevity, this collection of documents cannot directly confront the various questions that have been raised in useful depth and complexity. (The Epilogue addresses the historiography of these questions.) Instead, these documents provide a sample of the character and texture of information available to Americans and the sense that some made of it at the time.

Wandering Jews
Time, December 15, 1941

As news of actions against Jews in Poland and the Soviet Union began to leak out of Europe, private Jewish organizations and the American media began to reshape their visions of the past and present. The entry of the United States into the war also increased interest in what were now actions of a declared enemy. The Institute of Jewish Affairs in New York published *Jews in Nazi Europe,* which showed the worsening conditions for Jews from the 1930s through 1941. *Time* prominently published significant facts from this report in the story reproduced below, calling it "the first full balance sheet on what remains of Jewish life on the Continent." This was just before the Nazis set up the extermination camps to provide the *Endlösung,* or Final Solution, to the "Jewish problem."

— Not a Jew is left in Memel and Danzig.
— The number of Jews in Greater Germany has dropped from 760,000 to about 250,000 since the Nazis came to power.

"Wandering Jews," *Time,* Dec. 15, 1941, 6–7.

— Warsaw's ghetto had more than ten times as many deaths (4,290) as births (396) last June. In all Poland, Jewish deaths since the start of World War II have been five times the normal rate—300,000 in two years.

These were highlights of a 151-page report, *Jews in Nazi Europe,* released last week by Manhattan's Institute of Jewish Affairs. The volume covers 8,500,000 Jews in 16 countries, tots up the first full balance sheet on what remains of Jewish life on the Continent. Excerpts:

— Since Italy passed its racial laws in 1938, some 4,500 of its 57,000 Jews have become Christians "due to a desire to place children in Catholic schools and circumvent the economic restrictions imposed on Jews . . . also [in] the hope of emigration to Latin America, where many countries admit proselytes while barring Jews."

— Rumania's five-day Jewish pogrom last January was featured by "kosher butchery," a monstrous parody of the Jewish ritual for killing animals by throat-slitting. "All Jewish men from 18 to 50 years of age have been drafted for forced labor. Their daily food ration is one-eighth of that provided for a Rumanian soldier."

— Czecho-Slovakia had "no Jewish problem . . . prior to Munich." Afterwards the Nazis "Aryanized" an estimated $1,000,000,000 worth of Jewish property.

— "The Nazis boast that some 20,000 Jewish enterprises are already under Aryan control" in The Netherlands. The Dutch people do not support the anti-Semitic decrees forced on them by Germany.

— Before Hitler "half of the lawyers and one-fourth of the physicians of Berlin were Jewish" and in Vienna the 165,000 Jews (8.6% of the city) had "62% of the lawyers, 62.7% of the dentists, 47.2% of all physicians, 28.6% of the professors." In 1930 it is estimated that the Jews' share of the German income and aggregate wealth "was four times that of the Jewish population ratio. . . . Today there are no Jewish business enterprises in Germany, no Jewish lawyers, craftsmen, actors, or musicians. . . . With the exception of the manual labor which they perform upon a virtually slave basis, the Jews have been completely eliminated from the economic life of greater Germany."

Equally frank and detailed is the Institute's report on the Jewish refugee problem. Nearly a million European Jews had to flee their homes between 1933 and 1940. Principal havens: 330,000 to Russia (300,000 from the Nazi part of Poland at the start of World War I), 150,000 to England, France, Belgium, and The Netherlands (Nazis have caught up with them again in the last three), 135,000 to the U.S., 116,000 to Latin America, 110,000 to Palestine.

"Today," says the Institute,

opportunities for resettlement are choked off. . . . In the last analysis [refugee] rehabilitation rests on Palestine and the U.S. and, to a lesser degree, on certain South American countries. . . . Other likely countries are either closed to newcomers, or apply their laws exclusively against the Jews, directly or indirectly. [For example, in South America where the post-1933 immigration has swelled the Jewish population about 30%, Argentina will now admit Jews only if they have relatives in the country; Bolivia bars "Semitic elements"; Brazil admits few but Catholics; Chile, Bolivia, and Colombia clamped down after illegal visa scandals.] The era of . . . mass immigration that brought 2,460,495 Jews to the U.S. alone during the years 1881–1941 is now at an end. Apparently no country is willing to receive immigrants of this category in any sizable number.

MICHAEL WILLIAMS

Views and Reviews

Commonweal, December 26, 1941

The outbreak of war and reports such as *Time*'s did not end anti-Semitism in the United States or conspiratorial theories concerning Jewish power. It was a special problem among Catholic Americans who supported Father Coughlin's tirades (see pages 77–82). Some Catholic leaders recognized and deplored such hatred and actively worked to combat it. This short piece by Michael Williams, former editor of the *Commonweal,* a liberal Catholic magazine of relatively small circulation and a voice of reform in the American Catholic community, points to the severity of the problem. Monsignor Fulton J. Sheen, whom Williams mentions, was a well-known public spokesman revered by Catholics and non-Catholics alike as a voice of spiritual inspiration and solace.

. . . That the great majority of American Catholics, of all racial origins, will be loyal in thought, word, and deed now that the gigantic struggle for their country's fate has begun, and that the great majority of their spiritual leaders, the Bishops and the clergy, will speak and act as the Bishop of Hartford has already done, may be taken for granted. At the same time, the need for a great nationwide manifestation of patriotism on the part of all American Catholics, both clergy and laity alike, and the elimination of the pernicious influence of a small minority of false leaders, both clerical and lay, should be obvious.

Melancholy evidence of this lamentable fact has been provided by no less an authority on Catholic life and affairs than Monsignor Fulton J. Sheen, in his lecture at St. John's College, Brooklyn, on December 14, when he told his audience that when he spoke on November 17, to the Catechetical Congress in Philadelphia, in the course of one of the largest and most important annual Catholic meetings of our country, he was booed and hissed and heard himself branded as a "sell-out" and a "Judas" when he expressed his opinion that in the crisis of our national affairs at present it was the duty of Catholics to support the President of their country. He told of receiving literally hundreds of letters and telegrams attacking him for his speech. "One lady said she belonged to fourteen Catholic organizations," related Monsignor Sheen, "and not one percent of the membership of any of them supported the President." According to the press account of Monsignor Sheen's lecture in Brooklyn — which has notoriously been one of the principal infection points of the poisonous propaganda spread principally by Father Coughlin — Monsignor Sheen said at this point: "If this is true, I as a member of the Catholic Church denounce all of them." And then he went on to say that it might not be believable, but it was true that a number of people would like to see Hitler win the war because they hate Jews.

The prevalence of this blind spirit of hatred of Jews among American Catholics is also revealed this week in the syndicated column of Father Gillis — who denounces it — in the Catholic weekly press. Now of course it may be true that not all the American Catholics who cherish hatred of the Jews would, therefore, surrender their country to Hitler; nevertheless, the spreading of virulent anti-Semitism among Catholics in recent months and years is now an anti-national and, in my opinion, ultimately an anti-Catholic menace of the most sinister sort. I can well remember how when I was still the editor of *The Commonweal* I was told by a prominent German-American priest from the middle west that he was convinced that this paper must be financially controlled and directed by the Jews because of the anti-Hitler attitude displayed by myself and Dr. George N. Shuster and other editors and contributors. I asked the priest how he explained the famous castigation of Hitlerism contained in the encyclical letter of Pope Pius XI to the German Bishops. He solemnly informed me that the Jewish and Masonic influence in the Vatican itself was responsible for the Pope's attack on Hitler, "the man sent by Providence to uphold the Catholic Church against Communism."

That, of course, is a most fantastic example of the degree to which virulent anti-Semitism may extend even among our educated clergy; nevertheless, the doctrine that would hold a secret clique of Jews responsible for all the evils of our age, and which teaches that our own government is in the hands of such Jews, is far more widely spread among our Catholic people than is generally known. Our Church in this country has already suffered because of these horrible conditions. Every effort should now be made to repair the damage, and bring the full force of our immense majority of normal, strongly patriotic American Catholics into unimpeded support of their country and their Church.

REINHOLD NIEBUHR

Jews after the War

Nation, February 21 and 28, 1942

The growing body of information concerning the fate of Europe's Jews that began to emerge after December 1941 inspired a variety of reactions. Most Americans perceived such reports as one more indication of the evils of Nazism but saw the solution as winning the war. Some suspected that they contained exaggerations or were simply war propaganda. Reinhold Niebuhr, a prominent Christian theologian, a professor at Union Theological Seminary in New York, and a widely read columnist and author, provided one of the earliest and most telling commentaries.

Niebuhr states bluntly that the Nazis were bent on "extermination of the Jews," but he argues that winning the war would not be enough to secure the Jews' place in the postwar world. He addresses the long-term questions of anti-Semitism and the position of Jews in Christian Europe and America by grappling with some of the issues raised by Albert Jay Nock (whom he mentions; see pages 86–92), albeit from a very different perspective. Indeed, his discussions of "race" and ethnicity, as well as of a minority's relationship to a dominant culture, sound startlingly contemporary.

At the heart is Niebuhr's argument for a Jewish homeland both to preserve Jewish culture and to afford a choice for Jews who did not wish the cultural compromise of living in nations with a majority of Christians or people of other religions. He thus broaches the complicated and still

Reinhold Niebuhr, "Jews after the War," *Nation,* Feb. 21, 1942, 214–16; Feb. 28, 1942, 253–55.

pondered question, Who are the Jews—a nation, a religion, a race, or a culture?

Niebuhr also comes out squarely on the side of Zionism in its mission to create a separate Jewish homeland. At the time, Zionism was almost as controversial among Jews as it was among Christians. Despite endemic anti-Semitism, Jews were fiercely loyal Americans who sought to become an integral part of American life. Most American Jews who supported Zionism saw a new homeland as a place of refuge for *other* Jews. In addition, many worried that advocacy of Zionism might make them appear to be less loyal Americans.

Note the ways in which Niebuhr asks and answers the questions concerning the future of the Jews and the tensions inherent in the "universalism" of liberal democracies such as the United States. Also note what in retrospect seems to be something of a contradiction. Although he mentions the Nazi drive to eliminate Europe's Jews, rather than discussing ways to slow down that effort, he quickly moves on to discuss the postwar situation, this at a time when Allied victory was hardly ensured.

I

The position of the Jews in Europe and the Western world is by no means the least of the many problems of post-war reconstruction which must engage our minds even while our energies are being exhausted in achieving the prerequisite of any reconstruction, that is, the defeat of the Axis. It is idle to assume that this defeat will solve the problem of the Jews; indeed, the overthrow of Nazism will provide no more than the negative condition for the solution of any of the vexing problems of justice which disturb our consciences.

Millions of Jews have been completely disinherited, and they will not be able to obtain the automatic restoration of their rights. An impoverished Europe will not find it easy to reabsorb a large number of returned Jews, and a spiritually corrupted Europe will not purge itself quickly of the virus of race bigotry with which the Nazis have infected its culture. It must also be remembered that the plight of the Jews was intolerable in those parts of Europe which represented a decadent feudalism—Poland and the Balkans—long before Hitler made their lot impossible in what was once the democratic world.

The problem of what is to become of the Jews in the post-war world ought to engage all of us, not only because a suffering people has a claim upon our compassion but because the very quality of our civilization is involved in the solution. It is, in fact, a scandal that the Jews have had so little effective aid from the rest of us in a situation in which they are only the chief victims. The Nazis intend to decimate the Poles and to reduce other peoples to the status of helots; but they are bent upon the extermination of the Jews.

One probable reason for the liberal world's failure to be more instant in its aid to the Jews is that we cannot face the full dimensions of this problem without undermining the characteristic credos of the democratic world. Even the Jews are loath to bring the problem to our attention in all its tragic depth. We will not face it because we should be overwhelmed by a sense of guilt in contemplating those aspects of the problem which Hitler did not create but only aggravated. Some Jews have refused to face it in dread of having to recognize that the solutions provided by the liberal Jewish world have failed to reach the depths of the problem.

The liberal world has sought to dissolve the prejudice between Jews and Gentiles by preaching tolerance and good-will. Friends of the Jews have joined the Jews in seeking to persuade their detractors that the charges against them are lies. But this does not meet the real issue. The real question is, why should these lies be manufactured and why should they be believed? Every cultural or racial group has its own characteristic vices and virtues. When a minority group is hated for its virtues as well as for its vices, and when its vices are hated not so much because they are vices as because they bear the stamp of uniqueness, we are obviously dealing with a collective psychology which is not easily altered by a little more enlightenment. The fact is that the relations of cultural and ethnic groups, intra-national or international, have complexities unknown in the relations between individuals, in whom intelligence may dissolve group loyalties and the concomitant evil of group friction.

American theories of tolerance in regard to race are based upon a false universalism which in practice develops into a new form of nationalism. The fact that America has actually been a melting-pot in which a new amalgam of races is being achieved has given rise to the illusion that racial and ethnic distinction can be transcended in history to an indeterminate degree. Russian nationalism has the same relation to Marxist universalism as American nationalism has to liberal universalism. There is a curious, partly unconscious, cultural imperialism in theories of tolerance which look forward to a complete destruction of all racial distinctions. The majority group expects to devour the minority group by way of assimilation. This is a painless death, but it is death nevertheless.

The collective will to survive of those ethnic groups in America which have a base in another homeland is engaged and expressed in their homeland and need not express itself here, where an amalgam of races is taking place. The Finns need not seek to perpetuate themselves in America, for their collective will to live is expressed in Finland. But the Jews are in a different position. Though as an ethnic group they have maintained some degree of integrity for thousands of years, they are a nationality scattered among the nations. Does the liberal-democratic world fully understand that it is implicitly making collective extinction the price of its provisional tolerance?

This question implies several affirmations which are challenged by both Jewish and Gentile liberals; it is therefore important to make these affirmations explicit and to elaborate them. One is that the Jews are really a nationality and not merely a cultural group. Certainly the Jews have maintained a core of racial integrity through the ages. This fact is not disproved by the assertion that their blood is considerably mixed. There are no pure races. History develops new configurations on the bases of nature, but not in such a way as to transcend completely the natural distinctions. Who would deny that the Germans have a collective will to live, or think that this simple statement can be refuted by calling attention to the admixture of Slav blood in people of German nationality?

The integrity of the Jews as a group is of course not purely biological; it has also a religious and cultural basis. But in this Jews are not unique, for there are no purely biological facts in history. The cultural and religious content of Jewish life transcends racial particularity, as does the culture of every people, though never so absolutely as to annihilate its own ethnic core. The one aspect of Jewish life which is unique is that the Jews are a nationality scattered among the nations. I use the word "nationality" to indicate something more than "race" and something less than "nation." It is more than race by reason of the admixture of culture and less than nation by reason of the absence of a state. The Jews certainly are a nationality by reason of the ethnic core of their culture. Those Jews who do not feel themselves engaged by a collective will to live have a perfect right to be so disengaged, just as Americans of French or Greek descent need feel no responsibility for the survival of their respective nationalities. But Jews render no service either to democracy or to their people by seeking to deny this ethnic foundation of their life, or by giving themselves to the illusion that they might dispel all prejudice if only they could prove that they are a purely cultural or religious community.

The fact that millions of Jews are quite prepared to be *spurlos versenkt*,[1] to be annihilated, in a process of assimilation must affect the program of the democratic world for dealing with the Jewish question. The democratic world must accord them this privilege, including of course the right to express the ethos of their history in purely cultural and religious terms, in so far as this is possible, without an ethnic base. The democratic world must resist the insinuation that the Jews are not assimilable, particularly when the charge is made in terms of spurious friendship, as it is by Albert Jay Nock. They are not only assimilable but they have added to the riches of a democratic world by their ethnic and cultural contributions. Civilization must guard against the tendency of all communities to demand a too simple homogeneity, for if this is allowed complete expression it results in Nazi tribal primitivism. The preservation of tolerance and cultural pluralism is necessary not only from the standpoint of justice to the Jews but from the standpoint of the quality of a civilization.

---

[1] Literally, to have vanished without a trace, though Niebuhr translates it as "annihilated."

The assimilability of the Jews and their right to be assimilated are not in question; this conviction must prompt one-half of the program of the democratic world, the half which consists in maintaining and extending the standards of tolerance and cultural pluralism achieved in a liberal era. But there is another aspect of the Jewish problem which is not met by this strategy. That is the simple right of the Jews to survive as a people. There are both Jews and Gentiles who deny that the Jews have such a survival impulse as an ethnic group, but the evidence of contemporary history refutes them, as does the evidence of all history in regard to the collective impulses of survival in life generally. Modern liberalism has been blind to this aspect of human existence because its individualist and universalist presuppositions and illusions have prevented it from seeing some rather obvious facts in man's collective life.

One proof of the Jews' will to survive is, of course, that they have survived the many vicissitudes of their history. They have survived in spite of the fact that they have been a nationality scattered among the nations, without a homeland of their own, since the dawn of Western European history. They are a people of the diaspora. Modern assimilationists on both sides sometimes suggest that the survival of the Jews through the centuries was determined on the one hand by the hostility of the feudal world and on the other by the toughness of an orthodox religious faith; and they suggest that the liberal era has dissipated both the external and the internal basis of this survival. They assume that the liberal ideals of tolerance are infinitely extensible and that the breaking of the hard shell of a traditional religious unity will destroy the internal will to live.

The violent nationalism of our period proves the error of the first assumption. While we need not believe that Nazism or even a milder form of national bigotry will set the social and political standards of the future, it is apparent that collective particularities and vitalities have a more stubborn life than liberal universalism had assumed. The error of the second has been proved by the Jews themselves. For Zionism is the expression of a national will to live which transcends the traditional orthodox religion of the Jews. It is supported by many forces in Jewish life, not the least of which is an impressive proletarian impulse. Poor Jews recognize that privileged members of their Jewish community may have achieved such a secure position in the Western world that they could hardly be expected to sacrifice it for a Zionist venture. But they also see that for the great multitude of Jews there is no escape from the hardships a nationality scattered among the nations must suffer. They could, if they would, be absorbed in the Western world. Or they could, if they desired, maintain their racial integrity among the various nations. But they know that the price which must be paid for such survival is high. They know from their own experience that collective prejudice is not as easily dissolved as some of their more favored brothers assume.

These poorer Jews understand, out of their experience, what is frequently withheld from the more privileged—namely, that the bigotry of majority groups toward minority groups which affront the majority by diverging from the dominant type is a perennial aspect of man's collective life. The force of it may be mitigated, but it cannot be wholly eliminated. These Jews, therefore, long for a place on the earth where they are not "tolerated," where they are neither "understood" nor misunderstood, neither appreciated nor condemned, but where they can be what they are, preserving their own unique identity without asking "by your leave" of anyone else.

It is this understanding of a basic human situation on the part of the less privileged portion of the Jewish community which has given Zionism a particular impetus. There are of course individuals in the more privileged groups who make common cause with the less privileged because they have the imagination to see what their more intellectualist brothers have not seen. But on the whole Zionism represents the wisdom of common experience as against the wisdom of the mind, which tends to take premature flights into the absolute or the universal from the tragic conflicts and the stubborn particularities of human history.

The second part of any program for the solution of the Jewish problem must rest upon the recognition that a collective survival impulse is as legitimate a "right" as an individual one. Justice, in history, is concerned with collective, as well as with individual, rights. Recognition of the legitimacy of this right must lead, in my opinion, to a more generous acceptance of the Zionist program as correct in principle, however much it may have to be qualified in application.

The Jewish religionists, the Jewish and Gentile secularists, and the Christian missionaries to the Jews have, despite the contradictory character of their various approaches, one thing in common. They would solve the problem of the particularity of a race by a cultural or religious universalism. This is a false answer if the universal character of their culture or religion demands the destruction of the historical—in this case racial—particularism. It is just as false as if the command "Thou shalt love thy neighbor as thyself" were interpreted to mean that I must destroy myself so that no friction may arise between my neighbor and myself.

The author, who happens to be a Christian theologian, may be permitted the assertion, as a postscriptum, that he has his own ideas about the relation of the Christian to the Jewish religion. But he regards all religious and cultural answers to the Jewish problem which do not take basic ethnic facts into consideration as the expressions of either a premature universalism or a conscious or unconscious ethnic imperialism.

II

I offer "a" solution rather than "the" solution to the problem of anti-Semitism precisely because a prerequisite for any solution of a basic social problem is the understanding that there is no perfectly satisfactory formula. A perennial problem of human relations can be dealt with on many levels of social and moral achievements, but not in such a way that new perplexities will not emerge upon each new level. The tendency of modern culture to find pat answers and panaceas for vexing problems—one aspect of its inveterate utopianism—has confused rather than clarified most issues with which it has occupied itself.

I have previously suggested that the problem of the relation of the Jews to our Western democratic world calls for at least two different approaches. We must on the one hand preserve and if possible extend the democratic standards of tolerance and of cultural and racial pluralism which allow the Jews *Lebensraum*[2] as a nation among the nations. We must on the other hand support more generously than in the past the legitimate aspiration of Jews for a "homeland" in which they will not be simply tolerated but which they will possess. The type of liberalism which fights for and with the Jews on the first battle line but leaves them to fight alone on the second is informed by an unrealistic universalism. If its presuppositions are fully analyzed it will be discovered that they rest upon the hope that history is moving forward to a universal culture which will eliminate all particularities and every collective uniqueness, whether rooted in nature or in history. History has perennially refuted this hope.

The late Justice Louis D. Brandeis illustrated in his person and his ideas exactly what we mean by this double strategy. Brandeis was first a great American, whose contributions to our national life prove that justice to the Jew is also a service to democracy in that it allows democracy to profit from the peculiar gifts of the Jew—in the case of Brandeis and many another leader, the Hebraic-prophetic passion for social justice. But Brandeis was also a Zionist; his belief in the movement was regarded by some of his friends, both Gentile and Jewish, as an aberration that one had to condone in an otherwise sane and worthy man. Brandeis's Zionism sprang from his understanding of an aspect of human existence to which most of his fellow-liberals were blind. He understood

> that whole peoples have an individuality no less marked than that of single persons, that the individuality of a people is irrepressible, and that the misnamed internationalism which seeks the elimination of nationalities or peoples is unattainable. The new nationalism proclaims that each race or people has a right and duty to develop, and that only through such differentiated development will high civilization be attained.*

---

[2] Literally, living or vital space, ironic in its use here because Hitler had himself employed the word to describe the expansionist needs of the German nation.

*From an essay first published in 1916 and reprinted by the *Jewish Frontier* in its October 1941 issue.

Brandeis understood in 1916 what some of his fellow-Jews did not learn until 1933 and what many a Gentile liberal will never learn. "We Jews," he said, "are a distinct nationality, of which every Jew is necessarily a member. Let us insist that the struggle for liberty shall not cease until equal opportunity is accorded to nationalities as to individuals."

It must be emphasized that any program which recognizes the rights of Jews as a nationality and which sees in Zionism a legitimate demand for the recognition of these rights must at the same time support the struggle for the rights of Jews as citizens in the nations in which they are now established or may be established. This strategy is demanded, if for no other reason, because there is no possibility that Palestine will ever absorb all the Jews of the world. Even if it were physically able to absorb them, we know very well that migrations never develop as logically as this. I cannot judge whether Zionist estimates of the millions which a fully developed Palestine could absorb are correct. They seem to me to err on the side of optimism. But in any case it would be fantastic to assume that all Jews could or would find their way to Palestine, even in the course of many centuries.

It is more important, however, to consider what democracy owes to its own ideals of justice and to its own quality as a civilization than what it owes to the Jews. Neither democracy nor any other civilization pretending to maturity can afford to capitulate to the tendency in collective life which would bring about unity by establishing a simple homogeneity. We must not underestimate this tendency as a perennial factor in man's social life. Nor must we fail to understand the logic behind it. Otherwise we shall become involved in the futile task of seeking to prove that minority groups are not really as bad as their critics accuse them of being, instead of understanding that minority groups are thought "bad" only because they diverge from the dominant type and affront that type by their divergence. But to yield to this tendency would be to allow civilization to be swallowed up in primitivism, for the effort to return to the simple unity of tribal life is a primitive urge of which Nazism is the most consistent, absurd, and dangerous contemporary expression. In the case of the Jews, with their peculiar relation to the modern world and the peculiar contributions which they have made to every aspect of modern culture and civilization, any relaxation of democratic standards would also mean robbing our civilization of the special gifts which they have developed as a nation among the nations.

The necessity for a second strategy in dealing with the Jewish problem stems from certain aspects of the collective life of men which the modern situation has brought into tragic relief. The Jews require a homeland, if for no other reason, because even the most generous immigration laws of the Western democracies will not permit all the dispossessed Jews of Europe to find a haven in which they may look forward to a tolerable future. When I say the most "generous" immigration laws, I mean, of course, "generous" only within terms of political exigencies. It must be observed that the liberals of the Western world maintain a conspiracy of silence on this point.

They do not dare to work for immigration laws generous enough to cope with the magnitude of the problem which the Jewish race faces. They are afraid of political repercussions, tacitly acknowledging that their theories do not square with the actual facts. Race prejudice, the intolerance of a dominant group toward a minority group, is a more powerful and more easily aroused force than they dare admit.

A much weightier justification of Zionism is that every race finally has a right to a homeland where it will not be "different," where it will neither be patronized by "good" people nor subjected to calumny by bad people. Of course many Jews have achieved a position in democratic nations in which the disabilities from which they suffer as a minority group are comparatively insignificant in comparison with the prestige which they have won. A democratic world would not disturb them. Their situation would actually be eased to an even further degree if the racial survival impulse were primarily engaged in Palestine. Religious and cultural divergences alone do not present a serious problem, particularly under traditions of cultural pluralism. But there are millions of Jews, not only in the democratic world but in the remnants of the feudal world, such as Poland and the Balkans, who ought to have a chance to escape from the almost intolerable handicaps to which they are subjected. One reason why Jews suffer more than any other minority is that they bear the brunt of two divergences from type, religious and racial, and it is idle for Jews or Gentiles to speculate about which is the primary source of prejudice. Either would suffice, but the prejudice is compounded when both divergences are involved.

Zionist aspirations, it seems to me, deserve a more generous support than they have been accorded by liberal and democratic groups in Western countries. Non-Zionist Jews have erred in being apologetic or even hostile to these aspirations on the ground that their open expression might imperil rights painfully won in the democratic world. Non-Jewish liberals have erred equally in regarding Zionism as nothing but the vestigial remnant of an ancient religious dream, the unfortunate aberration of a hard-pressed people.

Whether the Jews will be allowed to develop a genuine homeland under their own sovereignty, within the framework of the British Empire, depends solely upon the amount of support which they secure in the two great democracies, for those democracies will have it in their power, if Hitler is defeated, to make the necessary political arrangements. The influence of the American government will be indirect but none the less effective — which is why American public opinion on this issue cannot be a matter of indifference. It is obviously no easy matter for British statecraft to give the proper assurances and to make basic arrangements for the future while it is forced to deal with a vast and complex Arab world still in danger of falling under the sway of the Nazis. Yet it must be observed that the Arabs achieved freedom and great possessions in the last war, and that this war, in the event of victory for the United Nations, will increase the extent and cohesion of their realm. The Anglo-Saxon hegemony that is bound to exist in the event of an Axis defeat will be in a position to see to it that Palestine is set aside for the Jews, that the present restrictions on immigration are abrogated, and that the Arabs are otherwise compensated.

Zionist leaders are unrealistic in insisting that their demands entail no "injustice" to the Arab population since Jewish immigration has brought new economic strength to Palestine. It is absurd to expect any people to regard the restriction of their sovereignty over a traditional possession as "just," no matter how many other benefits accrue from that abridgment. What is demanded in this instance is a policy which offers a just solution of an intricate problem faced by a whole civilization. The solution must, and can, be made acceptable to the Arabs if it is incorporated into a total settlement of the issues of the Mediterranean and Near Eastern world; and it need not be unjust to the Arabs in the long run if the same "imperial" policy which establishes the Jewish homeland also consolidates and unifies the Arab world. One may hope that this will not be done by making the Jewish homeland a part of an essentially Arab federation.

It must be noted in conclusion that there are both Jews and Gentiles who do not believe that Palestine is a desirable locus for a Jewish homeland though they do believe that a homeland must be created. They contend that there is as yet no evidence of Palestine's ability to maintain an independent economic existence without subsidies; that the cooperative agricultural ventures of the Jews, impressive in quality but not in size, offer no hope of a solid agricultural basis for the national economy; that the enmity of the Arab world would require the constant interposition of imperial arms; that the resources of Palestine could not support the millions whom the Zionists hope to settle there; and that the tendency to use Arab agricultural labor may once more create a Jewish urban caste. It is difficult to know to what degree such criticisms are justified. The fact that 25 per cent of the Jewish settlers in Palestine are engaged in agriculture tends to refute the argument that the Palestinian economy has no adequate agricultural base. The criticism that Palestine cannot, under the most favorable circumstances, absorb all the Jews who must find a new home and security after the war is more serious. However, even if fully borne out, it would not affect the thesis that the Jews require a homeland. It would simply raise the question whether a different, or an additional, region should be chosen. It is barely possible that a location ought to be found in Europe.

The whole matter is so important that it should be explored by an international commission, consisting of both Jews and Gentiles, both Zionists and non-Zionists. The Jews were the first, as they have been the chief, victims of Nazi fury. Their rehabilitation, like the rehabilitation of every Nazi victim, requires something more than the restoration of the *status quo ante*. We must consider this task one of the most important among the many problems of post-war reconstruction. We cannot, in justice either to ourselves or to the Jews, dismiss it from our conscience.

VARIAN FRY

The Massacre of the Jews

New Republic, December 21, 1942

By the end of 1942, as several of the extermination centers began operation, ghetto life in Poland deteriorated even further, Jews in the Western European countries under Nazi rule began to be organized for deportation east for annihilation, and wanton massacres on the battlefront continued. The American press reported the details of these stories as they were smuggled out of Europe through official and unofficial channels.

The State Department only reluctantly confirmed these events. Officials worried that such stories would be criticized as propaganda fabrications or that they would distract the public from the main task of winning the war. It is also clear that some officials directly involved in the handling of this information harbored anti-Semitism or simply resented pressure to report these things from outside the government. Yet the evidence was overwhelming, and on December 17, 1942, the Allied governments finally issued an official condemnation of the Nazi massacres. The statement was forthright but conservative, decrying the atrocities being committed and promising swift justice to the perpetrators at the end of the war.

The article that follows was written just before and published simultaneously with the Allied declaration. Its author, Varian Fry, is worthy of particular notice. Fry had been an American journalist in Germany during the 1930s (see pages 45–47) and an ardent anti-Nazi. When France fell to the Nazis in 1940, Fry volunteered to work for the Emergency Rescue Committee, a private organization in Vichy France (that part of the country collaborating with, but unoccupied by, the Germans). There he created an underground network to get refugees to neutral or Allied countries. Among those he helped rescue were the painters Marc Chagall and Max Ernst, the sculptor Jacques Lipchitz, the harpsichordist Wanda Landowska, and the philosopher Hannah Arendt. His work also brought him direct knowledge of Nazi actions and plans and impressed

Varian Fry, "The Massacre of the Jews," *New Republic,* Dec. 21, 1942, 816–19.

on him the truth of all that had been reported. By late 1941, his activities had become so notorious that the French expelled him, and he returned to the United States.

Note Fry's passion in "The Massacre of the Jews" and also his worries about the stories being misconceived as propaganda. Note also his sense of what the Allies could do in response.

There are some things so horrible that decent men and women find them impossible to believe, so monstrous that the civilized world recoils incredulous before them. The recent reports of the systematic extermination of the Jews in Nazi Europe are of this order.

We are accustomed to horrors in the historical past, and accept them as a matter of course. The persecution of the Jews in Egypt and the Roman Empire, the slaughters of Genghis Khan, the religious mania which swept Europe in the fifteenth and sixteenth centuries, the Indian massacres in America, and the equally brutal retaliations of the white men—all these we credit without question, as phenomena of ages less enlightened than our own. When such things occur in our own times, like the Armenian massacres, we put them down to the account of still half-barbarous peoples. But that such things could be done by contemporary western Europeans, heirs of the humanist tradition, seems hardly possible.

Our skepticism has been fortified by our experience with "atrocity stories" during the last war. We were treated, during that war, to many accounts of German atrocities. We were told of the rape of nuns, the forced prostitution of young Belgian girls, of German soldiers spearing infants on their bayonets, or deliberately and wantonly cutting off their hands. Later, when the bitterness of war had subsided, and Allied investigators were able to interview the populations of the formerly occupied countries, and scholars were let loose on the documents, most of these atrocities were found to have been invented. The natural reaction was to label all atrocity stories "propaganda" and refuse to believe them.

That habit of thought has lasted down to the present day. The Nazis have given us many reasons to change our thinking habits since they assumed power, but we have been slow to learn the new lesson. I remember how skeptical I was myself the first time a Nazi official told me that Hitler and Goebbels were bent on the physical annihilation of the Jews. On July 15, 1935, the S.A.[1] staged its first pogrom in Berlin. I was in Berlin at the time and witnessed the whole thing. I saw the S.A. men, unmistakable despite their mufti, throwing chairs and tables through the plate-glass windows of Jewish-owned cafés, dragging Jewish men and women out of buses and chasing them up the streets, or knocking them down and kicking

---

[1] *Sturmabteilung,* or storm troopers.

them in the face and belly as they lay prostrate on the sidewalk. And I heard them chanting their terrible song:

Wenn Judenblut vom Messer spritzt,
Dann geht es nochmal so gut!*

The next day, in a state of high indignation, I went to see "Putzi" Hanfstaengl, then chief of the Foreign Press Division of the Propaganda Ministry. On my way to his office, I learned that one of the victims of the previous night's bestiality had already died of his injuries. Yet, when Hanfstaengl told me, in his cultured Harvard accent, that the "radicals" among the Nazi Party leaders intended to "solve" the "Jewish problem" by the physical extermination of the Jews, I only half believed him. It was not much more than a year after the Blood Bath of June 30, 1934; yet even then I could not believe that there were men in positions of power and authority in western Europe in the twentieth century who could seriously entertain such a monstrous idea.

I learned better in November 1938, when the Nazi leaders openly encouraged the burning of synagogues, the pillage of Jewish homes, and the murder of their inhabitants.

One reason the Western world failed to rouse itself more promptly to the Nazi menace was surely this tendency to dismiss as impossible fantasy the many warnings the Nazis themselves gave us. We made the terrible mistake of judging the Nazis by our own standards, failing even after the war had begun to realize how completely they had renounced, if indeed they had ever espoused, those standards. Even today, after more than three years of the Nazi kind of war in Europe, and more than one year of direct experience with it ourselves, there are still far too many among us who do not understand the nature of the enemy — an enemy who will stop at literally nothing to achieve his ends. And his ends are the enslavement or annihilation not only of the Jews but, after them, of all the non-German peoples of Europe and, if possible, the entire world.

The program is already far advanced. According to a report to the President by leaders of American Jewish groups, nearly 2,000,000 European Jews have already been slain since the war began, and the remaining 5,000,000 now living under Nazi control are scheduled to be destroyed as soon as Hitler's blond butchers can get around to them. Of the 275,000 Jews who were living in Germany and Austria at the outbreak of the war, only 52,000 to 55,000 remain. The 170,000 Jews in Czecho-Slovakia have been reduced to 35,000. The figures for Poland, where the Nazi program has been pushed very rapidly, are uncertain. There were 3,300,000 Jews in Poland at the beginning of the war, but some 500,000 fled to Russia, leav-

---

*"When Jewish blood spurts from the knife,
Then everything will be fine again."

ing approximately 2,800,000 behind. By the beginning of the summer of 1942, this number had already been reduced to 2,200,000, and deportations and massacres since that time have been on an ever increasing scale. In the ghetto of Warsaw, in which 550,000 Jews once dwelt, there are today fewer than 50,000. In the city of Riga, Latvia, 8,000 Jews were killed in a single night. A week later 16,000 more were led into a woods, stripped, and machine-gunned.

It is not merely central and eastern Europe which are being "purged," or rendered "Judenrein," as the Nazis like to say. The Netherlands has already given up 60,000 of its 180,000 Jews. Of the 85,000 who once lived in Belgium, only 8,000 remain today, while of the 340,000 Jews of France, more than 65,000 have been deported. Even Norway has begun to ship her Jewish citizens eastward to the Nazi slaughter houses and starvation pens.

The methods employed by the Nazis are many. There is starvation: Jews all over Europe are kept on rations often only one-third or one-fourth what is allowed to non-Jews. Slow death is the inevitable consequence. There is deportation: Jews by the hundreds of thousands have been packed into cattle cars, without food, water, or sanitary conveniences of any sort, and shipped the whole breadth of Europe. When the cars arrive at their destination, about a third of the passengers are already dead. There are the extermination centers, where Jews are destroyed by poison gas or electricity. There are specially constructed trucks, in which Jews are asphyxiated by carbon monoxide from the exhausts, on their way to burial trenches. There are the mines, in which they are worked to death, or poisoned by fumes of metals. There is burning alive, in crematoria, or buildings deliberately set on fire. There is the method of injecting air-bubbles into the blood stream: it is cheap, clean, and efficient, producing clots, embolisms, and death within a few hours. And there is the good old-fashioned system of standing the victims up, very often naked, and machine-gunning them, preferrably beside the graves they themselves have been forced to dig. It saves time, labor, and transportation.

A few weeks ago a letter reached me from Paris. It had been smuggled over the demarcation line and two international borders and mailed in Lisbon. It told of the deportation of the Jews of Paris, which occurred in July. All Polish, Czech, German, Austrian, and Russian Jews between the ages of two and fifty-five were arrested. The women and children, to the number of 15,000, were herded into the notorious Vélodrome d'Hiver, where they were kept for a week, without any bedding but straw, with very inadequate food, and with virtually no sanitary facilities. Then they were packed into cattle cars and shipped to an unknown destination in eastern Europe. My informant, a member of the trade-union underground, tells me that some days later a French railway worker picked up a scrap of paper on the tracks. On it was written this message: "There are more than fifty women in this cattle car, some of them ill, and for days we have been refused even the most elementary conveniences."

Another letter, from a French Red Cross nurse who worked in the Vélodrome, tells exactly the same story, describing it as "something horrible, fiendish, something which takes hold of your throat and prevents you from crying out."

A German Social Democrat whom I know well sent me a long report on the deportations, written at the beginning of September. "I am an incorrigible optimist," he concluded, "but this time I see dark things ahead. . . . I am afraid not many of us will live to see the end of this war."

And a Frenchman, not himself a Jew, wrote a long report on the deportations and had it brought to me in a toothpaste tube. "We were at the Camp des Milles [near Marseilles] the day the last train left," he says.

> The spectacle was indescribably painful to behold. All the internees had been lined up with their pitifully battered valises tied together with bits of string. Most of them were in rags, pale, thin, worn out with the strain, which had dragged out for more than a week. Many of them were quietly weeping. . . . There was no sign of revolt: these people were broken. Their faces showed only hopeless despair and a passive acceptance of their fate.

Later, when Jews not already in concentration camps were being rounded up, he wrote:

> A large number of these desperate people, in just about all sections, tried to end their lives. In Marseilles, in the Cours Belsunce [the heart of the city], a refugee couple jumped out of the window at the very moment the police arrived to arrest them. . . . Many, realizing the danger they were in . . . disappeared from their homes and hid.

These are all letters I myself have received from persons I know, or know to be reliable. They concern only France. But the evidence for the other countries is of a similar, direct sort. There are, for instance, the two pathetic letters from Warsaw. I have seen photostats of them, and of the envelopes in which they were mailed, in the office of the American Jewish Congress. Written in German, they passed the German censor only because he did not understand the few Hebrew words in them, taking them, as he was intended to, for proper names. "I spoke to Mr. Jaeger," one of them goes. ("Mr. Jaeger" means the Germans.)

> He told me that he will invite all relatives of the family Achenu [Hebrew for "our brethren," i.e., the Jews], with the exception of Miss Eisenzweig [probably means those working in the iron mines], from Warsaw to his mansion "Kewer" [Hebrew for "tomb"]. Uncle Gerusch [Hebrew for "deportation"] also works in Warsaw; he is a very capable worker. My friend Miso [Hebrew for "death"] now

works with him. I am alone here; I feel very lonely. . . . Please pray
for me.

The New York office of the General Jewish Workers' Union of Poland has
received from a Polish Socialist underground worker known to it an account
of gas executions the details of which are as revolting as they are convincing.

In the office of the World Jewish Congress in Geneva there is an affidavit,
attested copies of which have been received here, recounting the extraordinary odyssey of a Polish Jew who was living in Brussels. On August 12 he
was arrested and deported to Rumania. There were seventy men in his cattle car, packed in like crowds in the subway during rush hour. After two and
a half days, their train stopped in Upper Silesia, and they were allowed to get
out of the car, have a short rest, and eat a little soup. Those too exhausted
to continue the journey were carried away, as were all boys between fourteen and twenty (to work, it was said, in the coal mines and the iron mills).
The others were then loaded back into the cars and shipped on to the
Ukraine. There they were asked whether they felt able to work or not. About
half said that they were not able to work. These were led away. The others
were given the uniforms of the Todt Organization and set to work building
fortifications. From where they were working they could hear the rumble of
big guns to the east, and once they saw a sign reading "Stalingrad—50 km."

The Jew from Brussels made friends with a young Bavarian officer, not
a Nazi, and learned from him that the men who had not been able to work
had all been immediately shot. Anyone who was sick for more than two
days was shot also, the officer said. In the end the officer helped the Jew
to hide himself in a train which was returning to the West. After many days
the Jew found himself on a siding at the Gare de l'Est in Paris. From there
he made his way to Switzerland, where he told his story.

This is the nature of the evidence. Letters, reports, cables all fit together.
They add up to the most appalling picture of mass murder in all human history. Nor is it only the Jews who are threatened. Polish authorities assert
that many hundreds of thousands of non-Jewish Poles have been slain with
equal callousness, and soberly warn that the entire Polish people may be
wiped out before this war is over. The decimation of the Greek people is a
matter of record. The Nazis are evidently quite indifferent to it, if they do
not actually welcome it. Thousands of French will die of hunger and cold
this winter, and thousands more will never be born, either because the
fathers who might have begotten them are being held in Nazi prison camps,
or because the mothers are too undernourished to carry them. The same
thing is true of many other countries of Europe. And by their executions
of "hostages" the Nazis are systematically destroying the potential leaders
of democratic movements in all the countries they have overrun.

We must face the terrible truth. Even though Hitler loses this war, he
may win it anyway, at least as far as Europe is concerned. There are reports,

apparently trustworthy, that the Nazis and the German army are prepared for eventual retreat, and that their plans call for the extermination of every living thing and the destruction of all physical property in the areas they may be forced to evacuate. When we remember that, even after the war of 1914–18 was hopelessly lost and the German army was retreating in confusion on the Western Front, it still found time, and the will, wantonly to destroy the factories and flood the mines in its path, we may well believe that this time it will be even more thorough, go even more berserk.

If this happens, we shall be confronted with the most frightful dilemma imaginable. Every man, woman, and child in Europe will become a hostage, a means of blackmail. If we continue the war, they will die. Yet if we do not continue the war, the Nazis will have won all they can then hope to win— time. Time to regroup their forces, divide ours and strike again.

Our only course then will be to overwhelm them so rapidly that they will not be able to carry out their threats. For that we shall need all the strength we can possibly muster, and all the courage. The Nazis will certainly hope to cut off our allies one by one by threatening the total annihilation of their peoples if they continue to oppose them. We and our allies must be prepared to face the challenge unflinchingly.

Meanwhile, there are some things which can be done now, slight as the chances are that they will have much effect in deterring Hitler and his followers from their homicidal mania. President Roosevelt could and should speak out again against these monstrous events. A stern warning from him will have no effect on Hitler, but it may impress some Germans like the officer who helped the Jew from Brussels to escape. A similar warning from Churchill might help, too. A joint declaration, couched in the most solemn terms, by the Allied governments, of the retribution to come might be of some avail. Tribunals should be set up now to begin to amass the facts. Diplomatic warnings, conveyed through neutral channels, to the governments of Hungary, Bulgaria, and Rumania might save at least some of the 700,000 to 900,000 Jews still within their borders. The Christian churches might also help, at least in countries like France, Holland, Belgium, Norway, the Pope by threatening with excommunication all Catholics who in any way participate in these frightful crimes, the Protestant leaders by exhorting their fellow communicants to resist to the utmost the Nazis' fiendish designs. We and our allies should perhaps reconsider our policy of total blockade of the European continent and examine the possibilities of extending the feeding of Greece to other occupied countries under neutral supervision. Since one of the excuses the Nazis now offer for destroying the Jews and Poles is that there is not enough food to go around, we might at least remove the grounds for the excuse by offering to feed the populations of the occupied countries, given proper guarantees that the food will not fall into the hands of the enemy.

If we do any or all of these things, we should broadcast the news of them day and night to every country of Europe, in every European language. There is a report, which I have not been able to verify, that the OWI has banned mention of the massacres in its shortwave broadcasts. If this is true, it is a sadly mistaken policy. We have nothing to gain by "appeasing" the anti-Semites and the murderers. We have much to gain by using the facts to create resistance and eventually rebellion. The fact that the Nazis do not commit their massacres in western Europe, but transport their victims to the East before destroying them, is certain proof that they fear the effect on the local populations of the news of their crimes.

Finally, and it is a little thing, but at the same time a big thing, we can offer asylum now, without delay or red tape, to those few fortunate enough to escape from the Aryan paradise. We can do this without any risk to ourselves, because we can intern the refugees on arrival, and examine them at leisure before releasing them. If there is the slightest doubt about any of them, we can keep them interned for the duration of the war. Despite the fact that the urgency of the situation has never been greater, immigration into the United States in the year 1942 will have been less than ten percent of what it has been in "normal" years before Hitler, when some of the largest quotas were not filled. There have been bureaucratic delays in visa procedure which have literally condemned to death many stalwart democrats. These delays have caused an understandable bitterness among Jews and non-Jews in Europe, who have looked to us for help which did not come.

My Marseilles correspondent, who is neither a Jew nor a candidate for a visa, writes that,

> in spite of the Nazi pressure, which she feels more than any other neutral, and in spite too of the reactionary tendencies of her middle class, the little country of Switzerland will [by accepting 9,000 refugees from Nazi terror since July] have contributed more to the cause of humanity than the great and wealthy United States, its loud declamations about the rights of the people and the defense of liberty notwithstanding.

This is a challenge which we cannot, must not, ignore.

HENRY MORGENTHAU

Diary Entry
December 3, 1942

It is clear from this entry in Secretary of the Treasury Henry Morgenthau's diary that the reports from Europe had been on Roosevelt's mind and had rekindled his prewar interest in finding havens and a homeland for Jews outside Europe. The president's remarks encouraged Morgenthau, but in retrospect how realistic do they seem?

I saw the President this morning and told him about my financing, and he was very much pleased.

Somehow or other he mentioned Palestine—I can't remember just how it came up—and so I said, "I am having a meeting at my house tonight to discuss Palestine at the suggestion of Sam Rosenman.[1]" The President said, "Listen, Henry, take my advice and go easy on that because I have pretty well made up my mind as to what I am going to do." I said that I would be very much interested in hearing about it. The President said, "Well, what I think I will do is this. First, I would call Palestine a religious country. Then I would leave Jerusalem the way it is and have it run by the Orthodox Greek Catholic Church, the Protestants, and the Jews—have a joint committee run it. They are doing it all right now and we might as well leave it that way." Then the President went on and said, "I actually would put a barbed wire around Palestine, and I would begin to move the Arabs out of Palestine." I asked him how he would do that and I said, "Would you have the Jews buy up the land?" He said, "No, but I would provide land for the Arabs in some other part of the Middle East, and I know there are plenty of places. Each time we move out an Arab we would bring in another Jewish family." I asked the President, "Would you propose that the majority should be Jews in Palestine?" and he said, "Yes, 90% of them should be Jews, but I don't want to bring in more than they can economically support, and I think that point has been reached." I said, "Well, what kind of a place would it be?" and he said, "It would be an independent nation just like any other nation—com-

---

"Concerning Placing Jewish Refugees," Morgenthau Diaries, Dec. 3, 1942, in *America and the Holocaust: Responsibility for America's Failure,* vol. 13, ed. David S. Wyman (New York: Garland Publishing, 1991), 8–9.

[1]Samuel Irving Rosenman (1896–1946), lawyer, friend, and advisor to President Roosevelt.

pletely independent. Naturally, if there are 90% Jews, the Jews would dominate the government." He said, "There are lots of places to which you could move the Arabs. All you have to do is drill a well because there is this large underground water supply, and we can move the Arabs to places where they can really live."

Then I said, "Well, Mr. President, so much for Palestine, but what about the two or three million Jews who are still in the heart of Europe?" He said, "Well, I have been working on that right along with Isaiah Bowman,[2] and I had a conversation sometime ago with Ilo, the President of the Republic of Colombia." The President said, "He has a very interesting idea. On the west side of the Andes, there is this virgin territory which President Ilo has visited, and what he is willing to do is to open up this country by way of highways over the Andes. He proposes that if there are 100 people, a third of them must be citizens of Colombia and the other two-thirds can be made up of refugees from Europe, but not more than 10% of any one group—of any one race or nationality—so that they will be assimilated." The President went on to say that this could be done not only in that part of the Upper Amazon which is Colombia but also in Ecuador. The President also said, "Then I am studying many other places in the world where the refugees from Europe can be moved." All I said when he had finished was, "Well, Mr. President, when we are back in Dutchess County, I wish you would keep me in mind because this is something in which I am very much interested and on which I would like to help," and he said he would. I asked whether this would cut across Herbert Lehman's[3] field, and he said, "No, the two of them will dovetail. Herbert has to do with feeding the people but when it comes to moving them out, that is something else."

I was surprised to find that the President was studying this thing with so much interest and had gone as far as he had in making up his mind on what he wants to do. It was most encouraging to me and most heartening. . . .

---

[2]Isaiah Bowman (1878–1950), geographer and educator; President of Johns Hopkins University.
[3]Herbert Henry Lehman (1878–1963), banker and Democratic political leader; governor of New York, 1933–42.

CHARLES CLAYTON MORRISON

Horror Stories from Poland

Christian Century, December 9, 1942

Unlike Varian Fry, most American editors and writers accepted the reports of Nazi genocide in their fullness only after the Allied declaration of December 17. Take the case of Charles Clayton Morrison, editor of the *Christian Century,* whose reaction to the overwhelming evidence of Nazi brutality was at first skeptical. In this piece, Morrison responds to a November 24 press conference held by Rabbi Stephen S. Wise, at which Wise announced that the State Department had confirmed reports that the Nazis had already killed two million Jews. Morrison both accepted that horrible things were happening and doubted some of the most awful realities. He tried to confirm the story with the State Department, and, when officials there remained noncommittal, he assumed Wise had exaggerated.

Beyond doubt, horrible things are happening to the Jews in Poland. It is even probable that the Nazis are herding all the Jews of Europe, so far as they can capture them, into Poland with the deliberate intention of exterminating them there. A responsible official of the Nazi foreign office once told an editor of this paper that Hitler's policy called for the "humane extermination" of the Jews. He was speaking in perfect English, and knew exactly what he was saying. There is probably little humaneness about what is going on in Poland, but plenty of extermination. The Nazis are loading upon themselves in that country a weight of guilt for which Christian Germany will, we hope, one day hold them to account. We question, however, whether any good purpose is served by the publication of such charges as Dr. Stephen S. Wise gave to the press last week. In the first place, although Rabbi Wise went out of his way to place the responsibility for his charges on the state department, that branch of the government has conspicuously refrained from issuing any confirmation. In the second place, Dr. Wise's figures on the numbers of Jews killed differ radically from those given out on the same day by the Polish government in exile. Whereas Dr. Wise says that Hitler has ordered all Jews in Nazi-ruled Europe killed by the end of

---

Charles Clayton Morrison, "Horror Stories from Poland," *Christian Century,* Dec. 9, 1942, 1518–19.

this year, the exiled Polish government claims only that orders have been issued for the extermination of half the Jews in Poland by the end of this year and that 250,000 had been killed up to the end of September. In the third place, Dr. Strasburger whose "underground" figures are used to support Rabbi Wise's charges is the same Polish leader who is campaigning in this country for the complete destruction of Germany. And in the fourth place, Dr. Wise's allegation that Hitler is paying $20 each for Jewish corpses to be "processed into soap fats and fertilizer" is unpleasantly reminiscent of the "cadaver factory" lie which was one of the propaganda triumphs of the First World War.

CHARLES CLAYTON MORRISON

Polish Atrocities Are Entered in the Books

Christian Century, December 30, 1942

Once the declaration of December 17 was made, Morrison could no longer entertain the notion that the reports from Poland and other locales were propaganda. Yet note the tone in which he accepts the facts of the case and the ways in which his reaction differs from that of Fry.

Extermination of a race has seldom, if ever, been so systemically practiced on a grand scale as in the present mass murder of Polish Jews by the Nazi power. A joint declaration by the governments of the eleven Allied nations, including governments in exile, was issued simultaneously in Washington and London on December 17, summarizing the essential facts, though without other statistical estimate than that "the number of victims of these bloody cruelties is reckoned in many hundreds of thousands," and reaffirming the "solemn resolution to insure that those responsible for these crimes shall not escape retribution." This statement serves two good purposes: first, as an expression of the horror and revulsion with which the conscience of the world reacts to this calculated and deliberate savagery; and second, as an indelible entry in the account with which the responsible perpetrators of the deeds will surely be confronted and for which they

Charles Clayton Morrison, "Polish Atrocities Are Entered in the Books," *Christian Century,* Dec. 30, 1942, 1611.

will have to settle. It is well to exercise some rhetorical restraint in speaking of a crime so vast and foul that language is bankrupt in attempting to characterize it adequately. The calm tone of the pronouncement does not reflect an absence of emotion but the presence of a cold determination not to expend in vain outcry one unit of emotional energy which can be better employed in bringing the war to such a conclusion that this gigantic crime can be stopped and the criminals punished. The right response to the Polish horror is a few straight words to say that it has been entered in the books, and then redoubled action on the Tunisian, Russian, Italian, and German fronts and on the production lines.

TOSHA BIALER

Behind the Wall (Life—and Death— in Warsaw's Ghetto)

Collier's, February 20 and 27, 1943

This article is notable in a number of ways. Written by an escapee of the Warsaw Ghetto, it is a rare wartime firsthand account (with photographs) of Jewish life in Nazi-occupied Poland. More extraordinary is that it was published in *Collier's,* one of the leading mass-circulation pictorial magazines of the era. The story thus reached millions of Americans only two months after the Allies had confirmed the mass killing of European Jews. It chronicles events in the Warsaw Ghetto from 1940 through the summer of 1942, when the Bialer family escaped.

The first thing we felt when the Polish war came to an end was overwhelming relief from aerial bombing. Only those who have been through air raids with no shelter to hide in will know what we felt. Gradually our men came home from the fighting—those who had escaped death or capture. Many people who had fled eastward during the campaign flocked back with some assurance that life would go on more or less as before.

There was little anxiety among the Jews in Warsaw. Naturally there would be the privations of war to contend with—hunger and cold and per-

Tosha Bialer, "Behind the Wall (Life—and Death—in Warsaw's Ghetto)," *Collier's,* Feb. 20, 1943, 17–18, 66–67; Feb. 27, 1943, 29–33.

Figure 4. One of the illustrations from the *Collier's* article on the Warsaw Ghetto. "Homeless, hungry children, some orphans and others hopelessly lost, have a hard time. These sleep in an abandoned newsstand."

haps even disease; and then, for us as well as for our Christian compatriots, there was the deep humiliation at having been defeated and overrun by another people. As Jews, we did not expect more than that. The fate of the Jews in Germany should have warned us.

A few weeks after the end of the war, the Gestapo swarmed in and began their work of destruction.

They very soon made their intentions clear. Toward the end of 1939 all Jews were ordered to wear the yellow arm band, and all Jewish stores to display a discriminating label. In certain streets with preponderantly Jewish population, posters were put up: "Infested Area!" "Beware! Thoroughfare Only!" This—as it was meant to—was an open invitation to all sorts of violence and plunder. The lawless elements of the city took full advantage of the opportunity to loot shops and private houses, break windows, and beat up persons wearing the stigmatizing arm band, encouraged at every point by officials of the secret police and led by the Storm Troopers who had accompanied the latter into the city. Searching for hidden arms was one of the most common excuses for the Gestapo to break into homes and commit any kind of outrage. On one such occasion my brother-in-law was arrested and dragged away in the middle of the night, and we never saw him again. Besides his wife, he left a little boy of six.

In March 1940, Jews under forty were called up for compulsory labor. Many fled from the country, many more were able to evade the order with bribes or by hiding. But a great number were seized and sent away. Only one man returned to Warsaw to tell the story of that expedition. The labor conscripts were taken to the Russian front and there put to work leveling ground for airfields and roads, working chest-deep in ice-cold water for days. The food was scant, and the accommodations were so flimsy they gave little or no shelter against the Russian winter. Many died from exposure and exhaustion. None of this group was ever heard of again.

Early in 1940 we were puzzled to see gangs of workmen engaged in constructing what seemed to be parts of a wall in various sections of the city. The strange thing was that these parts did not appear to belong to any recognizable pattern but were scattered all over. Many guesses were made, and the general conclusion was that the wall was a strategic measure, though directed against what or whom no one could imagine.

In the meantime, the Nazi administration was busy. All property, as well as stores, shops, and other business enterprises, were placed under German receivership. The receivers, appropriately enough, were Ukrainians or Poles of German stock, both our traditional antagonists. We were helpless against these open acts of robbery. Scorn and derision were added to willful confiscation: Jews were ordered to remove and transport the "requisitioned" objects. Old and ailing men were deliberately picked to carry the heaviest loads. They had to carry their heavy burdens down many flights of stairs, the use of the elevators being forbidden to them.

The Day of Atonement is the holiest day of the year in a Jewish community. In 1940 it fell on October 8th. On that day the Germans published an order declaring that all Jews were to move out of certain specified sections of Warsaw, and that non-Jews had to leave the sections that were not specified. The deadline for this move was October 31st.

The last week of October was a nightmare of congestion and confusion. Try to picture one third of a large city's population, six hundred thousand people, moving through the streets in an endless stream of humanity, pushing, pulling, wheeling, dragging, carrying all their belongings from every part of the city to one small section, crowding one another more and more as they converged. No cars, no horses, no help of any sort was available to us, by order of the occupying authorities. Every kind of obstacle was invented to hinder us in moving our belongings. Pushcarts were about the only method of conveyance we had, and these were piled high with household goods, furnishing much amusement to the German onlookers, who delighted in overturning the carts and seeing us scrambling for our effects. Many of the goods were confiscated arbitrarily without any explanation. Warsaw was an open highway, with the highwaymen in undisputed control. Everything that could not be transported in time was left behind after the moving and was declared ownerless and divided up among the Germans and their sympathizers.

In the ghetto, as some of us had begun to call it, half ironically and in jest, there was appalling chaos. Thousands of people were rushing around at the last minute trying to find a place to stay. Everything was already filled up but still they kept coming and somehow more room was found. The narrow, crooked streets of the most dilapidated section of Warsaw were crowded with pushcarts, their owners going from house to house asking the inevitable question: "Have you room?" The sidewalks were covered with their belongings. Children wandered, lost and crying; parents ran hither and yon seeking them, their cries drowned in the tremendous hubbub of half a million uprooted people.

The first days were spent in getting a foothold in our new surroundings, clearing up affairs, and trying to establish a design for living.

And then came the fifteenth of November, 1940, the day that none of us will ever forget.

That morning, as on every other, men and women set out on their way to work, storekeepers, employees, executives, most of whom worked in the non-Jewish sections. As they came to the various points where thoroughfares and streets crossed from the Jewish section into the non-Jewish districts, they ran against barbed wire strung across and guarded by German police who were stopping all traffic out of the Jewish section. Hastily they tried other streets, avenues, alleys, only to find in every case barbed wire or a solid brick wall, well guarded. There was no way out any more!

Quickly the news spread through the section. Other people came out of their houses and stared at the barricades, pathetically silent, stunned by the frightful suspicion that was creeping into their minds. Then, suddenly, the realization struck us. What had been, up till now, seemingly unrelated parts — a piece of wall here, a blocked-up house there, another piece of wall somewhere else — had overnight been joined to form an enclosure from which there was no escape. The barbed wire was the missing piece in the puzzle. Like cattle we had been herded into the corral, and the gate had been barred behind us. The Jewish section was sealed!

Despair swept over us like a cloud, blotting out all hope. This, then, was the fate that had been reserved for us — to be locked up here, our houses taken away, our means of support inaccessible, and left to starve or to perish from the diseases that accompany overcrowded conditions. So the ghetto talk had not been an idle rumor, a pretext to squeeze funds out of us. It had been a definite plan, carefully conceived and diligently pursued. . . .

The ghetto included the oldest, most deteriorated sections of the city, a district that had been an eyesore for years and should have been torn down long ago.

It comprised many blocks completely destroyed by bombing, without a habitable building left standing—rubble and ruins remaining as the Luftwaffe had left them, a danger to health and safety. With intentional foresight, not one park, not one playground or public garden was included in the area. There was no access to the river banks. The Jewish Hospital, modern and well equipped, erected and run on Jewish funds, had been left outside; so had the Liberal Jewish Synagogue and the Old People's Home. The ghetto was cut up into two sectors of unequal size, the main ghetto and the little ghetto, meeting at a narrow bottleneck, a plan calculated to cause us the most inconvenience and hardship possible. . . .

The Germans were set on our destruction. Herding us together was one step toward that aim, and the most effective one. By segregating us from the rest of the world, cutting us off from any outside interference, they could treat us like guinea pigs in an experimental laboratory, only in this case without an anesthetic. With cold logic they concluded that overcrowding; inadequate housing; insufficient food without nutrition; lack of sanitation, medicine, or recreation; and reduction to subhuman standards would produce starvation, disease, pestilence, factional strife resulting in deaths and mass suicide similar to their experience in Vienna, all of which would save them the trouble and ammunition required to massacre half a million people outright.

Against this unprecedented persecution, against the hardships of the present and the unimaginable evils of the future, we held grimly to one determination: the will to survive. . . .

We had no electricity any more. Carbide lamps and candles had to serve for lighting purposes, while electric appliances such as irons, heaters, cleaners, and the like became obsolete and so much scrap. We had no gas for cooking except from 1 A.M. to 6 A.M. The housewife at work all day could not possibly stay up so late or get up so early. Therefore we cooked over wood fires in small iron stoves. As the rooms naturally had no flues, the stove would fill them with choking smoke and cover everything with soot.

All radios were confiscated and telephones removed. Musical instruments, pianos in particular, were requisitioned. Streetcars no longer operated in the ghetto. They were replaced by an old horse-drawn wagon which rumbled through the main streets, stopping occasionally to lower a pair of steps for a passenger. . . .

The most vital problem for us was food. During those long months the word on every person's lips, the thought in every mind, was food—where to get it, how to get it, how much was there. For food a man would take the most fearful risks, would incur the most frightful punishments.

Because nothing could be grown in the ghetto, every bit of food had to be brought in from the outside. An Office of Provision was set up within the Jewish Council to receive what the Germans allotted to us and distribute it to the retailers. Our official bread ration was five pounds a month per person. Enough flour for this was delivered to the council, which then apportioned it to the bakers. The flour was dark and sticky, while the bread made from it tasted like turnips and was indigestible.

The diet forced upon us was calculated to starve us. It contained no fats, no eggs, no meat or fish, no fruits or vegetables, and was, therefore, almost completely lacking in calories and vitamins.

Naturally, in these circumstances we took matters into our own hands. A flourishing black market sprang up, supplied by highly organized smuggling, and this enabled us to keep from starving to death.

The smugglers were tough characters, reckless and unafraid. The penalty if caught was death, but there were always replacements to be found for their depleted ranks. Well organized and disciplined, they worked on a large scale. Moreover, the smugglers were fortunate in two respects: food was plentiful in the country around the capital, and they could generally count on the corruption and greed of the Germans. . . .

Small children were trained for this trade. They would creep through holes in the brickwork or climb over and jump down. Once on the outside they would run away on their errands. They made marvelous smugglers, for they could be taught easily and it was the sort of game their imaginations would seize upon with delight. They loved to outwit the sluggish Germans and were thoroughly familiar with every winding street and back alley through which they sped with their burdens. They were seldom caught, because children under fourteen did not have to wear the Jewish arm band.

Those who had no valuables left sold their last miserable belongings out on the sidewalks before their lodgings or hawked them through the streets. When these were gone, they sold their miserable bodies, their last strength, to menial services for a meal, for a piece of food. And those who had no more strength, died.

. . . The Germans began to hunt our men in the streets. They were caught like animals and carried away to slave at back-breaking jobs in the outside town. Late at night they were brought back and dumped inside the gates, drained of all strength. The less hardy never did return. We did not let our men go out on the streets unless it was absolutely necessary, and then they were preceded by a woman who would scan the surroundings and give a warning whenever she sighted the Gestapo. . . .

For our own sake and the sake of our families, we were terrified at any harm that might befall our jailers, because lightning reprisals would always strike at us. Day by day we saw friends and relatives murdered in retaliation for deeds in which they had no share, of which they had no knowledge. On one occasion a Polish policeman had been killed on duty. The Gestapo carried out an extensive search, in the course of which one building, at Nalewki 9, put up a stubborn resistance for several hours. When the defenders were finally overcome, fifty-three male inhabitants of that building were dragged out and summarily shot. . . .

There were tens of thousands of families who could not afford black-market prices and had to depend on the rationed goods for sustenance. Slow victims of undernourishment, these. Their teeth decayed and fell out, their hair and nails refused to grow, their eyes became great sunken hollows in fleshless faces, and their stomachs were repulsively bloated.

And, finally, there were many who had exhausted their funds entirely. These miserable travesties of human beings picked up what they could find in the streets and in garbage piles, consuming the rest of their strength in the awful fight against real starvation.

Disease and epidemic found an easy harvest. Tuberculosis took an increasingly heavy toll. Worst of all, spotted fever broke out and raged uncontrolled for months. Thousands upon thousands perished from this devastating plague, which played havoc with the conditions of filth and overcrowding in the ghetto.

It drained away the strength of our already overworked and weakened doctors and nurses. Our feeble medical resources were hopelessly unprepared to cope with its ravages. There were no hospitals in which to isolate the cases, no adequate means of disinfecting buildings. Cleanliness was impossible, and there was absolutely nothing to prevent the plague from spreading. We could only hope and pray that by some miracle it would pass us by. . . .

The ghetto had become a haunted town full of weird sights and unreal shapes. Death reigned in every house and on every street, was on every person's lips, had become the only industry. Everywhere undertaking establishments had sprung up, covering the entire ghetto, filthy little shops providing miserable coffins crudely put together. The carts that carried them to the gate were pushed or drawn by relatives of the dead. There were no horses to pull them. Undertaking was the only business left in the ghetto. The undertakers charged very little for the scant services they could perform, but even this was beyond the means of many people, who were therefore unable to bury their dead.

It is a gruesome feeling to be walking along an unlighted street at night and suddenly stumble against something which had once been a human being but is now a corpse rotting on the pavement covered over with a few newspapers held down by bricks. There were many of those piles in the streets that winter. They would lie there until the garbage truck passed on its round, often at irregular intervals.

Pitiful characters wandered about during the daytime, men and women wearing an old overcoat and, as far as could be seen, nothing underneath. In order to protect themselves, some had wrapped feather pillows around their waists and tied them fast with string, presenting a sadly grotesque appearance.

It became dangerous to walk in the street with a package. From nowhere robbers would jump you and seize it. Hurriedly they would tear off the wrapping and stuff the contents into their mouths without waiting to see what they were, in the hope of getting food. One poor man who tried this was badly fooled: the package contained bleaching soda. I saw another burglar fall down on the pavement and cover with his body the loot he had just snatched. The robbed woman screamed and attracted the attention of passers-by, who stopped to help. They beat and kicked the man, who lay still and took the punishment but refused to give up the package.

Such sordid scenes made us deeply ashamed of the level to which we had sunk. Gone were all decent standards of conduct, all civic virtues, all the dignity of man.

The only places we could gather during the daytime were the numerous small coffeehouses, whose growth had paralleled that of the undertaking shops. These places were a testament to the ineradicable optimism of our people. Most of the shopkeepers had long since sold out their stocks. As new merchandise was unobtainable, the stores would be forced to close down. But the owners believed firmly that the day of deliverance would come and wanted to be there when it did. So they converted their empty shops into coffeehouses. They served worthless substitutes: grain coffee, with candies and pastries purchased on the black market and adulterated by mixing and shortening. The coffeehouses were a haven where we could escape from the narrow confines of our one-room home, keep warm for a while, and find company. . . .

Nor could we observe the rites of our church in any strict sense of the word. The Liberal Synagogue was outside the ghetto, and we did not dare to use the Orthodox synagogues left inside. We were afraid to congregate in large numbers in a place of worship, as this would offer an opportunity to the Germans for massacre. Whatever rites we still observed were performed in private, with no more than the prescribed ten persons that in our creed form a congregation.

No schools were left in the ghetto. The Germans had decreed that Jewish children should receive no education whatsoever. We refused to let our children grow up to be ignorant savages, so we organized small groups into classes, with courageous men and women venturing to do the teaching.

Strange as it may seem, there were few suicides among the ghetto population. The determination to survive held strong to the bitter end. The Germans openly complained about this state of affairs, having hoped for a more rapid extermination. They drew unfavorable comparisons between our resistance and their experience in Vienna, where the Jewish population had killed themselves in an unparalleled wave of panic. They professed to be unable to understand why we continued to hang on, but I think that at the back of their minds they had some inkling of the truth: that we had no faith in the duration of their reign and were convinced beyond all doubt of their ultimate downfall and destruction.

Now that they had curbed us and reduced us to the minimum standards of existence, the Germans sent their soldiers "sight-seeing" in the ghetto. Individual soldiers could seldom obtain the necessary permit to enter, even if they had wanted to, either because of the danger they might encounter in the ghetto or because of jealousy between the Gestapo and the army. But their pleasure trips *en masse* were not only tolerated but systematically organized. They came rattling in on army charabancs, forty or fifty at a time, well fed, warmly clothed, broad-shouldered, and overbearing, and made the grand tour. With wide grins they took in our humiliation and misery. Pointing at us with disgust and scorn, they would tell one another: "Now you see how filthy those Jews are and how wise it was to shut them up together and let them stew in their own dirt." . . .

BEN HECHT

Remember Us

Reader's Digest, February 1943

This general description of the Jewish plight was published in the widely circulated *Reader's Digest,* excerpted from a longer piece in the much smaller circulation magazine the *American Mercury.* Ben Hecht (1893–1964) was a well-known novelist, journalist, playwright, and screenwriter. He was also an American Jew, who during the war became an active battler against anti-Semitism and an advocate of a Jewish state in Palestine.

This piece is revealing in a number of ways. Hecht quite accurately summarizes the millions of deaths that had already occurred by early 1943, but without mentioning the extermination centers that had been placed in operation in 1942. Note also that he indirectly makes the case for a Jewish state by showing how statelessness will make Jews invisible victims at the peace table after the war. Finally, despite his passionate commitments, Hecht makes no direct proposal for rescue in this article. Yet at the same time, he had signed and written part of a political advertisement that appeared in the *New York Times* on February 16, 1943, and that advocated paying ransom for Romanian Jews and sending them to Palestine.

When the time comes to make peace, the men of many countries will sit around the table of judgment. The eyes of the German delegates will look into the eyes of Englishmen, Americans, Russians, Czechs, Poles, Greeks, Norwegians, Belgians, Frenchmen, and Dutchmen. All the victims of the German adventure will be there to pass sentence—all but one: the Jew.

There are two reasons for this.

Ben Hecht, "Remember Us," *Reader's Digest,* Feb. 1943, 107–10.

First is the fact that the Jews have only one unity—that of the target. They have lived in the world as a scattered and diverse folk who paid homage to many cultures and called many flags their own. Under attack they have achieved falsely the air of "a race," "a people," and even "a nation."

The Germans have animated the myth of the Jewish menace beyond any of their predecessors and have tried to prove their case by presenting the world with a larger pile of Jewish corpses than has ever before been introduced into the ancient argument.

Despite this unity which death has given them, the peace will reveal that the Jews were a diversified and harmless political nobody who had in common little more than the rage of the Germans. They have no country to represent them at the judgment table.

The second reason why they will not be represented is even more practical. Outside the borders of Russia, there will not be enough Jews left in Europe to profit by representation were it given them. They will have been reduced from a minority to a phantom.

There will be no representatives of the 3,000,000 Jews who once lived in Poland, or of the 900,000 who once lived in Rumania, or of the 900,000 who once lived in Germany, or of the 750,000 who once lived in Hungary, or of the 150,000 who once lived in Czechoslovakia, or of the 400,000 who once lived in France, Holland, and Belgium.

Of these 6,000,000 Jews almost a third have already been massacred by Germans, Rumanians, and Hungarians, and the most conservative of the scorekeepers estimate that before the war ends at least another third will have been done to death.

These totals will not include Jews who died in the brief battles of the German blitzes; nor those who figure in the casualty lists of the Russians. Of the 3,000,000 Jews in Russia, more than 700,000 have entered the Soviet armies and fought and bled on all the valorous battlefields of the Muscovites. These are the lucky Jews of Europe and are not to be counted in the tale of their nightmare.

The millions who were hanged, burned, or shot did not die dreaming, like the valorous Greeks, Dutchmen, Frenchmen, and Czechs, of abasements to be avenged and homelands to be restored. These great sustaining powers in the human soul are unknown to the Jews. When they die in massacre they look toward no tomorrow to bring their children happiness and their enemies disaster. For no homeland is ever theirs, no matter how long they live in it, how well they serve it, or how many of its songs they learn to sing.

When plans for the new world are being threshed out at the peace conference, when guilts are being fixed and plums distributed, there will be nothing for the Jews of Europe to say to the delegates but the faint, sad phrase, "Remember us."

The dead of many lands will speak for justice, but the Jew alone will have no one to speak for him. His voice will remain outside the hall of judgment, to be heard only when the window is opened and the sad plaint drifts in:

"Remember us. In the town of Freiburg in the Black Forest two hundred of us were hanged and left dangling out of our kitchen windows to watch our synagogue burn and our rabbi being flogged to death.

"In Szczucin in Poland on the morning of September 23, which is the day set aside for our Atonement, we were in our synagogue praying God to forgive us. All our village was there. Above our prayers we heard the sound of motor lorries. They stopped in front of our synagogue. The Germans tumbled out of them, torches in hand, and set fire to us. When we ran out of the flames they turned machine guns on us. They seized our women and undressed them and made them run naked through the market place before their whips. All of us were killed before our Atonement was done. Remember us.

"In Wloclawek also the Germans came when we were at worship. They tore the prayer shawls from our heads. Under whips and bayonets they made us use our prayer shawls as mops to clean out German latrines. We were all dead when the sun set. Remember us.

"In Mogielnica, in Brzcziny, in Wengrow, and in many such places where we lived obeying the law, working for our bread and offering harm to no one, there also the Germans came with their bayonets and torches, debasing us first and then killing us slowly so they might longer enjoy the massacres.

"In Warsaw in the year 1941 we kept count and at the end of 12 months 72,279 of us had died. Most of us were shot, but there were thousands of us who were whipped and bayoneted to death on the more serious charge of having been caught praying to God for deliverance. Remember us.

"In the seven months after June 1941 there were 60,000 of us massacred in Bessarabia and Bukovina. There were more than that killed in Minsk. We hung from windows and burned in basements and were beaten to death in the market place, and it was a time of great celebration for the Germans.

"Remember us who were put in the freight trains that left France, Holland, and Belgium for the East. We died standing up, for there was no food or air or water. Those who survived were sent to Transnistria and there died of hunger slowly and under the watchful eyes of the Germans and Rumanians.

"We fill the waters of the Dnieper today with our bodies, thousands of us. And for a long time to come no one will be able to drink from that river or swim in it. For we are still there. And this, too, is held against us, that we have poisoned the waters with our dead bodies.

"Remember us who were in the Ukraine. Here the Germans grew angry because we were costing them too much time and ammunition to kill. They devised a less expensive method. They took our women into the roads and tied them together with our children. Then they drove their heavy motor lorries into us. Thousands of us died with German military cars running back and forth over our broken bodies.

"Remember us in Ismail when the Rumanians came. For two days they were busy leading all the Jews to the synagogue. We were finally locked inside it. Then the Rumanian Iron Guards blew us up with dynamite.

"In Ungheni, Rumania, the Germans accused us of crimes against the police. Three thousand of us were tried. The Germans followed us to our homes. They had been forbidden to waste bullets on us. We were old and unarmed but it took them two days to club us all to death with their rifle butts and rip us into silence with their bayonets.

"Remember, too, those of us who were not killed by the Germans but who killed themselves. Some say there were 100,000 of us, some say 200,000. No count was kept. Our deaths accomplished little, but it made us happy to die quickly and to know that we were robbing the Germans of their sport."

These are only a few of the voices. There are many more and there will be yet more millions.

When the German delegates sit at the peace table, no sons or survivors or representatives of these myriad dead will be there to speak for them. And by that time it will be seen that the Jews are Jews only when they fall under German rifle butts, before German motor lorries, and hang from German belts out of their kitchen windows. Once dead, it will be seen that the Jews are left without a government to speak for their avenging and that there is no banner to fly in their tomorrow.

Only this that I write — and all the narratives like it that will be written — will be their voice that may drift in through the opened window of the judgment hall.

Examples of Anti-Semitic Doggerel

Despite the efforts of sympathetic Christians and of outspoken Jews such as Ben Hecht, one of the paradoxes of America's entry into the war against Hitler was that anti-Semitism in America increased to its highest level in history. Inflamed by Father Coughlin (see pages 77–82) and other demagogues and taxed by war's unprecedented sacrifices, ordinary Americans sometimes succumbed to traditional anti-Semitic hatred, viewing Jews as crafty profiteers sending Christians to the slaughter. It is hard to gauge the precise impact that such views had on America's response to the reports of the mass killing of Jews in Europe, but clearly anti-Semitism blunted sympathy among Christians and paralyzed Christian and Jewish efforts to promote a more active government response.

Leonard Dinnerstein, *Antisemitism in America* (New York: Oxford University Press, 1994), 139–41. Dinnerstein's source for these verses is Lois J. Meltzer, "Anti-Semitism in the United States Army during World War II" (master's thesis, Baltimore Hebrew College, 1977).

These three examples of anti-Semitic verse circulated widely among civilians and servicemen. The common assumption then was that Jews as a group avoided military service or sought noncombat positions in the armed forces. This sentiment, which is expressed in particularly stark form in the first two examples, was untrue. Jews enlisted, served, died, and were decorated for valor in numbers at or above their percentage of the population.[1] For an example of the deepening that Nazi genocide brought to traditional anti-Semitism, one need only read the last line of "A Christmas Poem."

THE FIRST AMERICAN

The first American soldier to kill a Jap was Michael Murphy
The first American bomber to sink a battleship was Captain Colin Kelly
The first American to prove the effectiveness of a torpedo was Captain John
    Bulkley
The first American flier to bag a Jap plane was John O'Hare
The first American Coast Guard to detect a German spy was Ensign
    John Cullen
The first American to be decorated by the President of the United States
    for bravery was Lieutenant Patrick Powers
The first American to get new tires was Abe Cohen.

TO THE TUNE OF THE MARINE HYMN

From the shores of Coney Island
Looking eastward to the sea
Stands a kosher air-raid warden
Wearing a V for victory.

And the gentle breezes fill the air
With the hot dogs from Cohen's stand
Only Christian boys are drafted
From Coney Island's sands.

Oh, we Jews are not afraid to say
We'll stay home and give first aid
Let the Christian saps go fight the Japs
In the uniforms we made.

[1] See Mac Davis, *Jews Fight Too!* (New York: Jordan Publishing, 1944); Isaac E. Rontch, *Jewish Youth at War: Letters from American Soldiers* (New York: Marstin Press, 1945); and I. Kaufman, *American Jews in World War II,* 2 vols. (New York: Dial Press, 1947).

If the Army or the Navy
Ever gaze on heaven's scene
They will find the Jews are selling shoes
To the United States Marines.

So it's onward into battle
Let us send the Christian slobs
When the war is done and victory won
All us Jews will have their jobs.

If your son is drafted don't complain
When he sails across the pond
For us Jews have made it possible
All of us have bought a bond.

And when peace has come to us again
And we've licked that Hitler louse
You will find a Jew a-ruling you
In Washington's great White House.

A CHRISTMAS POEM

Oh little town of Bethlehem
For Christmas gifts see Abraham
At Christmas get a tree of pine
And buy the balls from Silverstein.
Down the chimney Santa drops
With toys bought from Isaac Blatz.
Ring out the old, ring in the New
And help fatten up some dirty Jew.
Hark! The herald angels sing,
Buy from Katz a diamond ring.
Our savior was born on Christmas day
Levy gives you six months to pay.
Peace on earth, good will to many
Hock your things with Uncle Benny.
Silent Night! Holy Night!
Damned if I don't think Hitler's right.

FREDA KIRCHWEY

While the Jews Die

Nation, March 13, 1943

Allied fortunes in the war directly affected the possibility of action to save Jews from certain death, and victory was in doubt through much of 1942. Yet two major battles in that year began to turn the tide in favor of the Allies. In Europe, the Soviet army finally stopped the German advance at Stalingrad and began a slow, costly, but ultimately triumphant counteroffensive. In the Pacific, American forces scored victories at Midway and in the Coral Sea, halting the previously unstoppable Japanese advance.

In this new atmosphere, commentators felt freer to criticize Allied conduct. Freda Kirchwey, the liberal editor of the *Nation* and a fierce opponent of fascism throughout the 1930s and early 1940s, made a special point of focusing attention on the fate of the Jews. This article is fascinating in that it raises questions concerning Allied conduct with which later historians would grapple beginning only in the late 1960s. Note Kirchwey's assessment of guilt and her contempt for British and American inaction. Note also her imagined dialogue with a well-meaning American. The forthcoming meeting mentioned, to have been convened in Ottawa, actually took place in Bermuda and is the subject of the two documents that follow this selection.

Jews in Europe are being killed because they are Jews. Other innocent people are being killed too — hostages, men and women who resist oppression, old people who consume food needed by German soldiers and workers. But only Jews are being killed without other excuse or cause than the fact that they belong to a single religious-racial group. Hitler has promised their total liquidation, and he is carrying out that promise as fast as his Mobile Extermination Squads can work. They work fast. Seven or eight thousand Jews a week are being massacred. The ghetto of Warsaw, two years ago the dumping ground for Jews from all over occupied Europe, is now depopulated. Every Jew is dead. In Cracow, where 60,000 Jews lived, 56,000 have been killed.

The ways in which these slaughters are conducted have been reported. The numbers have been verified. The story is old. But the killing goes on.

Freda Kirchwey, "While the Jews Die," *Nation,* Mar. 13, 1943, 366–67.

And as Hitler's armies are forced step by step back into Europe, the tempo of extermination quickens. He must hurry now lest the liberating armies arrive in time to rescue some fragment of the doomed race. It is not fantastic to believe that even when Hitler is overthrown, he will find profound compensation in leaving behind him a Europe "cleansed" of the hated Jew.

If this happens, no one living today will escape retribution for the crime. For the purge of the Jews is only positively a Nazi crime. In this country, you and I and the President and the Congress and the State Department are accessories to the crime and share Hitler's guilt. If we had behaved like humane and generous people instead of complacent, cowardly ones, the two million Jews lying today in the earth of Poland and Hitler's other crowded graveyards would be alive and safe. And other millions yet to die would have found sanctuary. We had it in our power to rescue this doomed people and we did not lift a hand to do it—or perhaps it would be fairer to say that we lifted just one cautious hand, encased in a tight-fitting glove of quotas and visas and affidavits and a thick layer of prejudice.

Today we hear something is going to be done. Secretary Hull has suggested a meeting at Ottawa of the executive committee of the Intergovernmental Committee on Refugees appointed at the Evian Conference in 1938. This group will undertake "preliminary exploration" of the problem of the Jews in occupied Europe. But the exploration, it seems, is to proceed along rather well-worn trails. For, as Mr. Hull assured the British government, the United States government feels "that it has been and is making every endeavor to relieve the oppressed and persecuted peoples. In affording asylum to the refugees, however, it is and must be bound by legislation enacted by Congress determining the immigration policy of the United States."

By all means let's have the conference. But let's remember that it wasn't called because our government felt impelled to do something about the greatest crime committed in our generation. Not a move of any sort was made until a delegation of prominent Jews called on Secretary Hull and the President of the United States on December 8 and presented them with verified accounts of the massacres in Poland which were simultaneously released to the press. The President and Mr. Hull promised action. But nothing happened until more than a month later, on January 20 to be exact, when Lord Halifax presented an aide-mémoire to Secretary Hull expressing the "concern" of the British government over the killings. And then it took another month for Secretary Hull to reply with the note quoted above. Hundreds of thousands of Jews fell into their self-dug graves while our government, with glacial slowness, moved toward a proposal to confer and to explore. And in view of this record of delay it is fair to wonder whether even this modest step would have been taken if a great mass-meeting of protest had not been called for March 1 in Madison Square Garden in New York— a meeting organized by the American Jewish Congress and sponsored by a group of important labor and liberal organizations. Mr. Hull's note to Lord

Halifax was dated February 25. It was made public the day after the mass-meeting took place.

Whatever the sequence of events, we must be glad that some voices were loud enough to penetrate the official armor. But let us not bank too much on the new "Evian" conference. The first one was held in 1938 while it was still possible to save the Jews of Europe. But Hitler is still busy with the job of exterminating 5,000,000 of them. Let us be hopeful—but not sanguine.

And let us also acknowledge the uncomfortable fact that if a group of American Jews had not demanded action, nothing, not even a conference, would have resulted from the horrors in Europe. Let us acknowledge that in shame. And let us ask ourselves what has come over the minds of ordinary men and women that makes it seem normal and indeed inevitable that this country should stolidly stand by and do nothing in the face of one of the world's greatest tragedies until the Jews themselves press for action.

But what on earth could we have done more than we did do? We let in refugees until people protested that jobs were being taken from good Americans by an invading army of aliens. We let them come in to the limit of the quotas—provided, of course, that they had money and good sponsors and respectable political views. We did our best—all that public opinion and Congress and our State Department would permit. And why should we do it all, anyhow? How about Palestine? Why don't the British let them in there? And how about South America and Canada and Australia?

This is the sort of question non-Jewish Americans ask when they are faced with Jewish suffering and the reproaches of their own conscience. But the questions are not impressive, and the answers are easy.

One answer is that we could have cut down those barbed-wire defenses strung along our shores. We could have suspended the immigration quotas for the duration of Hitler. We could have raised funds to support refugees who couldn't bring out any money. We could have chartered ships to bring them from Europe. We could have put any questionable individuals in detention camps or segregated them on a Caribbean island. We could have offered an example of decency and humanity to a world hungry for evidences of good feeling.

We could have done all this. But we wouldn't have had to be quite so generous. An easier answer was at hand. We could have made the resolutions of the Evian conference a reality instead of a hollow gesture. We could have entered into an agreement for common action with the other anti-Axis nations—an agreement to absorb all the victims of Hitlerism who were physically able to escape—each nation taking a quota decided upon with due regard to its size and wealth and capacity to absorb immigrants. If the United States had taken the lead in such a move, I am certain that no nation would have refused its cooperation. And under such a scheme, the burden on each would have been insignificant.

But nothing was done. Every nation established its own restrictions, the

United States admitting no more immigrants than in the days before the persecutions began. And so we come to the horrifying present.

The resolutions adopted by the mass-meeting at the Garden the other night were restrained and practical. Here they are, in summary:

1. Through neutral intermediaries, Germany and the governments of the states it dominates should be asked to release their Jewish victims and permit them to emigrate.
2. The United Nations should designate sanctuaries, in Allied and neutral states, for Jews whose release may be arranged for.
3. American immigration procedures should be revised in order that refugees may find sanctuary here within existing quotas.
4. Great Britain should be asked to receive a reasonable number of new refugees and accommodate them for the duration.
5. The United Nations should urge the Latin American republics to modify their immigration regulations sufficiently to provide refuge for agreed numbers of Nazi victims.
6. England should be asked to open the doors of Palestine for Jewish immigration.
7. The United Nations should provide financial guaranties to neutral states offering refuge to Jews from occupied territory.
8. The United Nations should organize the feeding through neutral agencies of victims forced to remain under Nazi oppression.
9. The United Nations should undertake the financing of the program here outlined.
10. The United Nations are urged to establish an intergovernmental agency to implement the program of rescue here outlined.
11. The United Nations are urged to appoint a commission forthwith to implement their declared intention to bring the Nazi criminals to justice.

This is a good program, though more moderate in several details than I would wish. How far it will influence the coming conference at Ottawa remains to be seen. One thing is certain. The United States—or the United Nations as a whole—will save only as many Jews as they are inflexibly determined to save. If the representatives of the anti-Axis powers meet in a mood of impatience, prepared to deal on a minimum basis with a difficult and irritating problem—if, in short, the mood of the past prevails—nothing will happen at Ottawa or after. Europe's remaining Jews will be saved only if their anguish has become unbearable to men and women who live in safety at a distance. They will be saved only if we recognize their fate as inextricably linked with our own.

From *Minutes of the American Delegation at the Bermuda Conference*

April 20, 1943

By January 1943, the governments in London and Washington were both under pressure from powerful organizations and public spokespersons, Christians and Jews, to seek ways for the Allies to help save some of Europe's Jews. The most obvious means, winning the war, was clearly years away, and each week the Nazis were murdering thousands. In response to the public outcry, the British Foreign Office suggested an informal meeting with American officials to see if they could find ways of at least ensuring the safety of those refugees from Nazism in neutral countries by getting them out of Europe. That conference was held on the island of Bermuda in April 1943.

Most historians have judged the Bermuda meeting to be a failure and even a cynical attempt to assuage public opinion without taking action. Some have pointed to the endemic anti-Semitic attitudes of key players in the State Department, most especially Assistant Secretary of State Breckenridge Long, and similar views among the British delegates, to explain an almost willful commitment to inaction at the conference. Others have asserted that the conferees faced the impossible task of coming up with solutions to an insoluble problem. Evidence supporting both interpretations emerges from the archives, although it is clear in this excerpt and in other sources that representatives of the United States and Britain came to the conference presuming that little could be done to save the Jews in Europe.

Following is an excerpt from the minutes of the opening session as recorded by the American delegation at Bermuda. The comments of the British delegation are of particular interest in their immediate framing of the questions to be discussed and those to be excluded from discussion and in their characterization of the victims of the Nazis. The British represented a united and conservative front against an American delegation of diplomats, politicians, and citizens who represented a variety of opinions. The Americans, for their part, represented the State Department's

---

"Minutes of the American Delegation at the Bermuda Conference," Apr. 20, 1943, in *America and the Holocaust: Responsibility for America's Failure,* vol. 13, ed. David S. Wyman (New York: Garland Publishing, 1991), 77–81.

and the public's strong determination to hold the line on immigration. The speakers included:

Richard Law, British parliamentary undersecretary of state for foreign affairs

Harold W. Dodds, president of Princeton University

Sol Bloom, Democratic congressman from New York and a Jew

R. Borden Reams, State Department member and secretary for the American delegation

---

CONFIDENTIAL MEMORANDUM FOR THE CHAIRMAN:

Mr. Law of the British Delegation presided at the Conference and began by saying that he thought it would be well to start by attempting to define the problem. He added that there are many exaggerated ideas about what can be done to solve the refugee problem. These comprise:

1. The suggestion that the United Nations make a deal with Hitler whereby he would be willing to release the Jews and other refugees in Germany and other occupied countries;
2. That we exchange Nazi prisoners and other persons in Allied hands for refugees; and
3. That we should send in food through the blockade to feed the peoples in Europe. He added that it seemed to the British Delegation that all of these problems are fantastic and that we could not embark on them without jeopardizing the course of the war.

Mr. Law continued that there are 15,000 or 20,000 refugees in Spain, about one half of which are Jews and one half non-Jews. There are also the children that we are trying to get out of the Balkans. There are the refugees in Persia and Greek refugees in Cyprus. He added that there was finally the question of the neutral countries: Switzerland, Spain, and Sweden. As regards the last, it is almost impossible for refugees to enter because of Nazi restrictions.

He continued that the view of the British Delegation is that it would be profitable to define the problem in these limited terms and forget the solutions proposed that are manifestly impossible and concluded it by suggesting that the Conference approach the problem in these limited terms.

At this time there was some discussion of the possibility of Portugal entering the picture as one of the neutral countries to which refugees might be admitted.

Dr. Dodds suggested that the Conference take up the three extreme proposals one by one.

The first proposal that the United Nations make a deal with Hitler was then opened for discussion.

Mr. Law stated that since this proposal involves negotiations with Hitler and since the British Delegation firmly believes that anything that the Nazis would agree to would be on the basis of some direct advantage to them this clearly was not practicable. In further discussing the matter, Mr. Law explained that it was thought in London that the most favorable thing that could be done in opening negotiations with Hitler would be the receipt of a blank negative to any proposals made by the United Nations—that this clearly was the hope in England. He added, however, that if Hitler accepted a proposal to release perhaps millions of unwanted persons, we might find ourselves in a very difficult position. For one thing, Hitler might send a large number of picked agents which we would be forced to take into our own countries. On the other hand, he might say, "Alright, take a million or two million." Then because of the shipping problem, we should be made to look exceedingly foolish.

Mr. Bloom then expressed the thought that we should at least negotiate and see what could be done. Dr. Dodds expressed the idea that we should not attempt to negotiate with the enemy countries. At this point a rather extended argument developed.

Mr. Bloom offered the suggestion that we propose that Hitler release each month the number of refugees that we find it possible to handle. Dr. Dodds replied that all of our facilities and more are being required to take care of those refugees outside of Germany.

A member of the British Delegation then said that he could not visualize that Hitler would agree to any release only of the refugees and would insist on an exchange. He would want a quid pro quo. He also observed that the matter should not be viewed just as a Jewish problem. If an approach was made to the German Government they might reply that they would agree but under conditions: "We will release X number of refugees if you will release to us X number of prisoners." He then went on to point out the difficulties already encountered with the German Government regarding exchange of prisoners and mentioned a specific instance—an exchange of British and German soldiers had broken down at the last minute through no fault of the British Government—and suggested that we might say that under these circumstances we could not make any approach to Germany. We cannot rely on anything he would promise. We would have to agree on what we could exchange for any refugees which were obtained. He would surely ask things that we could not give. Furthermore, the shipping problem is a real problem, and we have little prospect of any ships being allocated except for war purposes. He concluded that it was better not to agree to negotiate when on the face of it [we] cannot succeed and when it would lead to hopes among the refugees that cannot be realized.

Dr. Dodds then expressed the thought that Congressman Bloom was trying to explore the smart thing to do and discussed the advisability of two approaches, but concluded that it was much better not to begin to negotiate. Mr. Bloom then returned to his first point and argued that it was much more preferable to negotiate so that we could determine what the Germans were willing to do. He suggested that we be not too explicit as to what we could do and that it was better to leave the matter entirely open and conclude with a recommendation that we would try to do it if the opportunity arises. There then occurred an extended conversation between Dr. Dodds and Mr. Bloom, Dodds pointing out that Mr. Bloom's proposal was completely against the policy of our Government and that we were on record against negotiating on any terms with Nazi Germany. Bloom then began to recede from his former rather uncompromising position.

A member of the British Delegation then suggested that the question of potential refugees should be thoroughly discussed. Many of the potential refugees are empty mouths for which Hitler has no use. He would estimate that there must be 20 or 30 million people who are really a liability rather than an advantage to Hitler and whom he would therefore be glad to get rid of. Moreover, it would be relieving Hitler of an obligation to take care of these useless people. If Hitler would agree to release a large number of old people and children, we should be placed in a ridiculous position because we could only take between 500 and 1,000 a month. To open up negotiations and to have Hitler agree that we can take all we want and have us then to have to say that we cannot take them would place us in an impossible situation. Furthermore, we know that both our Governments would never agree to such a recommendation even if this Conference should recommend it to the Intergovernmental Committee.

Mr. Bloom then remarked that all he wanted was to somehow not close the door.

A British delegate then remarked that we can arrange to take more refugees from neutral countries, then possibly other refugees can enter such neutral countries from Germany.

Mr. Reams then interposed to say that there was no doubt whatever that the Department of State would oppose any negotiations with Germany.

Mr. Bloom then took up his original point and insisted that we should leave the possibility open of negotiating with Germany whether or not we actually made the recommendation that this be done.

After an extended argument on this point it was proposed that it be left for the moment and that the Conference should go on to the second point, which is the question of exchange of Nazi prisoners and others in allied hands for refugees. It was quickly decided that this proposal is out.

The third proposal to send food in through the blockade was then discussed. Mr. Bloom made extended remarks on this subject, spoke of the question of distribution of foodstuffs being highly important, but seemed to be generally against sending food.

A member of the British Delegation stated that there was considerable public opinion in England that food should be sent to many places such as occupied France, et cetera, et cetera. The only place food has actually been sent so far is to Greece. The feeling of the British Delegation is that this is really a question of blockade policy and that he did not see how this Conference could make any such recommendation.

Dr. Dodds then said that the question of sending food to occupied countries is entirely outside of our terms of reference and that we cannot make any recommendation about the Allied blockade. . . .

FREDA KIRCHWEY

A Program of Inaction

Nation, June 5, 1943

In this piece, Kirchwey responds to the result she had expected all along—that the Bermuda Conference would lead to no tangible actions to save Jewish lives.

The weeks following the end of the Bermuda conference on refugee problems have brought nothing but a series of excuses for the failure of the British and American governments to do anything effective to rescue the victims of Hitler's terror who still remain alive. Indeed, the conference itself seems to have been devoted almost entirely to the formulation of those excuses: You couldn't ask favors of Hitler or of any of the governments under his domination. There wasn't any available transportation even in ships coming back from the war fronts in ballast. The extermination of the Jews seemed only too likely, but still, among all the would-be refugees of Europe, how could one single out the Jews for special treatment? Then, where would they go? England had taken more than its share, and so had the rest of the empire. Palestine's gates had been closed by a White Paper. The quota system in the United States was immutable. The conferees would therefore concentrate most of their effort on the immediate problem of transferring to temporary places of settlement refugees who have succeeded in reaching neutral countries. The Nazi victims in occupied Europe would have to wait for an Allied victory. Wait—above the earth or under it.

What little has happened in recent weeks confirms the negative impression made by the conference. A Parliamentary debate on the results of the Bermuda meeting brought statements from both Mr. Eden, the Foreign

---

Freda Kirchwey, "A Program of Inaction," *Nation,* June 5, 1943, 796–97.

Secretary, and Osbert Peake, Under Secretary for the Home Office, agreeing that nothing much could be done for victims of fascist persecution until the war was won. At the same time the State Department announced that "a first contingent of refugees from a neutral country has been transferred to a temporary haven," but reiterated that "no negotiations with Hitler could be undertaken for the rescue of potential refugees from Nazi-occupied territory, since his entire record has left no doubt that he would only agree to such solutions as would be of direct aid to the Axis war aims."

The British and American governments are doubtless animated by both altruistic and interested motives in moving refugees from overcrowded neutral countries to settlements elsewhere, properly supervised and perhaps financed through some intergovernmental body. Such a project has the virtue of helping the refugees and at the same time relieving the pressure of unwelcome thousands on the gates of the United States and Britain—and Palestine. But the rescue of people who have already rescued themselves is at best a rather minor and tangential operation. The real job is a different one, and not all the alibis cooked up in a hundred conferences will justify its neglect.

We should examine the excuses formulated in Bermuda and decide for ourselves whether or not they are sufficient to justify inaction. Certainly it is unlikely that Hitler would yield to any pleas for the release of Jews now under his direct control. But since, in the past, he has been interested in getting rid of Jews and has not always insisted upon slaughtering them, it is barely possible that he might agree to an exodus from the ghettoes of Poland arranged through neutral intermediaries. It is not likely, but it is possible.

But assuming Hitler refused to relinquish his prey, there is still a definite chance that some of the lesser Axis governments might agree to do so. Hungary, Bulgaria, Rumania might well choose to dispose of a troublesome problem and at the same time curry favor with the powers that now appear the probable winners. If these Axis satellites would release the Jews within their borders, many hundreds of thousands could be saved.

But how could these hordes be transported? And where could they go? If Britain would ease the restrictions on immigration into Palestine, refugees admitted there could travel overland. This most desired of all solutions has been flatly refused. Not even to save lives will Britain go beyond the quotas established in 1939. Palestine ruled out, it still might be possible to establish settlements, temporary at least, in other parts of the Near and Middle East and in North Africa. Ships carrying war supplies to the Mediterranean could bring refugees back to Britain or the United States.

But this suggestion collides with one of the chief obstacles to a solution—the reluctance of Britain and the United States to admit more refugees. Britain has been far more generous in this matter than we have. The United States has multiplied the complications involved in getting a visa to such a degree that only a fraction of the existing quotas from Nazi-occupied countries are being filled. Without changing the law in any particular [way] we could take in more than 140,000 refugees immediately.

And today they could be used to help overcome our growing shortage of industrial man-power.

As for the difficulty, stressed both here and in London, of singling out the Jews for rescue and ignoring the 120,000,000 people who, according to Mr. Peake, would escape from enemy-occupied territories if they could, this is one of those stumbling-blocks set up to serve as an excuse for inaction. Whole populations neither can nor want to escape, however much they may hate the tyrant. The Jews alone represent a group detached by force from their homes and occupations, segregated physically as well as socially, marked as a whole for annihilation. It is disingenuous to pretend that because the entire population of occupied Europe cannot be evacuated, no effort should be made to save any special group.

The difficulties raised at the Bermuda conference are real. But they afford no valid excuse for a policy of sitting back and doing nothing. The process of extermination may be complete long before victory is won. The only hope lies in acting now. A determined effort should be made to carry out at least a limited program of rescue. Even the attempt would bring hope and comfort to the desperate millions marked for slaughter.

BILL DOWNS

Blood at Babii Yar—Kiev's Atrocity Story
Newsweek, December 6, 1943

Whatever the failure of the Bermuda Conference and the reactions to it, the killing did not stop, nor did the reporting of it in the American press. Here is *Newsweek*'s coverage of one of the most infamous massacres of the Holocaust, Babii Yar, placed prominently next to a story of vital interest to Americans—the Battle of Tarawa in the Pacific. Some details of the story bear notice. First, note that it was written by an American correspondent who was invited to an official Soviet press tour of the Babii Yar site. The reporter seems to have no doubt about what he saw, but the fact that in this and other cases inspection of atrocity sites had been organized by the Soviet authorities caused some people in the United States to doubt the veracity of the stories reported.

Bill Downs, "Blood at Babii Yar—Kiev's Atrocity Story," *Newsweek,* Dec. 6, 1943, 22.

Also of interest is the fact that the Soviet authorities at the time seemed to have identified the victims as Jews. After the war, in speeches and monuments and especially in regard to the massacres at Babii Yar, the official government line was to identify the victims only as "citizens." This denial of the victims' Jewish identity comported well with Stalin's anti-Semitism and an endemic strain of anti-Semitism in Russian culture, as well as with the Soviet ideal of a people given civic but not religious identity. This eerie eradication of Jewish identity was protested during the Soviet era by the poet Yevgeny Yevtushenko (1933–), a non-Jew, whose moving poem "Babii Yar" (1961) decried anti-Semitism and used as its major symbol the lack of Jewish identification at the Babii Yar monument. The poem was controversial in its challenge to the official story. Indeed, the fact that Yevtushenko's poem was tolerated at all was seen in the West as a loosening of Soviet control of artistic expression.

The first foreign witnesses this week returned to Moscow from what are probably the most terrible two acres on earth — a series of desolate ravines in the Lukyanovka district three miles northwest of Kiev. The name Babii Yar is going to stink in history. It is the name of the main ravine where the Russians estimate between 50,000 to 80,000 people were killed and buried during the 25 months of the German occupation. From what I saw, I am convinced that one of the most horrible tragedies in this Nazi era of atrocities occurred there between September 1941 and November 1943.

The press party was led by the Ukrainian author and poet Nikola Bazhan. The Ukrainian Atrocities Commission called three witnesses to meet us at the ravine. They were Efim Vilkis, 33, Leonid Ostrovsky, 31, and Vladimir Davidoff, 28 — all Jewish prisoners of war held in a prison camp across the road. Vilkis did most of the talking, interrupted occasionally by the other two.

The first act in the tragedy took place in September 1941, a few weeks after the Germans captured Kiev. One day they ordered all Jews to report at the Lukyanovka district and bring their valuables with them. Thousands of men, women, and children marched out to Lukyanovka, thinking they probably would be evacuated. Instead, Nazi SS troops led them to Babii Yar.

At the wide shallow ravine, their valuables and part of their clothing were removed and heaped in a big pile. Then groups of these people were led into a neighboring deep ravine where they were machine-gunned. When bodies covered the ground in more or less of a layer, SS men scraped sand down from the ravine walls to cover them. Then the shooting would continue. The Nazis, we were told, worked three days doing the job.

However, even more incredible was the action taken by the Nazis between Aug. 19 and Sept. 28 last. Vilkis said that in the middle of August the SS mobilized a party of 100 Russian war prisoners, who were taken to the ravines.

On Aug. 19 these men were ordered to disinter all the bodies in the ravine. The Germans meanwhile took a party to a nearby Jewish cemetery whence marble headstones were brought to Babii Yar to form the foundation of a huge funeral pyre. Atop the stones were piled a layer of wood and then a layer of bodies, and so on until the pyre was as high as a two-story house.

Vilkis said that approximately 1,500 bodies were burned in each operation of the furnace and each funeral pyre took two nights and one day to burn completely.

The cremation went on for 40 days, and then the prisoners, who by this time included 341 men, were ordered to build another furnace. Since this was the last furnace and there were no more bodies, the prisoners decided it was for them. They made a break but only a dozen out of more than 200 survived the bullets of the Nazi tommy guns.

As substantiating evidence, while walking over the mass graves, I saw bits of hair, bones, and a crushed skull with bits of flesh and hair still attached. Walking down the ravine, I constantly came across shoes, spectacle cases, and in one place found gold bridgework.

The most persistent question that presents itself is why the Nazis took such pains to cover this tragedy. Previously, the Germans made little effort to conceal their Jewish pogroms in any occupied territory. If in their retreat they intend to try to cover their crimes, this represents a new and significant policy which pre-supposes the possibility of defeat. The United Nations declaration regarding war criminals, which closely paralleled Soviet announcements on war crimes, thus can be said to have had its first real effect. . . .

ALFRED KAZIN

In Every Voice, in Every Ban
New Republic, January 10, 1944

As Allied advances made ultimate victory more certain, the slaughter of Jews went on unabated, and the frustration among those who urged direct and immediate action turned to desperation. In this piece, Alfred Kazin, one of America's foremost intellectuals and in 1944 at the begin-

Alfred Kazin, "In Every Voice, in Every Ban," *New Republic,* Jan. 10, 1944, 44–46.

ning of his career as a writer and critic, tries to make sense of the more general meaning of the Nazi slaughter and the Allies' seeming inability to confront it with more than words. Note the story of Shmuel Ziegelboim that begins the piece and Kazin's struggle to define the broader implications of Ziegelboim's suicide and what he sees as the failure of the Allies' response. Note that when Kazin speaks of the Polish government, he is referring to the government-in-exile headquartered in London.

On May 12 of this year, a man named Shmuel Ziegelboim, who was a Socialist, a Jew, and a Pole, was found dead by his own hand in a London flat. His wife and child had been killed by the Nazis in Poland; and no doubt he had had his fill of Polish politics—even (or especially) in London. I had never heard of Shmuel Ziegelboim before I read of his death; and so many Socialists, Jews, and Poles have died in these last few years that it is possible—conscience and memory being what they are even for one's own— that I would never again have thought of him had he not left a letter that was published in a negligible corner of *The New York Times*.

His letter was addressed in Polish to the President of Poland and to Sikorski, who was then Premier. What he wrote was this:

I take the liberty of addressing to you my last words, and through you to the Polish government and the Polish people, to the governments and peoples of the Allied states—to the conscience of the world.

From the latest information received from Poland, it is evident that the Germans, with the most ruthless cruelty, are now murdering the few remaining Jews in Poland. Behind the ghetto's walls the last act of a tragedy unprecedented in history is being performed. The responsibility for this crime of murdering the entire Jewish population of Poland falls in the first instance on the perpetrators, but indirectly it is also a burden on the whole of humanity, the people and the governments of the Allied states which thus far have made no effort toward concrete action for the purpose of curtailing this crime.

By the passive observation of the murder of defenseless millions, and of the maltreatment of children, women, and old men, these countries have become the criminals' accomplices. I must also state that although the Polish government has in a high degree contributed to the enlistment of world opinion, it has yet done so insufficiently. It has not done anything that could correspond to the magnitude of the drama being enacted now in Poland. From some 3,500,000 Polish Jews and about 700,000 other Jews deported to Poland from other countries—according to official statistics provided by the underground Bund organization—there remained in

April of this year only about 300,000, and this remaining murder still goes on.

I cannot be silent—I cannot live—while remnants of the Jewish people of Poland, of whom I am a representative, are perishing. My comrades in the Warsaw ghetto took weapons in their hands on that last heroic impulse. It was not my destiny to die there together with them, but I belong to them, and in their mass graves. By my death I wish to express my strongest protest against the inactivity with which the world is looking on and permitting the extermination of my people.

I know how little human life is worth today; but, as I was unable to do anything during my life, perhaps by my death I shall contribute to breaking down that indifference of those who may now—at the last moment—rescue the few Polish Jews still alive from certain annihilation. My life belongs to the Jewish people of Poland and I therefore give it to them. I wish that this remaining handful of the original several millions of Polish Jews could live to see the liberation of a new world of freedom, and the justice of true socialism. I believe that such a Poland will arise and that such a world will come.

I trust that the President and the Prime Minister will direct my words to all those for whom they are destined, and that the Polish government will immediately take appropriate action in the fields of diplomacy. I bid my farewell herewith to everybody and everything dear to me and loved by me.

—S. Ziegelboim

After the text, the newspaper report added: "That was the letter. It suggests that possibly Shmuel Ziegelboim will have accomplished as much in dying as he did in living."

I bring the matter up now because I have been thinking about the meaning of that letter ever since I clipped it out of *The Times,* and because I hope I can now write thoughtfully about it, since I no longer feel any hatred for the newspaper writer who added with such mechanical emotion that possibly "Shmuel Ziegelboim will have accomplished as much. . . ." Of course the newspaper writer did not believe that he had accomplished anything; nor did the Polish National Council, which released it to the world; nor do I. Shmuel Ziegelboim died because some men can find their ultimate grace only in the fulfilment of their will—even if their will, in 1943, is toward a death that has so desperate a symbolism. He died because the burden of carrying our contemporary self-disgust became too much even for a man who believed that a new world of freedom would come, "and the justice of true socialism." And he died because his wife and child were dead, and the millions in the great Jewish worlds of Poland, and the thousands of thousands of his comrades in the Jewish Labor Bund[1]—the disenchanted and dispossessed Jews who lived on air and were called *Luftmenschen,* but helped to defend Warsaw when the colonels fled.

I think I know how great and indirect a wish for immortality can go into any suicide. I shall believe that men want to die only when I hear of men living (or writing) in complete anonymity. I know something of the ultimate and forgivable egotism of any human spirit, and that the one thing we can never afford to lose is the promise of our identity. Shmuel Ziegelboim wrote at the end with the instinctive rhetorical optimism of those who feel that they are dying without too much division in themselves, and for something greater than their own ambitions. But I have wanted to believe, and now do believe, that Shmuel Ziegelboim died because he was finally unable to withstand the real despair of our time—which arises not out of the burning and the killing and the endless political betrayals, but out of a humiliation which some of us can still feel before so terrible a break in human solidarity. I think he died, as so many greater men have already died morally, because he was unable to believe in a future built on so unrecognized and unreported a human isolation and barbarism as we know today. Shmuel Ziegelboim came from a ghetto-driven, self-driven, but spiritually generous culture; and I honestly believe that he was thinking not only of his own people at the end, but of the hollowness of a world in which such a massacre could have so little meaning. In any event I should like to think that I am more "fortunate"—that is, relatively untouched and able to think about what freedom is. And that is why I bring the matter up now, as a token of what Shmuel Ziegelboim died for, and in an effort to say some very elementary things which liberals especially have not always cared to face.

I do not speak here of the massacre of the Jews, for there is nothing to say about it that has not already been said. I can add nothing, nor would I wish to add anything, to the private imprecations and the public appeals. I do not say that they are useless, for I do not dare to believe that anything here will be useless. It is merely that something has already been done— and not by the Nazis—which can never be undone, except as we seek to understand it and to grow human again (or expectant, or merely wise) through it. For the tragedy is in our minds, in the basic quality of our personal culture; and that is why it will be the tragedy of the peace. The tragedy lies in the quality of our belief—not in the lack of it, but in the unconsciousness or dishonesty of it; and above all in the merely political thinking, the desperate and unreal optimism, with which we try to cover up the void in ourselves. Yet I speak pragmatically: I am thinking of concrete situations. For Hitler will leave anti-Semitism as his last political trick, as it was his first; and the people who have been most indifferent to the historic *meaning* of the massacre of the Jews will be just those who will won-

[1] A Jewish socialist political group which was among those taking up armed resistance against the Nazis.

der why all the pacts and all the armies and all the formal justice will have done so little to give them their pre-Fascist "security" again. If liberal optimism is false now, it will seem cruel later, when in even a post-Hitler Europe men will see again (many of them know it now, but for other, for purely political, reasons) that fascism remains, even though fascists, too, can die.

The treatment of the Jews, historically, has always been a touchstone of the degree of imagination, of Christian confidence, really, which formally Christian countries have been able to feel in themselves. Historically, no massacre was ever unexpected, no act of cruelty ever so great that it violated the professions of a civilization—every civilization being what it was, even when the cathedrals rose highest. But surely there was never so much self-deception about our essential goodness or our dream of "social security," so little philosophic (or moral) searching of the lies our hopes build on our lack of community, as there is today. The real materialism of our time has nothing to do with our intellectual naturalism, which is indispensable to those who do not believe in magic; or to our complete technological reliance upon ourselves, which is what it is. The real materialism, the real heresy, is the blindness of those who, declining to believe that there is a prime cause in the heavens, believe bitterly that society is always the prime cause of what we are. It is the materialism that comes with passing the buck so persistently to everyone but yourself that you never know whom to blame, even when you are Koestler's Rubashov[2] in Lubyanka. It is the materialism of those who believe, as radicals, that you can begin by lying and making your victim lie (especially in public; a public life has a public apotheosis)—and that *then* you can build a brave new world based on the ultimate good sense of cooperativeness and the higher self-interest. It is the materialism of those who believe, as reactionaries, that you can build a tolerable society by appealing to an inner contempt among men for their "romantic"—and quite indestructible—hopes. It is the materialism of those who believe, as liberals, that you so fascinate men in a legality of good intentions, or even philanthropy, that you will

> By faith, and faith alone, embrace,
> Believing where we cannot prove. . . .

But it is above all the materialism of all those—not liberals, not radicals, certainly not reactionaries—who want only to live and let live, to have the good life back—and who think that you can dump three million helpless Jews into your furnace, and sigh in the genuine impotence of your undeniable regret, and then build Europe back again.

---

[2] N. S. Rubashov, main character of Arthur Koestler's *Darkness at Noon* (1941), is a fictional revolutionary and ex-commissar of the Soviet Union who finds himself in the Kremlin's Lubyanka prison awaiting trial for crimes he did not commit.

That is the central point—not a "moral" point which any true unbeliever need be afraid of for its own sake, but the coarsely shrewd point based on the knowledge that life is also a process of memory, and that where so great a murder has been allowed, no one is safe. I do not believe in ghosts; if I did, I could be falsely heroic and satisfyingly sentimental, and say that the blood of the Jews over Europe is like that Christ's blood which Marlowe's Faustus saw streaming in the firmament. For I know that the indifference—the historic contemporary indifference, with everything it suggests about our governments as well as ourselves: I do not forget the rulers in describing the ruled—is far more terrible than physical terror and far more "tangible" than conscience. And what I am saying is not that the peoples will be remorseful (did we do it?), but that they will be betrayed by the human practices encouraged by the massacre of the Jews. Something has been set forth in Europe that is subtle, and suspended, and destructive; and it will break the powerpacts, and the high declarations, and even the armies, since armies are only men. That something is all our silent complicity in the massacre of the Jews (and surely not of them alone; it is merely that their deaths were so peculiarly hopeless). For it means that men are not ashamed of what they have been in this time, and are therefore not prepared for the further outbreaks of fascism which are so deep in all of us. It means that we still do not realize why

In every Infant's cry of fear,
In every cry of every Man,
In every voice, in every ban,
The mind-forg'd manacles I hear.

Blake knew it, as we can still know it: the manacles are always forged by the mind. Can the mind still break them free? Can it?

FRED EASTMAN

A Reply to Screamers

Christian Century, February 16, 1944

Kazin's agonized meditation reflected in part his closeness, as a son of immigrant Eastern European Jews, to the cultures and peoples being destroyed by the Nazis. A rather striking contrast is the response of Fred Eastman to a similarly impassioned article by Arthur Koestler (1905–1983), the Hungarian Jewish journalist and novelist, whose *Darkness at Noon* (1941) has become one of the classic antitotalitarian novels of the century. In that piece, Koestler imagines himself (and, we might add, Kazin and Kirchwey) screaming for aid to the Jews of Europe while no one is listening. Eastman begins by sympathetically portraying Koestler's agony but then replying to it as an average American. The article speaks directly and, in its own way, agonizingly to the situation and may represent the feelings of a good many Americans at the time.

Of all the refugees from Hitler's terrorism probably none has been more articulate and eloquent than Mr. Arthur Koestler. This Hungarian-born newspaperman was sentenced to death in Spain, was reprieved, and later, after imprisonment in France, escaped to England. Then he began writing a series of novels documenting the atrocities being committed in Europe. All the time, to quote his own words, he has been "screaming about the killing, by hot steam, mass electrocution, and live burial of the total Jewish population of Europe." Many of these appalling atrocities he saw with his own eyes. "The greatest mass killing in history," he called it, claiming that nearly three million have been put to death. This, he insisted, goes on "daily, hourly, as regularly as the ticking of your watch."

In a recent article in the *New York Times* Mr. Koestler pictures himself as screaming for help in the midst of a nightmare. "There is a dream," he writes, "which keeps coming back to me at almost regular intervals; it is dark and I am being murdered in some kind of thicket or brushwood; there is a busy road at no more than ten yards' distance. I scream for help

---

Fred Eastman, "A Reply to Screamers," *Christian Century,* Feb. 16, 1944, 204–6.

but nobody hears me, the crowd walks past laughing and chatting." This nightmare, he goes on to say, is not a dream but a grim reality. He writes with photographs of these atrocities before him. People died to smuggle those photographs out of Poland. How can we be so indifferent about them? Do we not believe that these atrocities have been committed and that similar crimes are being enacted hourly even now? Or are we fooling ourselves by fantasy or disbelief, charging that such stories are "propaganda lies"?

Mr. Koestler's questions are agonizingly sincere and ably put. Someone should answer him, quietly and gently. I seem to have an inner urge to do it, although there are many others who could do it better. But I am probably a typical member of that crowd he thinks indifferent. I am a middle-aged father — a teacher by profession — with two sons in the service. Would Mr. Koestler and those who raise similar questions care to know why I, and those like me, have not stopped our work as we have heard his screams?

It is not because we are disbelieving or indifferent or without pity. The reports of the mass murders of Jews and countless others are too well authenticated to be denied. In all history there is no blacker crime. If we were disbelieving we would be fools. If we were indifferent we would be insane. If we were without pity we would be knaves. What then are the reasons for our not stopping our work and for not joining the screamers? Here are three of them, together with a plea.

In the first place, we were not taken by surprise. Like most of my fellows who endured through the First World War, I felt let down and disillusioned by its outcome. The politicians thought they could assure peace by political safeguards, leaving the whole tangle of economic interests and conflicting ideologies unsettled. I did not think so then, nor did my neighbors. We thought the "peace" would prove only a prolonged armistice and the renewal of the hostilities would be on a vaster and bloodier scale.

Two Earthquakes Converge

Moreover, even before World War I, we were conscious of the subterranean tremors of two great earthquakes. One was in the Orient, the other in Europe and America. As a boy I read in my father's library a little book entitled *Letters from a Chinese Official.* (I believe it was anonymously published, but later credited to G. Lowes Dickinson.) Its main point was a solemn warning that the West was selling arms to the East and teaching the Orientals by example that the way for a nation to get what it wants is to grab it. The "Chinese Official" bade us remember that there were a great many more Orientals than Westerners and should the former take both our guns and our example they might some day — and sooner than we thought — turn upon us. I do not know how many of my neighbors read that little book. But as long as I can remember we have all been shaking our heads and signing petitions to Congress against the sale of munitions to Japan. And we had misgivings about our own country's acquisition of the Philippines; it looked like a step toward American imperialism—a step bound to be resented by the Orient.

The other subterranean tremor presaged the coming of some kind of mighty conflict in Europe and America over philosophies of life. Not simply between scholars, but between the ordinary run-of-the-mill men like ourselves. We haven't been very articulate about it. But our writers and ministers, both Christian and Jewish, have been telling us for half a century that certain ideas were getting a grip on men's minds—ideas that were diametrically opposed to those upon which our schools and churches and our democracy were founded. Dominant among those ideas was the doctrine that man was not an immortal soul, made in the image of God and possessed of certain inalienable rights; instead he was a pawn of the state, made in his nation's image and possessed of no rights except those which had been conferred upon him by the state.

With growing apprehension we saw these ideas gradually take possession of the minds of a few professors and then eagerly seized upon by certain ambitious men—Hitler and others—as a new religion. We knew that our old religions, Hebrew and Christian, affirmed man's brotherhood and that this new one denied it; that our religious faith and our political democracy proclaimed the equality of men before the law, and that this new philosophy sneered at democracy, derided equality, and proclaimed the superior rights of a "master race." *Of course,* two such conflicting philosophies would one day come into head-on collision and blood would flow. Why should we be surprised when it happened?

Emotional Regurgitation

In the second place, the screamers do not tell us specifically what they want us to do. A Sunday school teacher once told her class of little girls the story of the Good Samaritan. She painted a vivid and gory picture of the man who had been beaten and robbed and left by the roadside to die. At that point she asked, "What would you do if you were to come along a road and find a poor man in such a condition?" One little girl answered, "I fink I would frow up." Surely the present case—the biblical instance multiplied by grisly millions—calls for something more than an emotional regurgitation.

Possibly some of the screamers want us to lash ourselves into a fury of hatred; but common sense has saved us from that. We know that hatred burns up the haters as well as the hated. We know that as soon as we begin to hate people, however wrong and guilty they may be, we throw away reason and judgment and the capacity to think straight about them or ourselves. Hatred is a Nazi technique—a technique that has boomeranged against them in every occupied country. Better let them have a monopoly upon it. My sons in the army tell me that few of our soldiers waste their energies in hatred; they feel that they have a job to do, a hard and distasteful job, and hating would only make it more hellish. My neighbors and I have heard more hatemongering from writers than from fighting men. Was it not Chesterton who said, "Hell hath no fury like a non-combatant"?

The Return from Violence

If it is not hating that the screamers want from us, what is it? Fighting? If this war isn't a big enough fight, just how much bigger would they make it? Our sons are in the service, our incomes are mortgaged for generations to come, and the casualty lists are mounting from week to week. If the spilling of blood and the conversion of our natural resources into instruments of destruction can stop the mass murders and the other depredations of Hitler's cohorts it is being done as rapidly as the generals of the United Nations can manage it.

There seems to be one other thing that some people, who claim to be more aroused about this mass killing of Jews in Europe than the rest of us, want. They seem to want more committees. They seem to feel that something has been accomplished when another committee has been formed, another list of sponsors printed in the press, generally another full-page advertisement printed in the *New York Times* and a few other papers appealing for funds, and another opportunity granted some congressmen and senators to issue publicity statements to the effect that the Jews must be saved. I am sure that Mr. Koestler is not among those who are seeking this. All that he has written indicates that he is too honest a person, too truly concerned in getting at the root-facts which constitute the tragedy of this generation, to be content with any such superficiality. I am sure that he wants something other than an emotional outburst, something more than a further extension of the war, something more than new committees. But what? Until I can be sure about that, I can see no reason to resort to screaming.

And there is still a third reason why my neighbors and I are not yet ready to join the screamers. Some of us have suspected all along, and most of us now begin to believe, that there will be a long-term task of building peace at the end of the fighting for which too much screaming now will unfit the screamers. What do we all seek after this war? Is it not peace and a reasonable amount of security for ourselves and for the rest of mankind? Is that not what we would see the Jews, as well as all the other tortured people of this present agony, obtain? Well, what are the chances of obtaining it if we approach the task emotionally exhausted and mentally confused by months or years of screaming?

Nazism Is More Than Nazis

If we are to have peace and security after military victory, we have got to overcome not simply the Nazis but Nazism—the state of mind which Nazism stands for, and which Mr. Koestler well knows is not confined to Germany. A bullet will kill a Nazi, but it will not kill Nazism. After the last shot is fired we then face the task of re-educating millions of minds which have been indoctrinated with false ideas, false values, and false loyalties. Some of those minds are in Germany; a lot of them are in Germany. But some of them are in the United Nations. Some of them—a lot of them if the testimony of my Jewish friends is to be accepted—are in the United States. You cannot shoot re-education into such minds. You cannot scream it in. It can only be done by persuasion and by offering concrete illustrations of a better way of living, together with opportunities to follow that way. Back of that persuasion there must be a lot of thinking. And underneath the thinking there must be a deep faith that man, through suffering, may yet learn mercy.

From *Final Summary Report of the Executive Director, War Refugee Board*
September 15, 1945

Although the State Department's conservatism on issues of rescue and immigration, reflected at the Bermuda Conference, dominated policy-making through 1943, the growing body of evidence of extermination and the increasingly strong voices for action in and out of government began to gain force. So did Allied successes on all fronts. By the beginning of 1944, despite setbacks and frustrations, victory was clearly in sight. Advocates for Europe's Jews grew bolder, and President Roosevelt became more receptive to their arguments. The turning point occurred when, after repeated frustration with the State Department in carrying out even modest attempts at rescue, several troubled officials in the Treasury Department submitted to Secretary Henry Morgenthau the "Report to the

---

"Final Summary Report of the Executive Director, War Refugee Board," Washington, Sept. 15, 1945, in *America and the Holocaust: Responsibility for America's Failure,* vol. 13, ed. David S. Wyman (New York: Garland Publishing, 1991), 127–54.

Secretary on the Acquiescence of This Government in the Murder of the Jews." It thoroughly documented the State Department's resistance to rescue proposals and collusion with a more severe British position, and it charged that the State Department was "guilty not only of gross procrastination and wilful failure to act, but even of wilful attempts to prevent action from being taken to rescue Jews from Hitler."[1]

Morgenthau was shocked and immediately took up the matter at the White House. He convinced Roosevelt that the charges were true, and on January 22 the president issued an executive order creating the War Refugee Board (WRB). He gave it the responsibility of rescuing and creating havens for "victims of enemy oppression." The board was run with input from the Departments of War, State, and Treasury, but in reality Treasury controlled matters. These excerpts from the board's final report indicate the kinds of actions that creative minds took once they were given the authority to do so and the frustrations they encountered. Note especially the board's sponsorship of Raoul Wallenberg, the Swedish banker/diplomat who is credited with saving thousands of Hungarian Jews from extermination.

The operations planned and developed by the Board to pull victims out of enemy hands to the safe neutral areas contiguous to Nazi territory involved complex problems of planning, organization, coordination, negotiation, and the use of unusual techniques. Full use had to be made of the resourcefulness, ingenuity, and contacts of resistance groups and underground operators. Evacuation from German-controlled territory for specially marked victims was not possible on an official and open basis. Funds and supplies were sent in to trusted agents in enemy areas to hide refugees from the Nazis, maintain and safeguard them, and transport them through underground channels to safety. Lesser German officials were bribed. False identification papers were supplied. Food was provided [to] families of the resistance groups who concealed and protected the refugees. Border officials were bribed to pass refugees. Exit and entrance visas were procured and transportation by boat or by rail was provided for evacuation to safe areas. Tens of thousands were rescued from the Nazis by these clandestine means.

The financing of rescue operations by means of funds transferred from the United States was made possible by an important change in policy of the Treasury and State Departments immediately prior to the establishment of the Board. It was decided that the United States Government, in

---

[1]David S. Wyman, *The Abandonment of the Jews: America and the Holocaust, 1941–1945* (New York: Pantheon Books, 1984), 187.

view of military developments favoring the Allied armies and because of the compelling humanitarian considerations, would permit established private agencies to transfer funds from the United States to their representatives in neutral countries to finance the rescue of persecuted peoples under Nazi control. A basic Treasury Department license under the Trading with the Enemy Act was devised to cover all such transfers. This license authorized the necessary communication with persons in enemy territory and the financing of rescue operations under specified controls and techniques designed to bring no financial benefit to the enemy. After the establishment of the Board all requests for licenses of this type were channeled through it and issued only upon its recommendation, ensuring coordination and government direction of all rescue programs.

The British Government formally objected to our government's new licensing policy, taking the position that our licenses afforded the enemy an opportunity to acquire foreign exchange for use in the prosecution of the war. The United States State Department, with the concurrence of the Board and the Treasury Department, replied that our government had concluded that the saving of lives far outweighed any possible danger involved in permitting the enemy to acquire relatively insubstantial quantities of foreign exchange and that we intended to continue the licensing policy we had been pursuing for several months. As a matter of fact, the controls specified in our licenses with respect to the acquisition of local currencies for use in enemy territory were so tight that of the more than twenty million dollars transferred to neutral areas for Board projects, only a trickle of free exchange seeped into enemy areas. Most of this went into the hands and private hoards of individual border guards. Throughout the existence of the Board no payment of ransom to the enemy was permitted to be made. . . .

. . . The Board's efforts to save the persecuted Jews in Hungary required the use of every resource and technique developed for the rescue of people in the hands of the enemy. Hungary, the last remaining refuge for Jews in Axis Europe, had an abnormal population of about one million Jews. When the German army overran Hungary in March 1944, all these Jews were in mortal danger. Reports soon came through of a wave of violent persecutions of the Jews in Hungary and the War Refugee Board geared its programs to the pressing emergency.

Direct rescue was difficult from Hungary, which was surrounded by Nazi-controlled territory. Intense psychological pressures were therefore exerted on the authorities and people of Hungary. Strong warnings and condemnations were issued by the President, by the Congress, the Secretary of State, Archbishop Spellman, and other prominent American Christians to the people of Hungary.

Appeals were made to the neutral governments to offer safe haven to Hungarian Jews and to inform the Nazis of their willingness to receive these suffering people. The governments of Sweden, Switzerland, Spain, and Portugal were urged to issue protective citizenship to Jews in Hungary claiming family or business ties with those countries. Many thousands were granted such special neutral protection.

Raoul Wallenberg, a young Swedish businessman, volunteered to proceed to Hungary for the War Refugee Board to aid in the rescue and relief of the persecuted Jews. The Swedish Government granted him diplomatic status and stationed him in Budapest for the sole purpose of rendering protection to these people. The Board furnished Wallenberg detailed plans of action, but made it clear that he could not act in Hungary as a representative of the Board. Wallenberg, supplied with funds from the Board and the American Jewish Joint Distribution Committee, carried on a relentless campaign in Hungary in behalf of the Jews. He issued Swedish protective passports by the thousands and hired extra buildings as official Swedish quarters to house several hundred rabbis and communal leaders under the protection of the extraterritoriality which attached to such buildings. He constantly pressed the Hungarian authorities for better treatment of Jews and succeeded in having thousands brought back to Budapest from the forced labor marches. In all, approximately 20,000 Jews received the safety of Swedish protection in Hungary. As a measure of the devotion of Wallenberg and as proof of the risks involved in his activities, the Board received word on April 4, 1945, that he was missing. Despite repeated attempts to trace his whereabouts he was reported dead early in June 1945.

The many warnings and appeals addressed to the Hungarian authorities by the United States and other democratic peoples resulted in the Horthy puppet government sending a message in July 1944 through the medium of the International Red Cross to the Governments of the United States and Great Britain stating that Hungary was willing to permit the emigration of certain categories of Jews. This offer in effect said "we will permit Jews to leave Hungary if the United States and Great Britain will take care of them." It was publicly accepted by the United States and at our insistence by the British Government, but no Jews were ever formally released by the German-controlled Horthy government.

Despite the difficulties in effecting direct rescue from Hungary, unremitting efforts were made to assist underground rescue operations by developing avenues of escape and finding havens of refuge in neutral and Allied territories. In addition, funds from America were transferred to Hungary via Switzerland and Sweden to keep Jews in hiding, to sustain them pending rescue or liberation, and to finance the rescue work of resistance groups in Rumania and Slovakia. These groups helped thousands to escape from Hungary through underground channels. Rescues were also developed through Yugoslav Partisan territory, which had well-established contacts with underground workers in Hungary. The flow of refugees through this channel was accelerated as the result of Board negotiations with Marshal Tito's representatives and the Allied military authorities in Italy. Relief supplies were provided for the maintenance of refugees in Yugoslavia and arrangements were made for evacuation from Yugoslavia to Italy by boat

Figure 5. Raoul Wallenberg. The most dramatic success of the War Refugee Board was its funding of Raoul Wallenberg's successful attempt to save thousands of Jews in Budapest during the summer of 1944. Wallenberg disappeared soon after the Red Army occupied Hungary in late 1944 and is believed to have died in a Kremlin prison.

or plane. Approximately 7,000 Jews were enabled to escape from Hungary by this route.

The Gestapo deported and killed the Jews in Hungary until the Russian armies defeated the Germans in that area. At that time there were only 100,000 Jews in all Hungary. Since the end of hostilities in Europe, however, thousands of Jews have returned to Hungary, either from their hiding places or from German labor camps.

EXTERMINATION CAMPS REVEALED

Majdanek, one of the major extermination camps and little more than a mile from the city of Lublin, Poland, was overrun by the Soviet army in late July 1944. A month and a half later, the Russians gave Western correspondents a tour of the camp facilities. The two documents that follow illustrate the various ways Americans reacted to the discovery of Majdanek.

RICHARD LAUTERBACH

Murder, Inc.

Time, September 11, 1944

This is a report by *Time*'s Moscow correspondent of his visit to Majdanek. Note the vivid details of the report and Lauterbach's description of his emotional reaction to the tour.

———————

. . . It was Sunday and the sun was hot. The Polish girls wore their best embroidered dresses to Mass and the men of Lublin chatted on street corners without a furtive, over-the-shoulder look. We drove out along the Chelm road about a mile from town. Dmitri Kudriavtsev, Secretary of the Soviet Atrocities Commission, said: "They called this 'the road of death.' " Kudriavtsev is a short man, with curly hair and a nice face. He has an even,

Richard Lauterbach, "Murder, Inc.," *Time,* Sept. 11, 1944, 36.

soft way of talking. You could not guess that he has pored over more horrors in the past three years than any living man.

Our car halted before a well-guarded gate. "This is Maidenek," Kudriavtsev said. I saw a huge, not unattractive, temporary city. There were about 200 trim, grey-green barracks, systematically spaced for maximum light, air, and sunshine. There were winding roads and patches of vegetables and flowers. I had to blink twice to take in the jarring realities: the 14 machinegun turrets jutting into the so-blue sky; the 12-ft.-high double rows of electrically charged barbed wire; the kennels which once housed hundreds of gaunt, man-eating dogs.

Gas Chambers

We got out to inspect the bathhouses. Said Kudriavtsev without emotion: "They came here first for a shower. Then the Germans said: 'Now you have had your wash. Go in there.' " He led us into one of four gas chambers. It was a solid grey concrete room, about 20 ft. square and 7 ft. high. A single large steel door sealed the entrance hermetically. There were three apertures, two for the pipes which brought in the gas, one, a thick glass peephole, protected by steel netting. It took about seven minutes for this "Zyklon B" to kill the occupants, as many as 250 at a time. Kudriavtsev was explaining: "The gas affects all parts of the organism. It is quicker when the body is warm, washed, and wet."

I took notes calmly, feeling little emotion. It was all so cold and bare. I wrote: "There are four chambers fed with these small, innocent, pale blue Zyklon crystals which give off cyanide when exposed to air. Two extra chambers for plain carbon monoxide. Maximum simultaneous capacity: 2,000." Kudriavtsev was still explaining: "On one day, Nov. 3, 1943, they annihilated 18,000 people — Poles, Jews, political prisoners, and war prisoners."

Death by Fire

We walked back into the sun. There was no horror left in Maidenek. It had evaporated with the Germans. We rode a little distance to some cabbage patches. The big, leafy cabbages were covered with a sooty, grey dust and next to them were high mounds of grey-brown stuff. "This," said Kudriavtsev, "is fertilizer. A layer of human bones, a layer of human ashes, a layer of manure. This is German food production. Kill people; fertilize cabbages."

The crematorium might have been a big bakeshop or a very small blast furnace. Here the Nazis carted the bodies, straight from the gas chambers. They cut them up scientifically. They put the chunks on iron stretchers, slid them on rollers into the five greedy mouths of the coke-fed ovens. They could disintegrate 1,900 people a day. "There was great economy," said Kudriavtsev. "These furnaces also heated the water for the camp."

We heard about a young Polish girl who had refused to undress for a shower. The degenerate, sadistic Mussfelt who ran the crematorium ordered her shoved into the furnace alive. Her hair burned quick and bright. Then she crisped up like bacon on an over-hot skillet.

Near the ovens were the remains of a room with a big stone table. Here gold fillings were extracted from the teeth. No corpse or piece of a corpse could be burned without a stamp on the chest: "Inspected for gold fillings."

Skulls and Buzzing Flies

Kudriavtsev led us to some large, open graves. Here were buried the bodies of the camp's personnel, hastily shot and buried on July 21 in the last hectic days before the Red Army closed in. The pits stank in the warm sun. There were skulls and a piece of a Red Army cap and a buzzing of large flies. Around the pits, in the grass, poppies were growing. Orange-red poppies. Big ones.

Back in the camp we saw a room full of passports and documents. Papers of Frenchmen, Russians, Greeks, Czechs, Jews, Italians, Belo-Russians, Serbs, Poles. Records left behind by some of the 1,500,000 of 22 nationalities who were brought to Maidenek.

820,000 Pairs of Shoes

We came to a large, unpainted warehouse. Not suspecting, I stepped up and went inside. It was full of shoes. A sea of shoes. I walked across them unsteadily. They were piled, like pieces of coal in a bin, halfway up the walls. Not only shoes. Boots. Rubbers. Leggings. Slippers. Children's shoes, soldiers' shoes, old shoes, new shoes. They were red and grey and black. Some had once been white. High heels, low heels, shoes with open toes. Evening slippers, beach sandals, wooden Dutch shoes, pumps, Oxfords, high-laced old-ladies' shoes. In one corner there was a stock of artificial limbs. I kicked over a pair of tiny white shoes which might have been my youngest daughter's.

The sea of shoes was engulfing. In one place the sheer weight had broken the wall. Part of the wall had fallen out, and with it a cascade of shoes. Kudriavtsev said: "There are 820,000 pairs here and 18 carloads of the best were shipped to Germany. You will see the receipts at the Gestapo warehouse."

Standing on the sea of shoes, Maidenek suddenly became real. It was no longer a half-remembered sequence from an old movie or a clipping from *Pravda* or chapters from a book by a German refugee living in Mexico City. The barbed wire had barbs which ripped flesh. The ashes on the big cabbages were the ashes of the brothers of the worn but pretty peasant women who had spoken to us that morning at Mass.

"The loudspeakers from the camp kept screeching Strauss waltzes," a Polish woman in Lublin said to me. "The *Beautiful Blue Danube* can never be beautiful to us again." She paused and repeated the words so many Poles and Russians had said that day: "I hope you Americans will not be soft with the Germans."

Biggest Atrocity Story Breaks in Poland
Christian Century, September 13, 1944

Note the startlingly different tone and insinuations of exaggeration and outright fabrication in this editorial as the *Christian Century* faced the issue of genocide again.

No atrocity story of the year is likely to top the latest concerning the alleged killing of 1,500,000 persons at the German concentration camp near Lublin, Poland. W. H. Lawrence of the *New York Times* was a member of the party of thirty journalists who were taken on a tour of the camp by a body called the Soviet-Polish Atrocities Investigation Commission. He described it as "a veritable River Rouge for the production of death." The victims were shipped there from all over Europe, the correspondents were told, were asphyxiated in gas chambers and their bodies cremated in huge furnaces. Chief evidence for the charge that 1,500,000 persons were killed in this manner was a warehouse "about 150 feet long" containing clothing of people of all ages who were said to have been done to death in the camp. As many as 18,000 persons a day were said to have been killed in the camp, although the capacity of the cremating furnaces was estimated to have been 1,900 per day. Maurice Hindus, who was another of the thirty correspondents, also reported the 1,500,000 figure. He said the warehouse contained 820,000 pairs of shoes. Many newspapers gave the Lublin charge the big headline of the day, but the parallel between this story and the "corpse factory" atrocity tale of the First World War is too striking to be overlooked. The story started in 1917 and was not fully discredited until 1925. There may or may not be a relation between the fact that the Lublin account came out immediately after it was charged by London Poles that the Russians had stopped their advance within artillery range of Warsaw and waited until the Germans had killed 250,000 Poles within the city who had risen to fight for their freedom in response to the call of the Polish government-in-exile.

"Biggest Atrocity Story Breaks in Poland," *Christian Century,* Sept. 13, 1944, 1045.

JAN KARSKI

Polish Death Camp

Collier's, October 14, 1944

The eerie sights at Maidanek were still only pale shadows of everyday events at that camp and other centers of mass murder such as Auschwitz or Treblinka. In late 1944, however, an eyewitness to killings at Belzec, site of one of the earliest experiments in extermination, published his accounts of what he saw. Jan Karski, a member of the Polish Underground, had been given the mission to witness conditions in the ghettos and at the extermination camps.

He was then sent abroad to Britain and the United States in 1943–44 to publicize, as an eyewitness, the privations of Poles and Polish Jews under the Nazis. He gained interviews with many important members of the British and American governments, including Franklin D. Roosevelt. In late 1944, he published *Story of a Secret State,* which became a Book-of-the-Month Club selection and sold thousands of copies in late 1944 and early 1945.[1] The book was a somewhat romanticized telling of his life in the underground. It included harrowing chapters on his visits to the Warsaw Ghetto and Belzec. The following selection from the book was featured in *Collier's* a month and a half before the book's publication.

As a member of the underground, I was ordered to leave Warsaw and report to the Polish government and the Allied authorities about conditions in Poland. My orders came from the delegate of the Polish government acting somewhere in Poland and from the commander in chief of the underground army. Jewish leaders confided to me their written report but they insisted that in order to be able to tell the truth I should see with my own eyes what actually happened to the Jews in Poland. They arranged for me to visit one of the Jewish death camps.

The camp was near the town of Belzec, about 100 miles east of Warsaw, and was well known all over Poland because of the tales of horror that were circulated about it. The common report was that every Jew who reached it, without exception, was doomed to death.

Jan Karski, "Polish Death Camp," *Collier's,* Oct. 14, 1944, 18–19, 60–61.
[1]Jan Karski, *Story of a Secret State* (Boston: Houghton Mifflin, 1944).

I was to go on a day when executions were scheduled. Information was easy to obtain because many of the Estonian, Latvian, and Ukrainian attendants who worked there under Gestapo supervision were in the service of the Jewish organizations—not from any humane or political consideration, but for money.

I was to wear the uniform of one of the Estonians, who would stay home while I went with his papers. I was assured that chaos, corruption, and panic prevailed in the camp to such an extent that there was no chance of my disguise being penetrated. Moreover, the whole expedition was perfectly organized in advance. I would go through a door habitually guarded only by Germans and Ukrainians, for an Estonian might sense a stranger in me.

The Estonian uniform itself constituted a pass, so that my papers would probably not be inspected. To make the camouflage more foolproof, still another bribed Estonian militiaman would accompany me. Since I knew German, I could talk with the German guards if it became necessary; and they, too, could be bribed.

The plan seemed simple and flawless. I agreed without any hesitation and without the slightest fear of being caught.

Early in the morning I left Warsaw in the company of a Jew who worked outside the ghetto in the Jewish underground movement. We arrived in Belzec shortly after midday and went directly to the place where the Estonian was supposed to be waiting. It was a little grocery store that had once belonged to a Jew. The Jew had been killed and since then it was being run, with the permission of the German authorities, by a local farmer who was, of course, a member of the underground.

My Estonian uniform was there waiting for me, but the man to whom it belonged had evidently decided it was more prudent to remain away. However, he had left me a complete outfit: trousers, long boots, a belt, a tie, and a cap. The idea of letting his personal papers be used had apparently given him qualms, too. Instead he had left me the papers of one of his colleagues who had probably returned to his native Estonia and had taken the opportunity to sell his papers. I was not surprised. Selling papers was an established business in Poland, not at all frowned upon. The uniform and the shoes fitted me but the cap came down to my ears. I stuffed it with paper. Then I asked my companion how I looked. He said I looked like a model Estonian militiaman.

An hour or two later the Estonian who was to accompany me arrived. He confirmed that the camp was so disorganized, chaotic, and indifferently managed that I could stroll about in perfect freedom. I was to stick to the place assigned me throughout the executions and in that way I would miss nothing. After the executions all the guards would be leaving the camp. I was to join them, mingling with the mob of mixed attendants but avoiding the Estonians. He reiterated the latter precaution solemnly, warning me that if I had any close contact with them it would be easy for them to recognize me as not "their man."

The camp was about a mile and a half from the store. We started walking rapidly, taking a side lane to avoid meeting people. It took about twenty minutes to get to the camp, but we became aware of its presence in less than half that time. About a mile away from the camp we began to hear shouts, shots, and screams.

"What's happening?" I asked. "What's the meaning of all that noise?"

"The Jews are hot," he said, grinning as though he had said something witty.

I must have glared at him, for he changed his tone abruptly.

"What could it be?" He shrugged. "They are bringing in a 'batch' today."

I knew what he meant and did not inquire further. We walked on while the noise increased alarmingly. From time to time a series of long screams or a particularly inhuman groan would set the hair on my scalp bristling.

"What are the chances of anyone's escaping?" I asked my companion, hoping to hear an optimistic answer.

"None at all," he answered, dashing my hopes to the ground. "Once they get this far, their goose is cooked."

"You mean there isn't a single chance of anybody's escaping from the camp, even with the way things are there?"

"Well, from the camp itself, maybe. But not alone. With a guard like me helping, it can be done. But it's a terrible risk," he said, wagging his head solemnly. "The Jew and I could both get killed."

We trudged on, the Estonian watching me out of the corner of his eye.

Dealer in Human Flesh

"Of course," he said craftily, "if a Jew pays well—very well—it can be done. But it is very risky, it has to be handled right . . ."

"How can they pay? They don't have any money on them, do they?"

"Say, we don't try to get money out of them. We ain't so dumb. We get paid in advance. It's strictly a cash proposition. We don't even deal with those in the camp"—he gestured contemptuously in the direction of the noise—"we do business with people on the outside, like you. If somebody comes to me and tells me that such and such a Jew is going to arrive and that he wants him 'cheated out'—well, if he is willing to fork out plenty of hard cash in advance, then I do what I can."

"Have you saved many Jews so far?" I asked.

"Not as many as I'd like, but a few, anyhow."

"Are there many more good men like you there who are so willing to save the Jews?"

"Save them? Say, who wants to save them?" He looked at me in bewilderment as though I were talking unheard-of nonsense. "But if they pay, that's a different story. We can all use some money."

I did not venture to disagree. It would have been hopeless to try to persuade him of anything different. I looked at his heavy, rather good-natured face and wondered how the war had come to develop such cruel habits in him. From what I had seen he seemed to be a simple, average man, not particularly good or bad. His hands were the calloused but supple hands of a good farmer. In normal times that was what he probably was—and a good father, a family man, and a churchgoer besides. Now, under the pressure of the Gestapo and the cajoleries of the Nazis, with everyone about him engaged in a greedy competition that knew no limits, he had been changed into a professional butcher of human beings. He had caught onto his trade well and discussed its niceties, used its professional jargon as coolly as a carpenter discussing his craft.

"And what are you here for?" The question was both shrewd and innocent.

"I'd like to 'save' some Jews too," I said with an air of conspiracy. "With your help, of course. That's why I've come to the camp, to see how everything works."

"Well, don't you go trying to do anything without us."

"Don't be silly. Why should I work without you? We both want to make money and we can help each other. We would be foolish to work against each other."

This satisfied him and I now had the status of a younger colleague.

The Approach to Horror

As we approached to within a few hundred yards of the camp, the shouts, cries, and shots cut off further conversation. I noticed an unpleasant stench that seemed to have come from decomposing bodies mixed with horse manure. This may have been an illusion. The Estonian was, in any case, completely impervious to it. He even began to hum some sort of folk tune to himself. We passed through a small grove of decrepit-looking trees and emerged directly in front of the loud, sobbing, reeking camp of death.

It was on a large, flat plain and occupied about a square mile. It was surrounded on all sides by a formidable barbed-wire fence, nearly two yards in height and in good repair. Inside the fence, at intervals of about fifteen yards, guards were standing, holding rifles with bayonets ready for use. Around the outside of the fence, militiamen circulated on constant patrol. The camp itself contained a few small sheds or barracks. The rest of the area was completely covered by a dense, pulsating, throbbing, noisy human mass—starved, stinking, gesticulating, insane human beings in constant agitated motion. Through them, forcing paths if necessary with their rifle butts, walked the German police and the militiamen. They walked in silence, their faces bored and indifferent. They looked like shepherds bringing in a flock to the market. They had the tired, vaguely disgusted appearance of men doing a routine, tedious job.

Into the fence a few passages had been cut, and gates made of poles tied together with barbed wire swung back to make an entrance. Each gate was guarded by two men who slouched about carelessly. We stopped for a moment to collect ourselves. I noticed off to my left the railroad tracks which passed about a hundred yards from the camp. From the camp to the track a sort of raised passage had been built from old boards. On the track a dusty freight train waited, motionless.

The Estonian followed my gaze with the interest of a person seeing what kind of an impression his home made on a visitor. He proceeded eagerly to enlighten me:

"That's the train they'll load them on. You'll see it all."

We came to a gate. Two German noncoms were standing there talking. I could hear snatches of their conversation. They seemed to be talking about a night they had spent in a near-by town. I hung back a bit. The Estonian seemed to think I was losing my nerve.

"Go ahead," he whispered impatiently into my ear. "Don't be afraid. They won't even inspect your papers. They don't care about the likes of you."

We walked up to the gate and saluted the noncoms vigorously. They returned the salute indifferently and we passed through.

"Follow me," he said, quite loudly. "I'll take you to a good spot."

We passed an old Jew, a man of about sixty, sitting on the ground without a stitch of clothing on him. I was not sure whether his clothes had been torn off or whether he, himself, had thrown them away in a fit of madness. Silent, motionless, he sat on the ground, no one paying him the slightest attention. Not a muscle or fiber in his whole body moved except for his preternaturally animated eyes, which blinked rapidly and incessantly. Not far from him a small child, clad in a few rags, was lying on the ground. He was all alone and crouched quivering on the ground, staring up with the large, frightened eyes of a rabbit. No one paid any attention to him, either.

The Jewish mass vibrated, trembled, and moved to and fro as if united in a single, insane rhythmic trance. They waved their hands, shouted, quarreled, cursed, and spat at one another. Hunger, thirst, fear, and exhaustion had driven them all insane. I had been told that they were usually left in the camp for three or four days without food or a drop of water. They were all former inhabitants of the Warsaw ghetto.

The Ultimate in Misery

There was no organization or order of any kind. None of them could possibly help or share with one another and they soon lost any self-control or any sense whatsoever except the bare instinct of self-preservation. They had become, at this stage, completely dehumanized. It was, moreover, typical autumn weather, cold, raw, and rainy. The sheds could not accommodate more than two to three thousand people and every "batch" included more than five thousand. This meant that there were always two to three thousand men, women, and children scattered about in the open, suffering exposure as well as everything else.

The chaos, the squalor, the hideousness of it all were simply indescribable. There was a suffocating stench of sweat, filth, decay, damp straw, and excrement. To get to my post we had to squeeze our way through this mob. It was a ghastly ordeal. I had to push foot by foot through the crowd and step over the limbs of those who were lying prone. It was like forcing my way through a mass of death and decomposition made even more horrible by its agonized pulsations. My companion had the skill of long practice, evading the bodies on the ground and winding his way through the mass with the ease of a contortionist. Distracted and clumsy, I would brush against people or step on a figure that reacted like an animal; quickly, often with a moan or a yelp. Each time this occurred I would be seized by a fit of nausea and come to a stop. But my guide kept urging and hustling me along.

In this way we crossed the entire camp and finally stopped about twenty yards from the gate which opened on the passage leading to the train. It was a comparatively uncrowded spot. I felt immeasurably relieved at having finished my stumbling, sweating journey. The guide was standing at my side, saying something, giving me advice. I hardly heard him. He raised his voice:

"Look here. You are going to stay here. I'll walk on a little farther. You know what you are supposed to do. Remember to keep away from Estonians. Don't forget, if there's any trouble, you don't know me and I don't know you."

I nodded vaguely at him. He shook his head and walked off.

I remained there perhaps half an hour, watching this spectacle of human misery. At each moment I felt the impulse to run and flee. I had to force myself to remain indifferent, to practice stratagems to convince myself that I was not one of the condemned. Finally, I noticed a change in the motion of the guards. They walked less and they all seemed to be glancing in the same direction—at the passage to the track which was quite close to me.

I turned toward it myself. Two German policemen came to the gate with a tall, bulky SS man. He barked out an order and they began to open the gate. It was very heavy. He shouted at them impatiently. They worked at it frantically and finally shoved it open. They dashed down the passage as though they were afraid the SS man might come after them, and took up their positions where the passage ended. The whole system had been worked out with crude effectiveness. The outlet of the passage was blocked off by two cars of the freight train, so that any attempt on the part of one of the Jews to break out of the mob would have been completely impossible.

The SS man turned to the crowd, planted himself with his feet wide apart and his hands on his hips, and loosed a roar that must have actually hurt his ribs. It could be heard far above the hellish babble that came from the crowd:

"Ruhe, ruhe! Quiet, quiet! All Jews will board this train to be taken to a place where work awaits them. Keep order. Do not push. Anyone who attempts to resist or create a panic will be shot."

He stopped speaking and looked challengingly at the helpless mob that hardly seemed to know what was happening. Suddenly, accompanying the movement with a loud, hearty laugh, he yanked out his gun and fired three random shots into the crowd. A single, stricken groan answered him. He replaced the gun in his holster, smiled, and set himself for another roar:

"Alle Juden, 'raus — 'raus!"

For a moment the crowd was silent. Those nearest the SS man recoiled from the shots and tried to dodge, panic-stricken, toward the rear. But this was resisted by the mob as a volley of shots from the rear sent the whole mass surging forward madly, screaming in pain and fear. The shots continued without letup from the rear and now from the sides, too, narrowing the mob down and driving it in a savage scramble onto the passageway. In utter panic they rushed down the passageway, trampling it so furiously that it threatened to fall apart.

Then new shots were heard. The two policemen at the entrance to the train were now firing into the oncoming throng corralled in the passageway, in order to slow them down and prevent them from demolishing the flimsy structure. The SS man added his roar to the bedlam.

"Ordnung, ordnung!" He bellowed like a madman.

"Order, order!" The two policemen echoed him hoarsely, firing straight into the faces of the Jews running to the trains. Impelled and controlled by this ring of fire, they filled the two cars quickly.

And now came the most horrible episode of all. The military rule stipulates that a freight car may carry eight horses or forty soldiers. Without any baggage at all, a maximum of a hundred passengers pressing against one another could be crowded into a car. The Germans had simply issued orders that 120 to 130 Jews had to enter each car. Those orders were now being carried out. Alternately swinging and firing their rifles, the policemen were forcing still more people into the two cars which were already overfull. The shots continued to ring out in the rear, and the driven mob surged forward, exerting an irresistible pressure against those nearest the train. These unfortunates, crazed by what they had been through, scourged by the policemen, and shoved forward by the milling mob, then began to climb on the heads and shoulders of those in the trains.

A Climax of Frightfulness

These latter were helpless since they had the weight of the entire advancing throng against them. They howled with anguish at those who, clutching at their hair and clothes for support; trampling on necks, faces, and shoulders; breaking bones; and shouting with insensate fury, attempted to clamber over them. More than another score of men, women, and children crushed into the cars in this fashion. Then the policemen slammed the doors across the arms and legs that still protruded, and pushed the iron bars in place.

The two cars were now crammed to bursting with tightly packed human flesh. All this while the entire camp reverberated with a tremendous volume of sound in which groans and screams mingled with shots, curses, and bellowed commands.

Nor was this all. I know that many people will not believe me, but I saw it, and it is not exaggerated. I have no other proofs, no photographs. All I can say is that I saw it, and it is the truth.

The floors of the car had been covered with a thick, white powder. It was quicklime. Quicklime is simply unslaked lime or calcium oxide that has been dehydrated. Anyone who has seen cement being mixed knows what occurs when water is poured on lime. The mixture bubbles and steams as the powder combines with the water, generating a searing heat.

The lime served a double purpose in the Nazi economy of brutality: The moist flesh coming in contact with the lime is quickly dehydrated and burned. The occupants of the cars would be literally burned to death before long, the flesh eaten from their bones. Thus the Jews would "die in agony," fulfilling the promise Himmler had issued "in accord with the will of the Fuehrer," in Warsaw in 1942. Secondly, the lime would prevent the decomposing bodies from spreading disease. It was efficient and inexpensive — a perfectly chosen agent for its purpose.

It took three hours to fill up the entire train. It was twilight when the forty-six cars were packed. From one end to the other the train, with its quivering cargo of flesh, seemed to throb, vibrate, rock, and jump as if bewitched. There would be a strangely uniform momentary lull and then the train would begin to moan and sob, wail and howl. Inside the camp a few score dead bodies and a few in the final throes of death remained. German policemen walked around at leisure with smoking guns, pumping bullets into anything that moaned or moved. Soon none were left alive. In the now quiet camp the only sounds were the inhuman screams that echoed from the moving train. Then these, too, ceased. All that was now left was the stench of excrement and rotting straw and a queer, sickening, acidulous odor which, I thought, may have come from the quantities of blood that had stained the ground.

The Last Incredible Journey

As I listened to the dwindling outcries from the train I thought of the destination toward which it was speeding. My informants had minutely described the entire journey. The train would travel about eight miles and finally come to a halt in an empty, barren field. Then nothing at all would happen. The train would stand stock-still, patiently waiting while death penetrated into every corner of its interior. This would take from two to four days.

When quicklime, asphyxiation, and injuries had silenced every outcry, a group of men would appear. They would be young, strong Jews, assigned to the task of cleaning out these cars until their own turn to ride in them should arrive. Under a strong guard they would unseal the cars and expel the heaps of decomposing bodies. The mounds of flesh that they piled up would then be burned and the remnants buried in a single huge hole. The cleaning, burning, and burial would consume one or two full days.

The entire process of disposal would take, then, from three to six days. During this period the camp would have recruited new victims. The train would return and the whole cycle would be repeated.

I was still standing near the gate, gazing after the no longer visible train, when I felt a rough hand on my shoulder. The Estonian was back again.

"Wake up, wake up!" he was scolding hoarsely. "Don't stand there with your mouth open. Come on, hurry, or we'll both be caught. Follow me and be quick about it."

I followed him at a distance, feeling completely benumbed. When we reached the gate he reported to a German officer and pointed at me. I heard the officer say, *"Sehr gut, gehen sie."* and then we passed through the gate.

The Estonian and I walked a while together and then separated. I walked to the store as quickly as I could, running when there was no one about to see me. I reached the grocery store so breathless that the owner became alarmed. I reassured him while I threw off my uniform, boots, stockings, and underwear. I ran into the kitchen and locked the door. In a little while my bewildered and worried host called out to me:

"Hey, what are you doing in there?"

"Don't worry. I'll be right out."

When I came out, he promptly entered the kitchen and called back in despair:

"What the devil have you been doing? The whole kitchen is flooded!"

"I washed myself," I replied, "that is all. I was very dirty."

Then I collapsed. I was completely, violently, rackingly sick. Even today, when I remember those scenes, I become nauseated.

VIEWS OF THE LIBERATIONS

Over the months after the discovery and tour of Majdanek, more information about the destruction of the European Jews continued to be reported. In late 1944 and the first three months of 1945, however, the power of such reports paled beside war news from both the European and Pacific fronts. The tide had turned in favor of the Allies, but fighting remained intense. American losses in the Pacific were heavy, and the enemy showed no sign of surrendering. For this reason, and no doubt because of the very unreality of the true number of Jews killed, the public continued seriously to underestimate the scale of Nazi murder. In November 1944, for instance, a Gallup poll found that only 12 percent of Americans doubted that the Nazis were murdering great numbers of people in concentration camps, but only 16 percent believed the figure to be two million or more, and 36 percent were sure that those killed in such circumstances numbered under one hundred thousand.[1]

Then, in April and May, two things happened that cracked the wartime stoicism and disbelief of the American people. Franklin Delano Roosevelt died on April 12, 1945, unleashing a period of heartfelt mourning not seen since the assassination and funeral of Abraham Lincoln. At roughly the same time, units of the American, British, and French armies began uncovering scenes of horror at German concentration camps such as Dachau, Buchenwald, and Bergen-Belsen.

Ironically, these were not extermination camps (although they still retain that popular reputation) but had once functioned as labor and detention camps, mostly for German dissidents and captured resistance members from the occupied countries in Western Europe. Although conditions were harsh by any standard and thousands died in captivity, these sites were considered mild compared to Auschwitz or Treblinka. Beginning in late 1944, however, the western camps became the destination points for a brutal transfer of surviving Jewish, Gypsy, and Slav prisoners from the extermination centers in Poland. Populations swelled with the sick and dying, just as the German infrastructure, battered by invasion, began to crumble. Food and water supplies dwindled, and administrative order began to break down.

The results by the spring of 1945 were horrific scenes of death by starvation and disease. American troops at Dachau and Buchenwald confronted piles of dead bodies and disease-ridden barracks where the dead and the barely living lay on crude wooden bunks amid their own filth. At Bergen-Belsen, the British walked into a typhus epidemic that had been killing thousands every day. So extensive were the deaths at this camp that the British had to dig mass graves and bulldoze bodies into them to sanitize the camp.

With the war in Europe near an end and emotions on edge because of Roosevelt's death, the eyewitness testimony, photographs, and newsreels of Allied soldiers as they confronted the dead and the emaciated survivors shook Americans as no news of Nazi genocide had done before. Now there could be no doubt, no avoiding the truth. Although these were not the scenes of the systematic killing of millions, the depravity displayed suddenly validated all that had been suspected or reported.

---

[1]George H. Gallup, "Nazi Atrocities," in *The Gallup Poll: Public Opinion, 1935–1971*, vol. 1 (New York: Random House, 1972), 472.

Figure 6. American medic confronts an open boxcar filled with dead prisoners at Dachau, early May 1945.

J. D. PLETCHER

The Americans Have Come—At Last!

1945

This vivid contemporaneous account of one American soldier typifies the experiences and reactions of GIs as they participated in the uncovering and liberation of the camps.

Capt. J. D. Pletcher, Berwyn, Ill., of the 71st Division Headquarters and Cpl. James DeSpain, Allegan, Michigan, arrived at Gunskirchen Lager the same morning the camp was found by elements of the Division. Capt. Pletcher's account of the scenes he witnessed follows.

When the German SS troops guarding the concentration camp at Gunskirchen heard the Americans were coming, they suddenly got busy burying the bodies of their victims—or rather, having them buried by inmates—and gave the prisoners who were still alive what they considered an extremely liberal food ration: One lump of sugar per person and one loaf of bread for every seven persons. Then, two days or a day and half before we arrived, the SS left. All this I learned from talking to inmates of the camp, many of whom spoke English. Driving up to the camp in our jeep, Cpl. DeSpain and I first knew we were approaching the camp by the hundreds of starving, half-crazed inmates lining the roads, begging for food and cigarettes. Many of them had been able to get only a few hundred yards from the gate before they keeled over and died. As weak as they were, the chance to be free, the opportunity to escape was so great they couldn't resist, though it meant staggering only a few yards before death came.

Then came the next indication of the camp's nearness—the smell. There was something about the smell of Gunskirchen I shall never forget. It was strong, yes, and permeating, too. Some six hours after we left the place, six hours spent riding in a jeep, where the wind was whistling around us, we could still detect the Gunskirchen smell. It had permeated our clothing, and stayed with us.

Of all the horrors of the place, the smell, perhaps, was the most startling of all. It was a smell made up of all kinds of odors—human excreta,

J. D. Pletcher, "The Americans Have Come—At Last!" in *The Seventy-First Came . . . to Gunskirchen, Witness to the Holocaust Publication Series*, no. 1 (Atlanta: Center for Research in Social Change, Emory University, 1979), 4–11.

foul bodily odors, smoldering trash fires, German tobacco—which is a stink in itself—all mixed together in a heavy, dank atmosphere, in a thick, muddy woods, where little breeze could go. The ground was pulpy throughout the camp, churned to a consistency of warm putty by the milling of thousands of feet, mud mixed with feces and urine. The smell of Gunskirchen nauseated many of the Americans who went there. It was a smell I'll never forget, completely different from anything I've ever encountered. It could almost be seen and hung over the camp like a fog of death.

As we entered the camp, the living skeletons still able to walk crowded around us and, though we wanted to drive farther into the place, the milling, pressing crowd wouldn't let us. It is not an exaggeration to say that almost every inmate was insane with hunger. Just the sight of an American brought cheers, groans, and shrieks. People crowded around to touch an American, to touch the jeep, to kiss our arms—perhaps just to make sure that it was true. The people who couldn't walk crawled out toward our jeep. Those who couldn't even crawl propped themselves up on an elbow, and somehow, through all their pain and suffering, revealed through their eyes the gratitude, the joy they felt at the arrival of Americans.

An English-speaking inmate offered to show us around the camp. We accepted his offer. Another inmate organizer asked me if he could climb on the jeep to say a few words to his people. We helped him up on the hood and he yelled for order. He spoke in his native tongue—Hungarian, I believe— and my guide interpreted for us. He was asking the inmates to remain in the camp and not clutter up the roads, some 3,000 had already left, and he wanted his fellow prisoners to help the Yanks by staying off the roads. He told them that the Americans were bringing food and water and medical help. After every sentence he was interrupted by loud cheers from the crowd. It was almost like a political speech. Everyone was hysterical with joy at being found by the Americans, yet in a frenzy of hunger, for they had had no food since the Germans left two days before, and not enough to keep anyone alive for months before.

During the talk of the man on our jeep hood, a tall, blondehaired man approached me. He spoke excellent English. He was an engineer, educated in New York. He had committed the crime of letting Jewish blood infiltrate into his family stream some generations back. As hungry as he was for food, he was hungry for news. He said the camp inmates had known all about the movements of the Yanks for the past five days. Every day they had known we were coming closer, and as we approached, the anticipation in the stinking hole of Gunskirchen heightened. Through the last few, foodless days, the inmates had lived on faith alone, he said. Faith that the Americans would come soon. He was vitally interested in knowing about all phases of the European War. He asked about the other armies, how far they had advanced, how fast they were moving, about the Russians. He eagerly listened to all the news I could give him.

The man on the jeep hood spoke for about five minutes. At the completion he asked the people to clear the road so that we might proceed.

Many of the more energetic waved the cheering crowds back to clear a path just wide enough for our vehicle.

All wanted to get close enough to see and many wanted to touch us as we moved slowly on. It was like a triumphal procession with the milling crowd cheering and waving their arms in exaltation.

The thousands of prisoners had been crammed into a few low, one-story, frame buildings with sloppy, muddy floors. Those who were able had come out of the buildings, but there were hundreds left in them — the dead, the near-dead, and those too weak to move. Sometimes, my guide said, it was so crowded in the buildings that people slept three-deep on the floor, one on top of the other. Often, a man would awake in the morning and find the person under him dead. Too weak to move even the pathetically light bodies of their comrades, the living continued sleeping on them.

I want to make it clear that human beings subjected to the treatment these people were given by the Germans results in a return to the primitive. Dire hunger does strange things. The inmates of Gunskirchen were a select group of prisoners — the intellectual class of Hungarian Jews, for the most part, professional people, many distinguished doctors, lawyers, representatives of every skilled field. Yet, these people, who would naturally be expected to maintain their sense of values, their human qualities, longer than any others, had been reduced to animals by the treatment of the Germans — the deliberate prolonged starvation, the indiscriminate murder on little or no provocation, the unbelievable living conditions gradually brought about a change in even the strongest.

The camp was littered with bodies. Since the Germans had left, the inmates had been unable to cope with the swiftly mounting death rate. As long as the SS men were in charge, they made the stronger inmates dig crude pits and bury the dead, not for sanitary reasons, but in an attempt to hide some of the evidence of the inhuman treatment given their prisoners.

For the thousands of prisoners in Gunskirchen, there was one 20-hole latrine. The rule of the SS men was to shoot on sight anyone seen relieving himself in any place but the latrine. Many of the persons in the camp had diarrhea. There were always long lines at the latrine and it was often impossible for many to reach it in time because of hours spent waiting. Naturally, many were shot for they could not wait in line. Their bodies were still lying there in their own filth. The stench was unbelievable.

Cpl. DeSpain and I both remarked later about the appearance of the inmates — that they all seemed to look alike. When men are reduced to skeletons, as these men were, they all resembled one another — the only difference being in their height and the color of their hair.

My guide explained that many of the new prisoners at Gunskirchen had recently been forced to march from the vicinity of Hungary to Gunskirchen. There was very little food. They died like flies. If they fell out and were too weak to continue, the SS men shot them. The air-line distance from the Hungarian border to Gunskirchen is 150 miles. The intervening territory is full of mountains and winding roads, so the actual distance these people walked was far greater than 150 miles. It is not hard to imagine the thousands of skeletons that mark their route.

The hunger in evidence is hard to imagine. We found huge animal bones in camp—the bones of a horse or cow the prisoners had found and smuggled into camp. Usually these prizes were eaten raw, the flesh torn from the bones and swallowed in great gulps.

Rarely did a prisoner have the strength to curb his hunger long enough to cook what food he got. Outside the gate of the camp was the carcass of a horse that had been killed by shellfire. There was a great, gaping wound in his belly. As we passed it, one of the inmates was down on his knees, eating off the carcass. It had been dead several days. The next day when we came back, the whole side had been sliced away. Though our troops got food to them as soon as possible, many could not wait. Of course, we quickly gave away all the rations and cigarettes we had. It was strange to see them eat the cigarettes instead of smoking them. Not one cigarette did I see smoked. They were all swallowed in a hurry.

American troops soon organized things. Water was hauled in German tank wagons. All horses and wagons in the vicinity were put on a food hauling detail. We found a German food warehouse three miles from Gunskirchen stocked with dried noodles, potatoes, soups, meats, and other food. German civilians took it to Gunskirchen under the supervision of American military government personnel, and before we could establish proper control some of the prisoners had gobbled down the food, gorged themselves, and died. A starving person must learn to eat all over again.

None of the inmates of Gunskirchen will ever be the same again. I doubt if any of us who saw it will ever forget it—the smell, the hundreds of bodies that looked like caricatures of human beings, the frenzy of the thousands when they knew the Americans had arrived at last, the spark of joy in the eyes of those who lay in the ditches and whispered a prayer of thanks with their last breaths. I felt, the day I saw Gunskirchen Lager, that I finally knew what I was fighting for, what the war was all about.

EDWARD R. MURROW

Broadcast Transcript from Buchenwald

April 15, 1945

Edward R. Murrow (1908–1965) was one of the most revered American broadcast journalists of all time. He gained his reputation first as a CBS reporter broadcasting from London during the Blitz, the period of German bombings in 1940 and 1941 that seriously damaged London and other English cities but also steeled the population against the Germans. Later, in a now famous series of television shows in the early 1950s, he bravely critiqued the reckless anticommunism of Senator Joseph McCarthy. Following is Murrow's report from the newly liberated concentration camp of Buchenwald. Heard by millions over CBS Radio, it amply illustrates Murrow's reportorial skill and moral sensibility.

During the last week, I have driven more than a few hundred miles through Germany, most of it in the Third Army sector—Wiesbaden, Frankfurt, Weimar, Jena, and beyond. It is impossible to keep up with this war. The traffic flows down the superhighways, trucks with German helmets tied to the radiators and belts of machine-gun ammunition draped from fender to fender. The tanks on the concrete roads sound like a huge sausage machine, grinding up sheets of corrugated iron. And when there is a gap between convoys, when the noise dies away, there is another small noise, that of wooden-soled shoes and of small iron tires grating on the concrete. The power moves forward, while the people, the slaves, walk back, pulling their small belongings on anything that has wheels.

There are cities in Germany that make Coventry and Plymouth appear to be merely damage done by a petulant child, but bombed houses have a way of looking alike, wherever you see them.

But this is no time to talk of the surface of Germany. Permit me to tell you what you would have seen, and heard, had you been with me on Thursday. It will not be pleasant listening. If you are at lunch, or if you have no appetite to hear what Germans have done, now is a good time to switch off the radio, for I propose to tell you of Buchenwald. It is on a small hill about four miles outside Weimar, and it was one of the largest concentration

Edward R. Murrow, *In Search of Light: The Broadcasts of Edward R. Murrow 1938–1961,* ed. Edward Bliss, Jr. (New York: Alfred A. Knopf, 1967), 90–95.

camps in Germany, and it was built to last. As we approached it, we saw about a hundred men in civilian clothes with rifles advancing in open order across the fields. There were a few shops; we stopped to inquire. We were told that some of the prisoners had a couple of SS men cornered in there. We drove on, reached the main gate. The prisoners crowded up behind the wire. We entered.

And now, let me tell this in the first person, for I was the least important person there, as you shall hear. There surged around me an evil-smelling horde. Men and boys reached out to touch me; they were in rags and the remnants of uniform. Death had already marked many of them, but they were smiling with their eyes. I looked out over that mass of men to the green fields beyond where well-fed Germans were ploughing.

A German, Fritz Kersheimer, came up and said, "May I show you round the camp? I've been here ten years." An Englishman stood to attention, saying, "May I introduce myself, delighted to see you, and can you tell me when some of our blokes will be along?" I told him soon and asked to see one of the barracks. It happened to be occupied by Czechoslovakians. When I entered, men crowded around, tried to lift me to their shoulders. They were too weak. Many of them could not get out of bed. I was told that this building had once stabled eighty horses. There were twelve hundred men in it, five to a bunk. The stink was beyond all description.

When I reached the center of the barracks, a man came up and said, "You remember me. I'm Peter Zenkl, one-time mayor of Prague." I remembered him, but did not recognize him. He asked about Benes and Jan Masaryk.[1] I asked how many men had died in that building during the last month. They called the doctor; we inspected his records. There were only names in the little black book, nothing more—nothing of who these men were, what they had done or hoped. Behind the names of those who had died there was a cross. I counted them. They totalled 242. Two hundred and forty-two out of twelve hundred in one month.

As I walked down to the end of the barracks, there was applause from the men too weak to get out of bed. It sounded like the hand clapping of babies; they were so weak. The doctor's name was Paul Heller. He had been there since 1938.

As we walked out into the courtyard, a man fell dead. Two others—they must have been over sixty—were crawling toward the latrine. I saw it but will not describe it.

In another part of the camp they showed me the children, hundreds of

[1]Eduard Benes (1884–1948) and Jan Masaryk (1886–1948) were leaders in pre-war democratic Czechoslovakia and remained active in the Czech government-in-exile during World War II. In exile, they became symbols of the survival of European democracy. After the war, they helped to create a new democracy in Czechoslovakia until the Communist takeover in 1948. In that same year, Benes died of natural causes soon after he heard of Masaryk's probable murder (staged as a suicide) by the Communists.

them. Some were only six. One rolled up his sleeve, showed me his number. It was tattooed on his arm. D-6030, it was. The others showed me their numbers; they will carry them till they die.

An elderly man standing beside me said, "The children, enemies of the state." I could see their ribs through their thin shirts. The old man said, "I am Professor Charles Richer of the Sorbonne." The children clung to my hands and stared. We crossed to the courtyard. Men kept coming up to speak to me and to touch me, professors from Poland, doctors from Vienna, men from all Europe. Men from the countries that made America.

We went to the hospital; it was full. The doctor told me that two hundred had died the day before. I asked the cause of death; he shrugged and said, "Tuberculosis, starvation, fatigue, and there are many who have no desire to live. It is very difficult." Dr. Heller pulled back the blankets from a man's feet to show me how swollen they were. The man was dead. Most of the patients could not move.

As we left the hospital I drew out a leather billfold, hoping that I had some money which would help those who lived to get home. Professor Richer from the Sorbonne said, "I should be careful of my wallet if I were you. You know there are criminals in this camp, too." A small man tottered up, saying, "May I feel the leather, please? You see, I used to make good things of leather in Vienna." Another man said, "My name is Walter Roeder. For many years I lived in Joliet. Came back to Germany for a visit and Hitler grabbed me."

I asked to see the kitchen; it was clean. The German in charge had been a Communist, had been at Buchenwald for nine years, had a picture of his daughter in Hamburg. He hadn't seen her for almost twelve years, and if I got to Hamburg, would I look her up? He showed me the daily ration — one piece of brown bread about as thick as your thumb, on top of it a piece of margarine as big as three sticks of chewing gum. That, and a little stew, was what they received every twenty-four hours. He had a chart on the wall; very complicated it was. There were little red tabs scattered through it. He said that was to indicate each ten men who died. He had to account for the rations, and he added, "We're very efficient here."

We went again into the courtyard, and as we walked we talked. The two doctors, the Frenchman and the Czech, agreed that about six thousand had died during March. Kersheimer, the German, added that back in the winter of 1939, when the Poles began to arrive without winter clothing, they died at the rate of approximately nine hundred a day. Five different men asserted that Buchenwald was the best concentration camp in Germany; they had had some experience of the others.

Dr. Heller, the Czech, asked if I would care to see the crematorium. He said it wouldn't be very interesting because the Germans had run out of coke some days ago and had taken to dumping the bodies into a great hole nearby. Professor Richer said perhaps I would care to see the small courtyard. I said yes. He turned and told the children to stay behind. As we walked across the square I noticed that the professor had a hole in his left shoe and a toe sticking out of the right one. He followed my eyes and said, "I regret that I am so little presentable, but what can one do?" At that point another Frenchman came up to announce that three of his fellow countrymen outside had killed three S.S. men and taken one prisoner. We proceeded to the small courtyard. The wall was about eight feet high; it adjoined what had been a stable or garage. We entered. It was floored with concrete. There were two rows of bodies stacked up like cordwood. They were thin and very white. Some of the bodies were terribly bruised, though there seemed to be little flesh to bruise. Some had been shot through the head, but they bled but little. All except two were naked. I tried to count them as best I could and arrived at the conclusion that all that was mortal of more than five hundred men and boys lay there in two neat piles.

There was a German trailer which must have contained another fifty, but it wasn't possible to count them. The clothing was piled in a heap against the wall. It appeared that most of the men and boys had died of starvation; they had not been executed. But the manner of death seemed unimportant. Murder had been done at Buchenwald. God alone knows how many men and boys have died there during the last twelve years. Thursday I was told that there were more than twenty thousand in the camp. There had been as many as sixty thousand. Where are they now?

As I left that camp, a Frenchman who used to work for Havas[2] in Paris came up to me and said, "You will write something about this, perhaps?" And he added, "To write about this you must have been here at least two years, and after that—you don't want to write any more."

I pray you to believe what I have said about Buchenwald. I have reported what I saw and heard, but only part of it. For most of it I have no words. Dead men are plentiful in war, but the living dead, more than twenty thousand of them in one camp. And the country round about was pleasing to the eye, and the Germans were well fed and well dressed. American trucks were rolling toward the rear filled with prisoners. Soon they would be eating American rations, as much for a meal as the men at Buchenwald received in four days.

If I've offended you by this rather mild account of Buchenwald, I'm not in the least sorry. I was there on Thursday, and many men in many tongues blessed the name of Roosevelt. For long years his name had meant the full measure of their hope. These men who had kept close company with death for many years did not know that Mr. Roosevelt would, within hours, join their comrades who had laid their lives on the scales of freedom.

Back in 1941, Mr. Churchill said to me with tears in his eyes, "One day the world and history will recognize and acknowledge what it owes to your President." I saw and heard the first installment of that at Buchenwald on Thursday. It came from men from all over Europe. Their faces, with more

---

[2]Agence Havas, the world's first news-gathering agency, founded in France in 1835. Its name changed to Agence Presse-France in 1944.

flesh on them, might have been found anywhere at home. To them the name "Roosevelt" was a symbol, the code word for a lot of guys named "Joe" who are somewhere out in the blue with the armor heading east. At Buchenwald they spoke of the President just before he died. If there be a better epitaph, history does not record it.

JAMES AGEE

From *Agee on Film*
May 19, 1945

James Agee (1909–1955) was an important writer in the 1930s and 1940s and a film reviewer for the *Nation.* His reputation grew immensely after his death and the republication in 1960 of what is now considered an American classic, *Let Us Now Praise Famous Men.*[1] This moving and poetic account of the rural poor during the depression, illustrated by the photographs of Walker Evans, sought to understand the humanity of its subjects across lines of class and race.

Agee's critique of the newsreels of liberated concentration camps— films Agee did not actually see—reveals a similar goal by warning against the use of such films as justification for a harsh peace with Germany. It also echoes common themes concerning fabricated atrocity stories used against the Germans during World War I and the legacy of the treaty terms forced on Germany after that war. One might consider whether Agee accurately gauged the actual motivations for showing the films and the reactions of audiences.

The recently released films which show Nazi atrocities are only part of what is rather clearly an ordered and successful effort to condition the people of this country against interfering with, or even questioning, an extremely hard peace against the people of Germany. The simple method is to show

James Agee, *Agee on Film* (New York: Grosset and Dunlap, 1958), 161–62.

[1]James Agee and Walker Evans, *Let Us Now Praise Famous Men* (Boston: Houghton Mifflin, 1941).

things more frightful than most American civilians have ever otherwise seen, and to pin the guilt for these atrocities on the whole German people. I am judging this to be so by what I have seen and read in the press and by the effect of the atrocity press and the atrocity films as it can be observed in everybody, by everybody. I have not felt it necessary to see the films themselves. I don't agree with those who will feel that this deprives me of the right to have some reactions and ideas of my own, in relation to the general matter; or that they are necessarily, for that reason, not worth putting on paper.

I cannot get my thoughts in order, yet, to write what I think needs writing, about such propaganda and the general reaction to it. But I do want to go on record against it, as I believe many other people would like to, before our voices become indistinguishable among those of the many confused or timid or villainous people who are likely after a while, when the shock wears off—and when it is safe or even stylish—to come somewhat to their senses. Briefly then: the passion for vengeance is a terrifyingly strong one, very easily and probably inevitably wrought up by such evidence, even at our distance. But however well aware I am of its strength, and that in its full immediate force and expression it is in some respects irrelevant to moral inquiry, I doubt that it is ever to be honored, or regarded as other than evil and in every direction fatally degrading and destructive; even when it is obeyed in hot blood or in a crisis of prevention; far worse when it is obeyed in cold blood and in the illusion of carrying out justice.

I think it has taken such strong hold on so many of us most essentially because we suspect the passion itself, and know that even if the passion were a valid one to honor there would be no finding victims, or forms of vengeance, remotely sufficient to satisfy it. We cannot bear to face our knowledge that the satisfaction of our desire for justice, which we confuse with our desire for vengeance, is impossible. And so we invent as a victim the most comprehensive image which our reason, however deranged, will permit us: the whole of a people and the descendants of that people: and count ourselves incomparably their superiors if we stop short of the idea of annihilation. And we refuse to grant that this war has proved itself lost—if indeed it ever could have been won—as surely in our own raging vengefulness as in that of the mob in the Milan square.[2] Indeed, we are worse than they and worse, in some respects, than the Nazis. There can be no bestiality so discouraging to contemplate as that of the man of good-will when he is misusing his heart and his mind; and there can be no trusting him merely because, in the long run, he customarily comes part way to, and resumes his campaign for, what he likes to call human dignity.

---

[2] The jeering crowd that, in late April 1945, killed Mussolini and his mistress and hanged them upside down for all to see.

Gazing into the Pit

Christian Century, May 9, 1945

The concluding selection is this somber editorial by the *Christian Century,* which ponders the magazine's own past disbelief and the meaning of the discovery of the camps. It bears comparison with the other selections in this section.

The horrors disclosed by the capture of the Nazi concentration camps at Buchenwald, Belsen, Limburg, and a dozen other places constitute one of those awful facts upon which a paper such as this feels under obligation to comment, but concerning which it is almost physically impossible to write. What can be said that will not seem like tossing little words up against a giant mountain of ineradicable evil? What human emotion can measure up to such bestiality except a searing anger which calls on heaven to witness that retribution shall be swift and terrible and pitiless? How can men (and, it is alleged, women) who have been capable of such deeds be thought of or dealt with save as vicious brutes who must be exterminated both to do justice and in mercy to the future of the race?

We have found it hard to believe that the reports from the Nazi concentration camps could be true. Almost desperately we have tried to think that they must be wildly exaggerated. Perhaps they were products of the fevered brains of prisoners who were out for revenge. Or perhaps they were just more atrocity-mongering, like the cadaver factory story of the last war. But such puny barricades cannot stand up against the terrible facts. The evidence is too conclusive. It will be a long, long time before our eyes will cease to see those pictures of naked corpses piled like firewood or of those mounds of carrion flesh and bones. It will be a long, long time before we can forget what scores of honorable, competent observers tell us they have seen with their own eyes. The thing is well-nigh incredible. But it happened.

What does it mean? That Germans are beyond the pale of humanity? That they are capable of a fiendish cruelty which sets them apart from all the rest of us? No, not that. For one thing, we read that a large portion of the victims in these concentration camps were Germans. We do not believe that the sort of Germans who were subjected to this torture under any conceivable circumstances would themselves have become torturers. For another thing, we have reason to know that mass cruelty in most revolting

---

"Gazing into the Pit," *Christian Century,* May 9, 1945, 575–76.

forms has not been confined to Germany. We have seen photographs that missionaries smuggled out of raped Nanking. We have read the affidavits of men who escaped from the Baltic states and eastern Poland. We know what horrors writers like Dallin and William Henry Chamberlin[1] believe would be revealed if the prison camps in the Soviet Arctic were opened to the world's inspection. We know, too, the frightful things that have happened in this country when lynching mobs ran wild—things so horrible that they can only be told in whispers.

No, the horror of the Nazi concentration camps is the horror of humanity itself when it has surrendered to its capacity for evil. When we look at the pictures from Buchenwald we are looking, to be sure, at the frightful malignity of Nazism, this perversion of all values which in its final extremity is actually intent, as Hitler himself has said, on reducing all European life to "ruin, rats, and epidemics." But in the Nazis and beyond them we are looking into the very pit of hell, which men disclose yawning within themselves when they reject the authority of the moral law, when they deny the sacredness of human personality, when they turn from the worship of the one true God to the worship of their own wills, their own states, their own lust for power.

Buchenwald and the other memorials of Nazi infamy reveal the depths to which humanity can sink, and has sunk, in these frightful years. They reveal the awful fate which may engulf all civilizations unless these devils of our pride and of our ruthlessness and of the cult of force are exorcised. And they reveal that the salvation of man, the attainment of peace, the healing of the nations is at the last a religious problem. The diplomats may mark out what boundary lines they please, the victorious armies may set up what zones of occupation they will, but if man continues his self-worship, the pit yawns for us all.

The foul stench of the concentration camps should burden the Christian conscience until Christian men cannot rest. The conventional ministry of past years is no ministry for these days when mankind totters on the brink of damnation. The puny plans which denominations have been making are so inadequate to this crisis that they are nearly irrelevant. Unless there is a great upsurge of testimony to the power of the Christian gospel to save men from the sin which is destroying them and their institutions, all the reconstitution of church paraphernalia now being planned will be so much building on sand. In this crisis the gospel cannot be preached dispassionately, tentatively, or listlessly—not and save civilization from the pit. A time has come when the Christian must proclaim his gospel "like a dying man to dying men."

---

[1]David J. Dallin (1889–1962) and William Henry Chamberlin (1897–1969), two American scholars of the Soviet Union who emphasized the predatory, totalitarian, and murderous aspects of Stalinist Russia.

For we are dying men—dying, all of us and our institutions and our civilization, in the sins which have reached their appalling climax in the torture chambers of Europe's prison camps. Only faith in the God and Father of Jesus Christ, the God who sent his Son to reveal a common and all-inclusive brotherhood, can save us. Our contempt for the sacredness of life, our worship at the shrine of our own power, has gone so far that it has taken these horrors to shock us into awareness of the tragic fate toward which we are stumbling.

In God's providence, has not the World Council of Churches become a living hope for such a time as this? So far, progress toward the formation of the World Council has been cautious, following familiar patterns, a matter of negotiations and treaties among sovereign denominations. The goal has seemed largely to be the attainment of an organization. Is not the agony of mankind a call to the World Council to forget everything but the proclamation of the Christian evangel?

Should it not be the business of the World Council now to gather from all lands Christians who will go everywhere, pointing to the encroachments of human depravity which have been laid bare, proclaiming to men and nations, "Except ye repent, ye shall all likewise perish"? Let the council gather for this common task Niemöller[2] and the Christian leaders with him who have withstood the Nazi scourge, as many of them as may emerge from imprisonment; let it gather Bishop Berggrav[3] and the noble pastors of Norway; let it gather every Christian in the world who sees the peril and knows the means of escape, and let it send them forth with such an evangel as has not stormed this sin-stricken world since the days of the first apostles. Buchenwald and the other concentration camps spell doom. But it is not simply the doom of the Nazis; it is the doom of man unless he can be brought to worship at the feet of the living God.

---

[2]Martin Niemöller (1892–1984), German Lutheran pastor who preached against the Nazis in the 1930s and eventually was incarcerated in various concentration camps before being liberated in 1945.

[3]Eivind Berggrav (1884–1959), Norwegian Lutheran bishop, who resisted the Nazi occupation of his country and wrote extensively about the Christian duty to resist an evil state.

Epilogue: The Changing Historical Perspective

In 1945, few doubted a simple and dramatic rendering of the facts: America and the Allies had been surprised by the genocidal record of Nazism, which they discovered late in the war and really only believed after seeing the awful scenes in the liberated camps. Newsreel images seemed to tell it all: outraged American officials and soldiers viewing the remains of concentration camp atrocities and ministering to emaciated survivors. America saw itself as a shocked and innocent liberator; it saw the Nazis as the polar opposite—evil incarnate.

For almost twenty-five years after the end of the war, this basic image remained in place, obscuring the more complicated story of America's relation to the Holocaust. The reasons were clear. First, the politics of the cold war allowed for little questioning of any less-than-heroic roles played by America during the Second World War. Second, few Americans wished to replay the horrid details of Nazi genocide. Third, no new generation of Americans had yet come along to challenge the image that those who fought the war had created of themselves.

All of this began to change in the 1960s. The reopening of public consideration of the Holocaust in general came with the Eichmann trial in 1961–62. Adolf Eichmann, an SS officer who had been one of the key architects and implementers of what the Nazis called the *Endlösung,* or Final Solution, of the "Jewish problem," had escaped capture after the war and settled unobtrusively in Argentina. A decade and a half later, Israeli commandos kidnapped him and brought him to Israel, where he was put on trial for crimes against the Jewish people. He was convicted and hanged.

For most Americans, the Eichmann trial only confirmed, albeit in horrid detail, a story already known. Yet Hannah Arendt, herself a refugee from Hitler's Germany and by then an important force among American intellectuals, shocked a great many by taking a different angle on the trial. In *Eichmann in Jerusalem* (1962), she argued that Eichmann's life and crimes illustrated "the banality of evil," thus challenging the simple demonizing of the Nazis and suggesting a more universal susceptibility to evil. Eichmann, she suggested, was an ordinary man acting from ordinary motives. Like any bureaucrat, he wished to please the higher-ups so as to advance his career. That meant doing his job well, no matter that it involved the slaughter of millions.

Arendt also charged that the Jewish communities of Europe had contributed to their own destruction by cooperating, as individuals and as communities, with the implementation of Nazi deportation and extermination plans in the hope that cooperation would lead to leniency. Right or wrong, Arendt shattered an agreed-on moral and historical tale and sent scholars back to the archives.

Arendt's work did not deal directly with Allied culpability, but her rejection of past images of the Nazis and her suggestion of complicity even on the part of the victims sent shock waves through the intellectual community. In a more stable cultural atmosphere, the debate that grew out of Arendt's work might not have moved beyond scholarly and small-circulation intellectual journals. Yet the trial's reminders of all that had happened and Arendt's unsettling reflections came at the beginning of a period of major national self-scrutiny, one in which virtually every aspect of America's self-image was examined assiduously by often unfriendly cultural commentators. Sociologists, philosophers, historians, poets, writers, and popular musicians all weighed in with visions of a culture in crisis, blinded by hypocrisy and illusion concerning its history and values.

The driving events in this self-examination were the civil rights movement and the Vietnam War. Within this environment the Holocaust emerged as a reference point for ultimate evil. Allusions to Nazi genocide began to appear in songs such as Tom Paxton's "Last Train to Nuremberg" (1962) and Bob Dylan's "With God on Our Side" (1963). Sylvia Plath evoked memories of Nazi cruelty in "Daddy" (1963), one of her most famous poems. Popular films such as *Judgment at Nuremberg* (1961) and *The Pawnbroker* (1965) explored related psychological and moral issues in greater detail than ever before.

Crucial works also appeared in Europe and were soon translated and published in America. *The Deputy,* a play by the young German drama-tist Rolf Hochhuth, raised a storm of controversy upon its American pre-miere in 1966 because of its indictment of the Vatican and the Western democracies for their inaction during the Holocaust. A French survivor of the camps, Jean-François Steiner, reiterated one of Arendt's themes in his novel *Treblinka* (1967). Steiner condemned key members of the Jew-ish community and camp inmates for their complicity with the Nazis in rounding up, transporting, and preparing other Jews for extermination. *Treblinka's* publication in America caused enormous controversy.

By the end of the 1960s, the term *Holocaust* had become entrenched in the vocabulary of the nation and the world, attesting to a need for some way to name and then interpret the rediscovered record of Nazi slaughter. This endeavor involved more than simply looking back at German crimes. Instead, these crimes became a reference point for ex-ploring American society and its shortcomings. Thus the battle over civil rights, which involved a recovery of black history and the history of white racism as well as demonstrations and legislation, was often framed in moral and historical reference to Nazi racial doctrines. With the esca-lation of the U.S. role in Vietnam, the antiwar movement often compared American use of napalm and atrocities such as the My Lai massacre to Nazi war crimes. This perspective was summed up in the popular Ger-manized spelling *Amerika* in the political graffiti of the era.

In such an atmosphere of increased questioning of American values, motives, and hidden history, historians began to look anew at the ways in which the Roosevelt administration and the American people had grappled with the reports of genocide in Europe and had evaluated op-portunities to aid its victims. The journalist Arthur D. Morse's *While Six Million Died* (1967) accused the Allies of being "bystanders" to the ex-termination of European Jews because they had turned a deaf ear to pleas for rescue and more open immigration policies. David Wyman's *Paper Walls* (1968) tracked, in more thorough and devastating fashion, how public anti-Semitism and the resistance of anti-Semites in the State Department had combined to close off America to Jewish refugees. Henry Feingold, in *The Politics of Rescue* (1970), homed in on what he saw as the anti-Semitism of Breckenridge Long, a key player in the State Department, and his power to block immigration efforts in the early 1940s. Saul Friedman's *No Haven for the Oppressed* (1973), which dis-puted the anti-Semitic portrait of Long drawn by Wyman and Feingold, nonetheless emphasized the lack of help given Jewish refugees by the United States. Friedman argued that for most Americans, the question of refugees had paled in comparison to the depression and the war. He noted that various rescue plans, especially during the war, might have involved bargaining with the enemy—something for which no official wished to be held accountable. And he blamed the American Jewish community for inaction.

One question closely related to that of immigration and rescue policymaking haunted scholars: When did Americans at various levels of government or in the press come to know of Germany's policy toward the Jews and the Final Solution? The question had a peculiar poignancy because of the popular refrain at the time of the liberation of the camps in 1945: "We didn't know!" The victorious Allies had scoffed at these words when used by Germans. Yet many citizens in the Allied countries and soldiers in the field had had precisely the same reaction to the newsreels and photographs of Bergen-Belsen, Buchenwald, and Dachau.

Walter Laqueur's *The Terrible Secret: Suppression of the Truth about Hitler's Final Solution* (1980) noted that as early as 1942, definitive information about the Nazis' use of killing sites in Poland had leaked out to the West. Indeed, by December of that year, the Allies had made general proclamations decrying the killings and pledging punishment with Allied victory. He recounted the personal visits of Jan Karski to leaders in London and Washington, where Karski had conveyed his eyewitness accounts of conditions in the Warsaw Ghetto and exterminations at Belzec. Laqueur focused on the reaction of Supreme Court justice Felix Frankfurter, a Jew and Roosevelt confidant, to Karski's revelations. "I know that what you have to say is true," Frankfurter said, "but I don't believe it." The perspective of knowing and believing—of assimilating such "unbelievable" information—gave Laqueur one way of understanding the lack of action.

Deborah Lipstadt, in *Beyond Belief: The American Press and the Coming of the Holocaust, 1933–1945* (1986), documented the extent to which Hitler's plans for and actions against the Jews had been reported in the American press from the beginning of the Nazi regime through the end of the war. She demonstrated that virtually everything of importance had been reported in the press, but often with conflicting interpretations, back-page placement, and sometimes skeptical commentary. Clearly, however, the "discovery" of the camps at the end of the war should not have been surprising to the public, save for the awful shock of having to face directly the nightmarish scenes depicted by press photographers and Signal Corps cameramen.

This new view of America and the Holocaust reached a wide audience with the publication of David Wyman's *The Abandonment of the Jews* (1984). Wyman's conclusion that the United States had been a "passive accomplice" to Nazi genocide was built on his own previous work and that of others, but it also took into account much new research. Its pointed moral judgments and clearly expressed disappointment in the Roosevelt administration and American Jews caught the mood of post-Watergate, post-Vietnam America so well that, unlike any other book on the topic, it skyrocketed to the *New York Times* bestseller list. Wyman did not mince words:

> The Nazis were the murderers, but we were the all too passive accomplices. . . . Germany's control over most of Europe meant that even a determined Allied rescue campaign probably could not have saved as many as a third of those who died. But a substantial commitment to rescue almost certainly could have saved several hundred thousand of them, and done so without compromising the war effort. (p. ix)

Behind Wyman's indictment lay a powerful question for contemporary America: "Would the reaction be different today? Would Americans be more sensitive, less self-centered, more willing to make sacrifices, less afraid of differences now than they were then?" (p. xii).

No one reading the Wyman book could come away without an almost sickening sense of moral failure. Even the War Refugee Board, which helped finance Raoul Wallenberg's spectacularly successful intervention on behalf of thousands of Hungarian Jews, fell into Wyman's category of "too little, too late."

Wyman's work and that of others struck a moral nerve of the nation, and especially of the Jewish community, for Wyman greatly expanded on Saul Friedman's earlier work concerning the ineffectiveness of the Jewish community in America in relation to the Holocaust. He demonstrated the lack of unity among major Jewish organizations and charged that timidity and internecine feuds had diminished what should have been a stronger and more focused campaign for government action. Nor was Wyman the only critic of American Jewish organizations. In a public act of self-scrutiny, the controversial American Jewish Commission on the Holocaust investigated the question and published its highly critical findings as *American Jewry during the Holocaust* (1984). Rabbi Haskel Lookstein gave an only slightly less harsh reading in his study of the American Jewish press during the Holocaust, *Were We Our Brothers' Keepers? The Public Response of American Jews to the Holocaust, 1938–1944* (1985).

Such interpretations were offset by an alternative view, which emerged in Richard Breitman and Alan Kraut's *American Refugee Policy and European Jewry, 1933–1945* (1987). These historians of the refugee question before and during World War II noted that "sweeping judgment may seem morally appropriate, in view of the magnitude of the tragedy, but it obliterates important distinctions of behavior among individuals and among governments" (p. 2). In response to Wyman's claim that the Allies' refusal to bomb the railroad tracks leading to Auschwitz proved indifference, these authors (who agreed with Wyman that they should have been bombed) pointed out that some opposition to this strategy materialized in Jewish circles because they thought that many prisoners might be killed in the bombing raids.

As for Wyman's contention that the State Department's resistance to liberalizing immigration quotas and processes was a product of anti-Semitism, Kraut and Breitman argued that it was a result of the bureaucratic vision of the immigration office in the Department of State. The department saw itself as protecting the nation from possible spies and unsupportable refugees during a time of economic downturn. Kraut and Breitman also pointed out that the number of Jewish refugees admitted between 1933 and 1945—about one hundred thousand from Germany and Austria alone—was not so shameful considering that the demand reached its peak during the Great Depression.

Wyman asserted that many Jews might have been saved had the Roosevelt administration taken part in various plans for trading trucks for Jews or other secret negotiations initiated by third parties. Kraut and Breitman noted that America was locked in a total war with Germany, with any leverage it might have had being built around military might. It would have been exceedingly difficult and controversial to negotiate with the enemy using military materiel as a reward. At the very least, any negotiations with the Germans would have been chancy affairs.

Others contributed to a modification of the most extreme criticism of American policymakers and American Jews. The eminent Holocaust scholars Martin Gilbert and Lucy Dawidowicz cautioned that criticism of the Allies and Jewish communities had become overdrawn. Henry Feingold, who early on had helped lay the foundation for the critical barrage, later evolved a more moderate position. Like Kraut and Breitman, Feingold came to see the influence of politics and the limits of statecraft, more than anti-Semitism, as primary explanations for the government's cautiousness. Feingold also found it more appropriate to explain Jewish actions in the context of American Jewish history than to use what he viewed as anachronistic standards to find them morally wanting. The evolution of Feingold's thought can be followed conveniently in a collection of his essays, *Bearing Witness: How America and Its Jews Responded to the Holocaust* (1995).

Such attempts to move from moralizing to historical subtlety hardly prepared the way for the most recent entry into the debate, William D. Rubinstein's *The Myth of Rescue: Why the Democracies Could Not Have Saved More Jews from the Nazis* (1997). No matter what conclusion historians have drawn concerning the motivations of policymakers and the historical realities that shaped Allied responses to Nazi genocide, most have agreed that at least some thousands more Jews might have been saved and that the inaction of the Roosevelt administration was in retrospect a historical tragedy. Yet Rubinstein begins his book with a simple statement:

> The argument of *The Myth of Rescue* is that no Jew who perished during the Nazi Holocaust could have been saved by any action which the Allies could have taken at the time, given what was actually known about the Holocaust, what was *actually* proposed at the time and what was realistically possible. (p. x)

His point-by-point refutation of past historians combines valuable correctives and overargued generalizations, but with little new research. Rubinstein's book has all the strengths and weaknesses of a clever case in forensic debate.

Now that the question of America's and the Allies' relationship to the Holocaust has in a sense come full circle, perhaps the relevance of the documents in this volume can be seen in greater relief. They do not answer the questions posed by Rubinstein or by Wyman before him. Instead, they tell us much about the world in which Americans thought and acted as the tragedy of the European Jews was taking place.

Chronology of Events
Related to the Holocaust
(1933–1945)*

1933

January 30 Adolf Hitler becomes chancellor of Germany.

March 22 Nazis create Dachau concentration camp to detain Gypsies and "reeducate" political prisoners.

April 1 Anti-Jewish boycott of businesses and attacks on Jewish citizens occur in the streets of Germany. Jews are barred from the civil service and universities. In the United States, there are protests and a call for a boycott of German goods.

1935

September 15 Nuremberg Laws are enacted in Germany, formally restricting Jewish rights and further limiting their role in the economy.

November 15 Racial definitions of Jews are created in Germany.

1936

July/August Olympics are held in Berlin. Despite a strong movement to boycott the games, the U.S. team participates.

1937

July 15 Nazis establish Buchenwald concentration camp near Weimar.

1938

March 12–13 *Anschluss* makes Austria part of Germany. Jews are hunted down, jailed, and humiliated. Thousands go into hiding or flee to France, Britain, and the United States.

---

*Adaptation of time line available from Simon Wiesenthal Center at its Web site: http://www.wiesenthal.com/resource/timeline.html.

July 6 President Franklin Roosevelt calls the Evian Conference on Jewish refugees, but no solutions result.

September 30 At the Munich Conference, Britain and France agree to Hitler's occupation of the Sudetenland (part of Czechoslovakia) in exchange for "peace in our time." Jews in the Sudetenland are immediately attacked and restricted.

October 28 Seventeen thousand Polish Jews living in Germany are expelled to the Polish border and live there under horrible conditions.

November 7 Herschel Grynszpan, son of expelled Polish Jews, retaliates by killing German diplomat Ernst vom Rath in Paris.

November 9–10 Nazis use Rath's murder as a pretext for *Kristallnacht,* a countrywide (including Austria and the Sudetenland) attack on Jews and their homes, synagogues, and businesses. Jews themselves are fined for the destruction, their insurance policies are canceled, and thirty thousand men are thrown into concentration camps to be held for ransom.

1939

January 30 In a Reichstag speech, Hitler accuses "world Jewry" of plotting war against him and predicts the end of European Jews in case of war.

March 15 Germans take over the rest of Czechoslovakia.

May–June Hamburg-America Line ship *St. Louis* sails for Cuba with more than nine hundred Jewish refugees but is refused entry in Havana and in the United States.

August 23 Molotov-Ribbentrop Pact, a nonaggression pact between the Soviet Union and Germany, is signed.

September 1 Germany invades Poland, and World War II begins.

October 28 First Polish ghetto is established.

1940

April 9 Germany invades Denmark and southern Norway.

May 10 Germany invades Holland, Belgium, Luxembourg, and France.

May 20 Nazis establish concentration camp at Auschwitz.

June 22 France surrenders.

August 8 Battle of Britain begins.

November 16 Warsaw Ghetto is sealed.

1941

April 6 Germany attacks Yugoslavia and Greece.

June 22 Germany invades the Soviet Union. *Einsatzgruppen* follow army to carry out killing of Jews.

September Americans step up the debate over entry into the war. President Roosevelt declares unrestricted warfare on Nazi forces in the Atlantic to protect shipping. Charles Lindbergh's Des Moines speech decries interventionism and blames the British, Jews, and Roosevelt administration for U.S. move toward war.

September 28–29 Massacre at Babii Yar.

October Nazis establish Auschwitz II (Birkenau) for the extermination of Jews. Gypsies, Poles, Russians, and others also are murdered at the camp.

December 7–8 Japanese attack Pearl Harbor. United States declares war on Japan.

December 8 Nazis establish Chelmno extermination camp.

December 10 Germany declares war on United States.

1942

January 20 At the Wannsee Conference in Berlin, formal plans to kill all of Europe's Jews are made.

March 17 Nazis establish Belzec extermination camp. Soon after, Jan Karski visits in disguise and reports to the Polish Underground.

May Nazis establish Sobibor extermination camp.

July 22 Nazis establish Treblinka concentration and killing center.

Last half of year Jews from Belgium, Croatia, France, the Netherlands, Germany, Greece, Norway, and Poland are deported to killing centers. Jewish resistance in Poland begins in earnest.

December Confirmation of massive killings received in London and Washington. Allies issue declaration promising retribution after the war.

1943

January Germans surrender at Stalingrad.

April Warsaw Ghetto revolt begins; ends in June.

1944

March 19 Germany occupies Hungary.

May 15 Nazis begin deporting Hungarian Jews. By June 27, 380,000 are sent to Auschwitz.

June 6 D-day: Allied invasion at Normandy.

July 24 Russians liberate Majdanek and invite Western journalists to tour the site.

1945

January 17 Evacuation of Auschwitz.

April 6–May 8 U.S. Army units discover Ohrdruf concentration camp and begin a series of liberations that include Buchenwald, Dachau, Mauthausen, Bergen-Belsen (British troops), and many other smaller camps.

April 30 Hitler commits suicide.

May 8 V-E Day: Germany surrenders.

Questions for Consideration

1. In what ways have these primary sources altered your thoughts about America's relation to the Holocaust?

2. How would you list anti-Semitism in importance among the factors that shaped American responses to the plight of Europe's Jews?

3. In what ways have these sources changed your sense of the general values and ideas in American society during the 1930s and 1940s?

4. Given the sources in this collection, how would you explain the fact that many Americans, when confronted with the newsreels and pictures of the liberated camps, claimed not to have been aware of the Nazis' genocide?

5. In what ways do American responses to human rights crises or acts of genocide overseas today seem different from those in the 1930s and 1940s? In what ways do they seem similar?

6. Consider your own intellectual, moral, and emotional responses to particular selections, especially those that report atrocities or make arguments about how individuals and governments might act. In what ways do your own reactions allow you to understand the various ways in which Americans may have read these reports at the time?

7. As you read the various commentaries (as opposed to straight reports) on the fate of the Jews in Europe, which arguments do you feel are the strongest? Which have revealed to you new angles on the topic?

8. In what ways do you think the vision of minorities in mainstream America was different (compared to today) in the 1930s and 1940s? Are there any similarities?

Selected Bibliography

GENERAL WORKS ON THE HOLOCAUST

Gilbert, Martin. *The Holocaust: A History of the Jews of Europe during the Second World War.* New York: Holt, Rinehart & Winston, 1985.

Hilberg, Raul. *The Destruction of the European Jews.* 2d ed. New York: Holmes & Meier, 1985.

Yahil, Leni. *The Holocaust: The Fate of European Jewry, 1932–1945.* New York: Oxford University Press, 1990.

AMERICA, THE ALLIES, AND THE HOLOCAUST

Abzug, Robert H. *Inside the Vicious Heart: Americans and the Liberation of Nazi Concentration Camps.* New York: Oxford University Press, 1985.

Breitman, Richard, and Alan Kraut. *American Refugee Policy and European Jewry, 1933–1945.* Bloomington: Indiana University Press, 1987.

Dinnerstein, Leonard. *America and the Survivors of the Holocaust.* New York: Columbia University Press, 1982.

Feingold, Henry. *Bearing Witness: How America and Its Jews Responded to the Holocaust.* Syracuse, N.Y.: Syracuse University Press, 1995.

———. *The Politics of Rescue: The Roosevelt Administration and the Holocaust, 1938–1945.* New Brunswick, N.J.: Rutgers University Press, 1970.

Friedman, Saul S. *No Haven for the Oppressed: United States Policy toward Jewish Refugees, 1938–1945.* Detroit: Wayne State University Press, 1973.

Gilbert, Martin. *Auschwitz and the Allies.* New York: Holt, Rinehart & Winston, 1981.

Laqueur, Walter. *The Terrible Secret: Suppression of the Truth about Hitler's Final Solution.* Boston: Little, Brown, 1980.

Lipstadt, Deborah. *Beyond Belief: The American Press and the Coming of the Holocaust, 1933–1945.* New York: Free Press, 1986.

Loftus, John, and Mark Aarons. *The Secret War against the Jews: How Western Espionage Betrayed the Jewish People.* New York: St. Martin's Press, 1994.

Morse, Arthur. *While Six Million Died: A Chronicle of American Apathy.* New York: Random House, 1967.

Penkower, Monty Noam. *The Jews Were Expendable: Free World Diplomacy and the Holocaust.* Urbana: University of Illinois Press, 1983.

Rubinstein, William D. *The Myth of Rescue: Why the Democracies Could Not Have Saved More Jews from the Nazis.* New York: Routledge, 1997.

Wyman, David S. *The Abandonment of the Jews: America and the Holocaust, 1941–1945.* New York: Pantheon Books, 1984.

————. *Paper Walls: America and the Refugee Crisis, 1938–1941.* Amherst: University of Massachusetts Press, 1968.

————, ed. *America and the Holocaust.* 13 vols. New York: Garland Publishing, 1990–91.

AMERICAN JEWS AND THE HOLOCAUST

Bauer, Yehuda. *American Jewry and the Holocaust: The American Jewish Joint Distribution Committee, 1939–1945.* Detroit: Wayne State University Press, 1981.

Finger, Seymour Maxwell, ed. *American Jewry during the Holocaust.* New York: Holmes & Meier, 1984.

Lookstein, Haskel. *Were We Our Brothers' Keepers? The Public Response of American Jews to the Holocaust, 1938–1944.* New York: Hartmore House, 1985.

Lowenstein, Sharon R. *Token Refuge: The Story of the Jewish Refugee Shelter at Oswego.* Bloomington: Indiana University Press, 1986.

SPECIAL TOPICS

Brinkley, Alan. *Voices of Protest: Huey Long, Father Coughlin, and the Great Depression.* New York: Alfred A. Knopf, 1983.

Dinnerstein, Leonard. *Antisemitism in America.* New York: Oxford University Press, 1994.

Genizi, Haim. *American Apathy: The Plight of Christian Refugees from Nazism.* Ramat Gan, Israel: Bar-Ilan University Press, 1983.

Mandell, Richard D. *The Nazi Olympics.* New York: Macmillan, 1971.

Ross, Robert. *So It Was True: The American Protestant Press and the Nazi Persecution of the Jews.* Minneapolis: University of Minnesota Press, 1980.

Wood, E. Thomas, and Stanislaw M. Jankowski. *Karski: How One Man Tried to Stop the Holocaust.* New York: John Wiley & Sons, 1994.

Acknowledgments

Photo Credits
Page 35, Robert F. Wagner Labor Archives, New York University; page 69, Reprinted by permission of GRM Associates, Inc., Agents for *The Pittsburgh Courier*. From the book issue of July 11, 1936 of *The Pittsburgh Courier*. Copyright © 1936, 1964 by *The Pittsburgh Courier;* page 78, Underwood & Underwood/Corbis-Bettmann; page 84, Hulton-Deutch Collection/Corbis; page 100, UPI/Corbis-Bettmann; page 139, from Tosha Bialer, *Collier's*, February 20 and 27, 1943; page 178, The National Archives/Corbis; page 193, Hulton-Deutch Collection/Corbis.

Text Credits
James Agee, excerpt from *Agee on Film* (New York: Grosset and Dunlap, 1958), pp. 161-162. Originally published in *The Nation* (May 19, 1945). Copyright 1945 by The Nation Company, L. P. Reprinted with the permission of *The Nation*.

"The Official Decrees and Measures against the Jews," "Execution of Decrees," "The Effect of the Anti-Jewish Measures," "Acts of Violence against Jews Since Hitler Became Chancellor," and "The Nazi Anti-Jewish Campaign" from *The Jews in Nazi Germany: The Factual Record of their Persecution by the National Socialists*. Reprinted with the permission of The American Jewish Committee.

Robert E. Asher, "A Jew Protests against Protesters" from *The Christian Century* (April 12, 1933). Copyright 1933 by the Christian Century Foundation. Reprinted with the permission of the publishers.

Bermuda Conference, excerpt from the Minutes of the American Delegation (April 20, 1943) in David S. Wyman (ed.), *America and the Holocaust: Responsibility for America's Failure, Volume 13*. Copyright © 1991. Reprinted with the permission of Garland Publishing, Inc.

Reverend L. M. Birkhead, "Nazis Ask World to Combat Jews" from *The New York Times* (July 28, 1935). Reprinted with the permission of the Associated Press.

Richard Breitman and Alan M. Kraut, "Exchange between Raymond Geist and George Messersmith, December 5, 1938 and December 20, 1938" from *American Refugee Policy and European Jewry, 1933–1945*. Copyright © 1987 by Richard Breitman and Alan M. Kraut. Reprinted with the permission of Indiana University Press.

Richard L. Cary, "Letter to Clarence E. Pickett, June 28, 1932" and "Letter to Clarence E. Pickett, July 23, 1933" from Jack Sutters (ed.), *Archives of the Holocaust: An International Collection of Selected Documents, Volume 2*. Copyright © 1990. Reprinted with the permission of Garland Publishing, Inc.

"Biggest Atrocity Story Breaks in Poland" from *The Christian Century* (September 13, 1944). Copyright 1944 by the Christian Century Foundation. Reprinted with the permission of the publishers.

Bill Downs, "Blood at Babii Yar—Kiev's Atrocity Story" from *Newsweek* (December 6, 1943). Copyright 1943 by Newsweek Inc. Reprinted with the permission of *Newsweek*.

Fred Eastman, "A Reply to Screamers" from *The Christian Century* (February 16, 1944). Copyright 1944 by the Christian Century Foundation. Reprinted with the permission of the publishers.

"Editor Holds Riots Inspired by Nazis" from *The New York Times* (July 26, 1935). Copyright 1935 by The New York Times Company. Reprinted with the permission of *The New York Times*.

"FDR Creating War Incidents, Lindbergh Says" from *Chicago Daily Tribune* (September 11, 1941). Copyright 1941. Reprinted with the permission of Knight-Ridder Newspapers/Tribune Information Services.

"The Forbidden Theme" from *The Christian Century* (September 24, 1941). Copyright 1941 by the Christian Century Foundation. Reprinted with the permission of the publishers.

Varian Fry, "The Massacre of the Jews" from *The New Republic* (December 21, 1942). Reprinted with the permission of *The New Republic*.

"Gazing into the Pit" from *The Christian Century* (May 9, 1945). Copyright 1945 by the Christian Century Foundation. Reprinted with the permission of the publishers.

"Germany: Hitler Decrees Swastika Reich Flag; Bars Intermarriage; Relegates Jews to Dark Ages" from *Newsweek* (September 21, 1935). Copyright 1935 by Newsweek, Inc. Reprinted with the permission of *Newsweek*.

"Germany: Jews Begin to Feel a Soft Spot in the Iron Heel" from *Newsweek* (September 28, 1935). Copyright 1935 by Newsweek, Inc. Reprinted with the permission of *Newsweek*.

Ben Hecht, "Remember Us" from *Reader's Digest* (February, 1943). Copyright 1943 by The American Mercury. Reprinted with the permission of the Estate of Ben Hecht.

Holloway cartoon, "The Black Eagles" from *The Pittsburgh Courier* (July 11, 1936). Reprinted by permission.

Jan Karski, "Polish Death Camp" from *Collier's* (October 14, 1944). Copyright 1944 by Jan Karski. Reprinted with the permission of the author.

Alfred Kazin, "In Every Voice, in Every Ban" from *The New Republic* (January 10, 1944). Reprinted with the permission of *The New Republic*.

Freda Kirchwey, "While the Jews Die" from *The Nation* (March 13, 1943). Copyright 1943 by The Nation Company, L. P. Reprinted with the permission of *The Nation*.

Freda Kirchwey, "A Program of Inaction" from *The Nation*. Copyright 1943 by The Nation Company, L. P. Reprinted with the permission of *The Nation*.

Richard Lauterbach, "Murder, Inc." from *Time* (September 11, 1944). Copyright 1944 by Time, Inc. Reprinted with the permission of *Time*.

"Lindbergh's Nazi Pattern" from *The New Republic* (September 22, 1941). Reprinted with the permission of *The New Republic*.

Walter Lippmann, "Hitler's Speech" from *The Los Angeles Times* (May 19, 1933). Copyright 1933 by New York Tribune, Inc. Reprinted with the permission of Los Angeles Times Syndicate.

Louis Lochner, "Letter to Betty and Bobby, Berlin, November 28, 1938" from "Round Robins from Berlin: Louis P. Lochner's Letters to His Children, 1932–1941" from *Wisconsin Magazine of History* 50, no. 4 (Summer 1967): 324. Reprinted with the permission of The State Historical Society of Wisconsin.

James Marshall, excerpts from "The Anti-Semitic Problem in America," from *The Atlantic Monthly* (June/July 1941). Reprinted by permission.

"Mass Meeting Protests Hitler's Anti-Jewish Program" from *The Christian Century* (April 26, 1933). Copyright 1933 by the Christian Century Foundation. Reprinted with the permission of the publishers.

Henry Morgenthau, diary entry for November 16, 1938 ["Concerning Placing Jewish Refugees"] from David S. Wyman (ed.), *America and the Holocaust: Responsibility for America's Failure, Volume 13*. Copyright © 1991. Reprinted with the permission of Garland Publishing, Inc.

Henry Morgenthau, diary entry for December 3, 1942 ["Concerning Placing Jewish Refugees"] from *America and the Holocaust: Responsibility for America's Failure, Volume 13*. Copyright © 1991. Reprinted with the permission of Garland Publishing, Inc.

Charles Clayton Morrison, "Horror Stories from Poland" from *The Christian Century* (December 9, 1942). Copyright 1942 by the Christian Century Foundation. Reprinted with the permission of the publishers.

Charles Clayton Morrison, "Polish Atrocities Are Entered in the Books" from *The Christian Century* (December 30, 1942). Copyright 1942 by the Christian Century Foundation. Reprinted with the permission of the publishers.

"Murder of a People" from *The Nation* (December 19, 1942). Copyright 1942 by The Nation Company, L. P. Reprinted with the permission of *The Nation*.

Edward R. Murrow, "Broadcast Transcript from Buchenwald, April 15, 1945" from *In Search of Light: The Broadcasts of Edward R. Murrow 1938–1961,* edited by Edward Bliss, Jr. Copyright © 1967 by the Estate of Edward R. Murrow. Reprinted with the permission of Alfred A. Knopf, Inc.

"N.A.A.C.P. Asks A.A.U. to Abandon Olympics" from *The Pittsburgh Courier* (December 14, 1935). Reprinted by permission.

Reinhold Niebuhr, "Jews after the War" Parts I and II from *The Nation* (February 21 and 28, 1942). Copyright 1942 by The Nation Company, L. P. Reprinted with the permission of *The Nation*.

Albert Jay Nock, excerpts from "The Jewish Problem in America" from *The Atlantic Monthly* (June/July 1941). Reprinted by permission.

Clarence E. Pickett, "Letter to J. S. Conning, May 5, 1932" and "Letter to Gilbert L. Mac-Master, March 30 (typed April 3), 1933" from Jack Sutters (ed.), *Archives of the Holocaust: An International Collection of Selected Documents, Volume 2.* Copyright © 1990. Reprinted with the permission of Garland Publishing, Inc.

Captain J. D. Pletcher, "The Seventy-First Came...to Gunskirchen Lager" from *Witness to the Holocaust Publication Series #1.* Reprinted with the permission of the Center for Research in Social Change, Emory University.

"Refugees" from *Time* (July 18, 1938). Copyright 1938 by Time, Inc. Reprinted with the permission of *Time*.

"Statement of Non-Jewish Advocates of Boycott" from *The New York Times* (October 25, 1935). Copyright 1935 by The New York Times Company. Reprinted with the permission of *The New York Times*.

Frances Strauss, excerpts from "The Intermarriage," from *The Atlantic Monthly* (June/July 1941). Reprinted by permission.

"Topics of the Times: Refugee Ship" from *The New York Times* (June 8, 1939). Copyright 1939 by The New York Times Company. Reprinted with the permission of *The New York Times*.

"Wandering Jews" from *Time* (December 15, 1941). Copyright 1941 by Time, Inc. Reprinted with the permission of *Time*.

War Refugee Board, excerpt from "Final Summary Report of the Executive Director, War Refugee Board" (Washington, September 15, 1945), in David S. Wyman (ed.), *America and the Holocaust: Responsibility for America's Failure, Volume 13.* Copyright © 1991. Reprinted with the permission of Garland Publishing, Inc.

Michael Williams, "Views and Reviews" from *The Commonweal* (December 26, 1941). Copyright 1941 by Commonweal. Reprinted with the permission of the publishers.

Index

225